Praise for Our History Is the

"*Our History Is the Future* is a revelatory history of Indigenous resistance that helps us not only understand our past but change our present." Rebecca Nagle (Cherokee), author of *By the Fire We Carry*

"A touching and necessary manifesto and history featuring firsthand accounts of the recent Indigenous uprising against powerful oil companies . . . With an urgent voice, Estes reminds us that the greed of private corporations must never be allowed to endanger the health of the majority. An important read about Indigenous protesters fighting to protect their ancestral land and uphold their historic values of clean land and water for all humans." *Kirkus*

"This book offers a first draft of history that will serve as the last word for years to come. Combining the literary skill of the poet, the rich contextual knowledge of the historian, and the sharp edge of experience, Nick Estes has crafted a powerful account of the Standing Rock resistance, situating it in a struggle lodged deep in time and across the full reach of global solidarities." Philip J. Deloria, author of *Playing Indian*

"*Our History Is the Future* brings the history of Native American anti-imperialism to the center of the study of racial capitalism while renewing the focus on political economy in Indigenous Studies; it brings the experience of the camp at Standing Rock to the study of history, and deep learning to the ongoing fight for sovereignty; it is a book by a young scholar that draws brilliantly on the wisdom of centuries of struggle. In short: you should read it." Walter Johnson, author of *River of Dark Dreams: Slavery and Empire in the Cotton Kingdom*

"In addition to providing a thorough and cogent history of the long tradition of Indigenous resistance, *Our History Is the Future* is also a personal memoir and homage to the Oceti Sakowin; an entreaty to all their relations that demands the 'emancipation of the earth.' Estes continues in the legacy of his ancestors, from Black Elk to Vine Deloria: he turns Indigenous history right-side up as a story of self-defense against settler invasion. In so doing, he is careful and judicious in his telling, working seamlessly across eras, movements, and scholarly literatures, to forge a collective vision for liberation that takes prophecy and revolutionary theory seriously. The book will be an instant classic and go-to text for students and educators working to understand the 'structure' undergirding the 'event' of the Dakota Access Pipeline. This is what history as Ghost Dance looks like." Sandy Grande, author of *Red Pedagogy: Native American Social and Political Thought*

"This extraordinary history of resistance counters the myth of Indigenous disappearance and insignificance while calling into question the very notion that resistance itself is impossible in a world saturated by capital and atrophying inequality. This is a radical Indigenous history in its finest form—that connects individual lives to global scales of political articulation while remaining attentive to intellectual formation and coalitional politics from the nineteenth century to the present. Estes draws from multiple archives and intellectual traditions and seeks not only to connect past to present but also to transform futures and possibilities for justice." Audra Simpson, *Mohawk Interruptus: Political Life Across the Borders of the Settler States*

"Nick Estes is a forceful writer whose work reflects the defiant spirit of the #NoDAPL movement. *Our History Is the Future* braids together strands of history, theory, manifesto and memoir into a unique and compelling whole that will provoke activists, scholars and readers alike to think deeper, consider broader possibilities and mobilize for action on stolen land." Julian Brave NoiseCat, 350.org

"Fearless and inspiring, Nick Estes delivers a powerful rebuke of Euro-American Manifest Destiny with an Indigenous perspective that is inclusive and ideologically precise. This book correctly, if not necessarily, focuses its energy on the natural evolutionary and revolutionary pathway of Oceti Sakowin resistance. Respectful, brilliant, and insightful, This book should be considered a key ingredient to achieve the universal Native construct of balance—something we must all have to ensure our continued existence." Marcella Gilbert, Lakota Water Protector, Warrior Women Film Project

"*Our History Is the Future* establishes Nick Estes as one of the leading scholars of our time. This dynamic book offers a careful, deeply researched, and even-handed account of the events at Standing Rock, placing them in a long continuum of Oceti Sakowin resistance. This is a war story that links the #NoDAPL movement in the present to anti-colonial and anti-capitalist struggles in the past to demonstrate the possibilities of liberated futures." Jordan T. Camp, author of *Incarcerating the Crisis: Freedom Struggles and the Rise of the Neoliberal State*

"It is customary to hail a bold young author as the voice of their generation. In *Our History Is the Future*, Nick Estes gives voice to many generations; those who've come before and those still to come. The book slips through time, evoking the scent of campfire that once indicted Indigenous people in the nineteenth century—a smoke that still lingers on twenty-first-century Water Protectors and marks them as enemies of the state. This utterly astonishing book imparts the long history of Indigenous people, their relatives, and their struggle for liberation against capitalist North America's settler colonial violence. The long memory of the people, Estes shows, cannot be clipped by the oblivion of empire. The people do not forget." Christina Heatherton, co-editor of *Policing the Planet: Why the Policing Crisis Led to Black Lives Matter*

"A mindful and dynamic text. Nick Estes's narrative power gives dynamism and detailed realism to some of the most formative movements of our time. The book is expansive in its isolation and focus. The book embodies resistance and shows the true effort it takes to maintain it." Terese Mailhot, author of *Heart Berries*

OUR HISTORY IS THE FUTURE

Standing Rock versus
the Dakota Access Pipeline,
and the Long Tradition
of Indigenous Resistance

NICK ESTES

Chicago, Illinois
Haymarket Books

This paperback edition published by Verso 2023
First published by Verso 2019

This edition published in 2024 by
Haymarket Books
P.O. Box 180165
Chicago, IL 60618
www.haymarketbooks.org

ISBN: 979-8-88890-082-6

Distributed to the trade in the US through Consortium
Book Sales and Distribution (www.cbsd.com) and
internationally through Ingram Publisher Services
International (www.ingramcontent.com).

This book was published with the generous
support of Lannan Foundation, Wallace Action
Fund, and Marguerite Casey Foundation.

Special discounts are available for bulk purchases
by organizations and institutions. Please email
info@haymarketbooks.org for more information.

Cover artwork by Yatika Fields.
Cover design by Rachel Cohen.

Printed in Canada by union labor.

Library of Congress Cataloging-in-Publication data is available.

10 9 8 7 6 5 4 3 2 1

CONTENTS

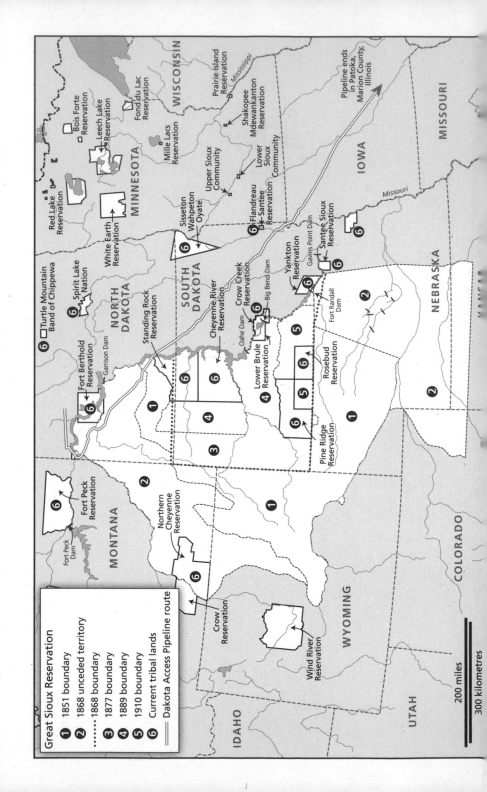

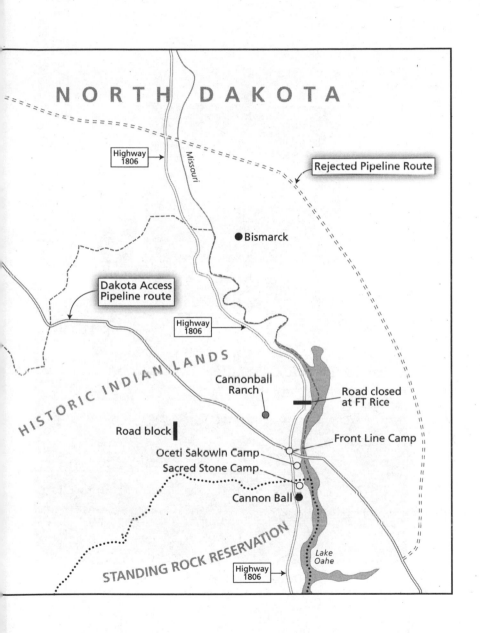

October 2016. Photo by author.

Prologue

PROPHETS

Thanksgiving is the quintessential origin story a settler nation tells itself: "peace" was achieved between Natives and settlers at Plymouth, Massachusetts, where *Mayflower* pilgrims established a colony in 1620, over roast turkey and yams. To consummate the wanton slaughter of some 700 Pequots, in 1637 the governor of the Massachusetts Bay Colony, William Bradford, proclaimed that Thanksgiving Day be celebrated "in honor of the bloody victory, thanking God that the battle had been won." Peace on stolen land is borne of genocide.

It was Thanksgiving 2016. We had spent a bitterly cold night at a Wyoming gas station off I-80, among a half-dozen other cars loaded with camp supplies and Water Protectors. Everyone was up before sunrise, hoping the interstate would reopen after the overnight freeze. Among them were Natives and non-Natives from the Pacific Northwest and West Coast, sporting fatigues and signature black and tan Carhartt jackets with patches declaring: "WATER IS LIFE." "This is Trump country—we gotta hit the road!" one of the Water Protectors exclaimed, half-jokingly, to the packed truck stop bathroom. Outside, white men glared at us from their dually pickups. Wyoming is an oil, gas, and coal state, and it was sending its police to fight the modern-day Indian war that we were on our way to help resist. We filed into our cars and took the on-ramp toward Standing Rock.

This was my fourth and final trip to Oceti Sakowin Camp, the largest of several camps that existed at the confluence of the Cannonball and Missouri Rivers, north of the Standing Rock Indian Reservation, from April 2016 to February 2017. Initially, the camps had been established to block construction of Energy Transfer Partners' $3.8 billion Dakota Access Pipeline (DAPL), a 1,712-mile oil pipeline that cut through unceded territory of the 1868 Fort Laramie Treaty and crossed under Mni Sose (the Missouri River) immediately upstream from Standing Rock, threatening the reservation's water supply.

This was not just about Standing Rock water: The pipeline crossed upriver from the Fort Berthold Indian Reservation on the Missouri River, transporting oil extracted from that reservation's booming fracking industry. It cut under the Mississippi River at the Iowa–Illinois border, where a coalition of Indigenous peoples and white farmers, ranchers, and environmentalists in Iowa opposed it. And it crossed four states— North Dakota, South Dakota, Iowa, and Illinois. But it was Standing Rock and allied Indigenous nations, including Fort Berthold, who had put up the most intense resistance.

After North Dakota Governor Jack Dalrymple declared a state of emergency on August 19, 2016—to safeguard the pipeline's final construction—the movement surged. Dalrymple deployed the National Guard and invoked powers under the Emergency Management Assistance Compact (EMAC) that are normally used only during natural disasters, such as floods, fires, and hurricanes. EMAC also allows for state, municipal, and federal law enforcement agencies to share equipment and personnel during what are declared "community disorders, insurgency, or enemy attack." In April 2015, Maryland Governor Larry Hogan had also used EMAC powers to crush a Black-led uprising for justice for Freddie Gray, a Black man killed by Baltimore police. This time it was an Indigenous nation that was declared the threat.

The encampments were about more than stopping a pipeline. Scattered and separated during invasion, the long-awaited reunification of all seven nations of Dakota-, Nakota-, and Lakota-speaking peoples hadn't occurred in more than a hundred years, or at least seven generations. Oceti Sakowin,

dubbed the "Great Sioux Nation" by settlers, once encompassed territory that spanned from the western shores of Lake
Superior to the Bighorn Mountains. Only in stories had I heard
about the Oceti Sakowin uniting, its fire lit, and the seven tipis
or lodges—each representing a nation—arranged in the shape
a buffalo horn. Historically, this reunification had happened in
times of celebration, for annual sun dances, large multi-tribal
trading fairs, and buffalo hunts. But the last time was also in a
time of war—to resist invasion. Now, the gathering had become
what the passengers of our car—Carolina, an Indigenous
immigration lawyer, Dina, an Indigenous writer, and I—liked
to call "Indian City"; at its peak, the camp was North Dakota's
tenth-largest city. Its population surpassed 10,000 people,
possibly reaching as many as 15,000.

The camp was at a standstill when we arrived, and
completely encircled by law enforcement employing hundreds
of miles of concertina wire, road blocks, and twenty-four-
hour aerial surveillance, in what resembled a military occupation. In an effort to sow division, TigerSwan, a private security contractor hired by DAPL to assist North Dakota law
enforcement, infiltrated the camps and planted false reports
on social media and local news comparing Water Protectors
to jihadist insurgents. The #NoDAPL movement was "an
ideologically driven insurgency with a strong religious component," they claimed, in documents released by the *Intercept*.[1]
The effects were devastating, and many of the planted stories
continue to circulate as truth, the divisions cleaved still fester-
ing. And because of the violent police crackdown on protests,
including the infamous October 27 raid on the 1851 Treaty
Camp, a hiatus had been placed on high-risk direct actions
like placing bodies before earthmovers.

So the next day—Black Friday—we went to the mall. In
Bismarck, North Dakota, shoppers, mostly white, flooded the
Kirkwood Mall, eager to cash in on holiday discounts. Our
plan was to disrupt Black Friday shopping, in unison with

other Black Friday actions, to keep the message of #NoDAPL in the news and the fire burning in people's hearts and minds. Back at camp, I had run into a childhood friend, Michael, and his partner Emma, and we had packed into his car. Through traffic was entirely blocked on Highway 1806, the fastest route to reservation border towns Mandan and Bismarck, and military checkpoints choked off business to Prairie Knights Casino—a major employer in the reservation and source of revenue for Standing Rock—and hampered residents' access to off-reservation jobs and groceries. What resembled an economic embargo and, in different circumstances, could be considered an act of war against a sovereign nation, added an extra half hour to forty-five minutes to our drive.

The mall was packed. Bismarck police, all of them white, guarded the entrances with AR-15 rifles. Once inside, our goal was to create a prayer circle in the mall's large food court, without getting caught; this meant we would have to "blend in." That's hard enough for Natives in a sea of whites.

Our cover was blown. A white woman cried out: "They smell like campfire!" Shoppers stopped and looked. She pointed to a group of women—faces wind and sun-burnt, jackets and skirts unwashed—heading toward the mall's restrooms. Two cops, their AR-15s slung over their shoulders, approached, and grabbed and twisted one of the women's arm. She was dark-skinned, and her black hair was neatly braided to her waist. I waited to hear her arm pop from dislocation or fracture, as the cop slammed her face-first on the thin carpet.

"I'm trying to go to the bathroom!"

"Shut the fuck up!"

Soon all four of them were sitting on the ground with their hands zip-tied behind them, and then the cops dragged them away. The smell of fire, a central aspect of camp life—ceremony, planning, cooking, eating, sleeping, singing, storytelling, and keeping warm—had given them away. "Oceti" in "Oceti Sakowin," after all, means "council fire." In another time, they might have been accused of "smelling like an Indian" because fire is central to Lakota ceremonial life; but now, smoke also indicated that one had come from the #NoDAPL camps.

"What's your problem?" asked a white man, approaching the cops. With a leg sweep, he was also facedown, with a knee on his neck and knee on his spine.

"Quit resisting!" the officer shouted. They didn't bother to pick him up, instead dragging him belly-first across the ground.

"He smelled like campfire," shrugged the cop who had thrown him down.

Eventually, we formed a prayer circle—before cops began tackling, punching, and kicking us too. A man's crutches were taken from him, and he hobbled on one foot as another cop tackled him. White men from the crowd began holding Water Protectors for the police or throwing them into the police line.

"Go back to the reservation! Prairie niggers!" one of them screamed in our faces.

White children looking on also screamed, though they seemed more scared of the police than of the Water Protectors. A woman got caught between the police and our retreating line, and cops grabbed her by the hair and dragged her to the ground crying. Her partner stepped in and was kneed several times in the face. A woman began running as we made our way through the exit doors and was tackled on the pavement by a cop.

We had flinched each time they nabbed one of us from the crowd, expecting the now-familiar chemical shower of CS gas or pepper spray—another odor that was mixed in with the smoke, and that, in a single attack, could dull a person's sense of smell for days, sometimes weeks. But the presence of white shoppers and their families—unwanted collateral damage—protected us from being shot or sprayed. Instead, the cops used their hands and feet. Thirty-three were arrested. After Michael, Emma, and I escaped, we rendezvoused at the car.

Michael turned to me, his hands shaking. "Now I know what it's like to be hunted."

At camp, the smell of campfire brought us back to another world—an older world, an Indigenous world always thought to be on the brink of extinction, a place at once familiar to Native peoples and radically unfamiliar to settlers. In the twilight hours, Water Protectors told stories and shared the prophetic visions of a better world, not just in the past, but one currently in the making, as purple-grey smoke filled the spaces between tipis, tents, and lines of cars and trucks.

The camps had attracted Indigenous and non-Indigenous people from across North America. On my first day in camp, in August, I dug compost holes with my Ojibwe relative Josh—a cook from Bismarck—and built a cook shack at the camp's main kitchen with my Diné relative Brandon and a Palestinian network administrator, Emad, from Yankton, South Dakota—himself a refugee from the US-backed Israeli colonization of his homelands. My Palestinian comrade Samia once called our sacrosanct duty at camp an "intifada on the plains," because she saw it as an uprising against the same occupier. The cook shack, pieced together with genuine solidarity and gnarly fallen trees, survived a brutal Northern Plains winter and helped feed thousands.

I also knew Michael, a white kid from my small hometown of Chamberlain, South Dakota, along the Missouri River. I grew up in a single-parent, single-income household, in a mobile home literally on the wrong side of the tracks. Michael's parents made ends meet by working at the Catholic-run Indian boarding school where my father and his siblings had their Lakota culture and language beaten from them. Along with other kids like us, both Native and white, the two of us bonded over skateboarding, punk rock, and left politics—everything we felt rebelled against the pervasive, and often violent, conservatism of our hometown.

Politicians and media attempted to play up divisions in the camps, depicting white Water Protectors as "hippies" who treated the movement like "Burning Man." Those elements existed, and some Native people played along. But such portrayals gloss over meaningful solidarities. For example, our national camp, Kul Wicasa, welcomed everyone. Our camp's leader, my friend and Tahansi (cousin) Lewis Grassrope, helped create the Oceti Sakowin Horn, inviting not only Indigenous, but also non-Indigenous peoples to participate. (Our families had shared political commitments that went back generations. In the 1930s his great-grandfather Daniel Grassrope, a traditional headman, and my great-grandfather Ruben Estes, a translator, traveled together to Washington, DC, to encourage Congress to pass the 1934 Indian Reorganization Act.)[2] Lewis knew the importance of allies.

Two years earlier he and I had spent cold nights in poorly insulated tipis protesting our own nation. Of all the tribal councils, that of the Lower Brule Sioux Tribe was the only to cast support for TransCanada, the company building the Keystone XL Pipeline. Our protest camp had little to no help from our own people, nor from the outside world. There were no television cameras or social media live streams, and there was no Mark Ruffalo. But now the world had come to #NoDAPL. A white woman named Maria, a local reporter and a friend from Chamberlain, embedded herself in the camp as a cook, feeding thousands. Abe, a white military veteran from Colorado, ran our camp security. In Chicago, my comrades Kofi from #BlackLivesMatter and Renae, a Nuu-chah-nulth revolutionary socialist, led solidarity delegations. And there were many more.

Political elites and corporate media have frequently depicted poor whites and poor Natives as irreconcilable enemies, without common ground competing for scarce resources in economically depressed rural areas. Yet, the defense of Native land, water, and treaties brought us together. Although not perfect, Oceti Sakowin camp was a home to many for months. And the bonds were long lasting, despite the horrific histories working against them.

Chamberlain is a white-dominated border town next to the Lower Brule and Crow Creek Indian reservations. The

7

settlement began as Fort Kiowa, across the river, a notorious trade hub whose early history is depicted in the 2015 blockbuster film *The Revenant* with great historical accuracy, despite its tired trope of a white savior "playing Indian." The film shows the nineteenth-century fur trade's organized plunder of not only the river ecosystem, but entire nations of people, and its apocalyptic death-world of rape, genocide, poaching, trespass, theft, and smallpox. In the final scene, the main protagonist, Hugh Glass, a real historical figure, approaches Fort Kiowa, where he sees Native women and children begging outside the gates and being bought and sold inside by drunk white traders. These river trade forts were the first "man camps": large, usually temporary, encampments of men working in extractive industries, from the fur trade to oil and gas development, where rates of sexual and domestic violence, and murders and disappearances of Native women and girls are intensified. As Ihanktonwan elder and member of the Brave Heart Society Faith Spotted Eagle has pointed out, "history teaches us that during times of crisis violence escalates;"[3] indeed, the proliferation of violence against the land has been directly related to attacks on Indigenous women's bodies.

This region—our homeland—is also part of He Sapa, the Black Hills, or *the heart of everything that is*. He Sapa is the beating heart of the Lakota cosmos, where we emerged from red earth, took our first breath, and gained our humanity as Oyate Luta: the "Red People," or the "Red Nation." During the last ice age, massive glaciers carved up the land. After the ice retreated, it left rolling hills and tunneling valleys that became buffalo roads, where herds that once blackened the plains traveled during seasonal migrations to and from water. The buffalo followed the stars, and the people followed the buffalo. To honor our relations, we called ourselves "Pte Oyate" (the Buffalo Nation), and "Wicahpi Oyate" (the Star Nation). In these ebbs and flows of migration, all roads led to

Mni Sose, which translates to "roiling water," for the once-astir and often-muddy river. Many Lakotayapi nouns, like "Mni Sose," indicate not merely static, inanimate form, but also action. In this landscape, water is animated and has agency; it streams as liquid, forms clouds as gas, and even moves earth as solid ice—because it is alive and gives life. If He Sapa is the heart of the world, then Mni Sose is its aorta. This is a Lakota and Indigenous relationship to the physical world. What has been derided for centuries as "primitive superstition" has only recently been "discovered" by Western scientists and academics as "valid" knowledge. Nevertheless, knowledge alone has never ended imperialism.

The US military understood this vital connection to place and other-than-humans in the 1860s when it annihilated the remaining 10 to 15 million buffalos in less than two decades. A century later another branch of the military, the US Army Corps of Engineers, constructed five earthen rolled dams on the main stem of the Missouri River, turning life-giving waters into life-taking waters. A river that was once astir was now choked and plugged. After World War II, the United States also aimed to "get out of the Indian business": to terminate federal responsibilities to Indigenous peoples that had been guaranteed through treaties, to relocate Indigenous peoples off their reservations, and to sell off remaining lands and resources to private industry and white settlers. The Pick-Sloan Plan, a basin-wide multipurpose dam project—which aimed to provide postwar employment, hydroelectricity, flood control, and irrigation to white farming communities and far-off cities—worked in tandem with Indian termination and relocation. With the flooding of the fertile river bottomlands, people were forced off the reservation. Remaining lands were largely uninhabitable, making relocation the only option for many. Thirty percent of Missouri River reservation populations were removed; 90 percent of commercial timber was destroyed; thousands of acres of subsistence farms and gardens were flooded; and 75 percent of wildlife and plants indigenous to the river bottomlands disappeared.

Oglala visionary and prophet Nicholas Black Elk, himself a Catholic, compared the invasion of white Christians as akin to the biblical flood. But unlike the Genesis flood that receded after 150 days, Black Elk's apocalyptic deluge had no end. It has worked continuously to eliminate Indigenous peoples and their other-than-human relatives from the land, thereby severing their relationship *with* the land. According to the vision Black Elk described to poet John Neihardt in 1931, white men came like an endless wall of floodwater, creating "a little island," or a reservation, "where we were free to try to save our nation, but we couldn't do it." Constantly hounded as fugitives, escaping from one patch of dry land to the next, the people "were always leaving our lands and the flood devours the four-leggeds as they flee." The four-leggeds were bears, elk, deer, buffalos, wolves, and so forth—some of whom are presently extinct in the lands of the Oceti Sakowin. The Department of the Interior is tasked with managing the diminished lands and territories of both wildlife and Indians, survivors of an ongoing holocaust. "All of our religion of the old times that the early Indians had was left behind them as they fled and the water covered the region," Black Elk lamented. "Now, as I look ahead, we are nothing but prisoners of war."⁴ His "we" included the four-leggeds.

Over the last 200 years, the US military has waged relentless war on the Oceti Sakowin as much as it has on their kinship relations, such as Pte Oyate (the buffalo nation) and Mni Sose (the Missouri River). What happened at Standing Rock was the most recent iteration of an Indian War that never ends. DAPL was originally meant to cross the Missouri River upstream from Bismarck, a city that is 90 percent white. But the Army Corps rerouted it to cross downstream, citing a shorter route, fewer water crossings, and reduced proximity to residential areas. Now, it crossed the river just upstream from an 84 percent Native residential area—a suggestion made not by Dakota Access, but by the Army Corps, which went so far as to guide companies funding the pipeline to create environmental justice studies that would find no "disproportionate risk to a racial minority."[5]

In fact, the Army Corps had been one of the main driving forces behind choking the Missouri River after World War II. In 1946, without authorization from Congress, the Army Corps modified the Garrison Dam project to protect the small majority-white town of Williston, North Dakota, from flooding. Nothing was done, however, to protect against the flooding of the Fort Berthold Indian Reservation. The 212-foot dam flooded 152,360 acres of reservation lands, dislocating 325 families (80 percent of the tribal membership) and destroying 94 percent of their agricultural lands.[6] In 1955, the Army Corps selected the Big Bend dam site on Lower Brule and Crow Creek reservation lands, without notifying either tribal council. Six different sites were considered, four of which would not have flooded the agency town of Lower Brule. The reservation site was chosen for hydraulic reasons but also because its location wouldn't flood the upriver town of Pierre, the white-dominated state capital of South Dakota, or its neighboring town of Fort Pierre.[7] Big Bend Dam flooded and dislocated both reservation communities for the second time, forcing some families who had moved to higher ground to relocate yet again. The first flood took out the Crow Creek Agency (the combined headquarters of the Crow Creek and Lower Brule tribes). A quarter of Lower Brule's population was removed during the first deluge, and half during the second.

My grandparents, Joyce and Andrew Estes—both Kul Wicasa from Lower Brule—fought the construction of the Pick-Sloan dams in the 1950s and 1960s. The dams flooded nearly all of my great-grandmother Cornelia Swalla's allotment. My grandfather, a World War II veteran and, according to my father, Ben, a Lakota code talker, returned from the war to find his homelands and nation under threat from the very government he fought to defend. Our lands, and lives, were targeted not because they held precious resources or labor to be extracted. In fact, the opposite was true: our lands and lives were targeted and held value because they could be wasted—submerged, destroyed. Grandpa Andrew, nicknamed "Brown" for his dark complexion, later gifted his mother Cornelia's remaining allotted lands to the Lower Brule Sioux Tribe so that our nation could rebuild the inundated Lower Brule town site. In 1937, my great-grandfather Ruben Estes, Cornelia's husband and the first tribal chairman, opposed the state of South Dakota's attempt to build dams on the Missouri River without Lower Brule's consent. The old ones called Ruben "Tongue" because, after butchering his cattle, he gave away all the meat to elders and the hungry, keeping only the tongues for himself. My ancestors were tribal historians, writers, intellectuals, and fierce Indigenous nationalists at a time when Indians weren't supposed to be anything but drunk, stupid, or dead. They were also Water Protectors, treaty defenders, and humble people of the earth, and they fought for and took care of Mni Sose as best as they could.

In 1963, my grandfather Frank Estes, who was named after Franklin Delano Roosevelt in honor of the "Indian New Deal," wrote and published the first book on Lower Brule, *Make Way for the Brules*.[8] His book was a study of Indigenous movement before and during the reservation period. It was a response to the forced removals caused by the Fort Randall and Big Bend Dams and a challenge to the confinement narrative that Native people should just stay "home" in prisoner of war camps, now called "reservations," out of sight and out of mind. In 1971, my grandfather George Estes, with Richard Loder, cowrote *Kul-Wicasa-Oyate*—a more extensive history of Lower Brule Sioux Tribe, including the reconstitution of communities and families after surviving forced removal by the US military to our river reservation homeland in the nineteenth century, as well as the two forced relocations caused by the Pick-Sloan dams in the twentieth century.

My grandfather Andrew, who had an eighth-grade education, wrote in the preface of *Kul-Wicasa-Oyate* what would have been a fitting epigraph for this book about our nation's history of the defense of our land, our water, and our people:

My people's history has been lost or destroyed since the coming of the white man. My people, in many ways, have been lost and destroyed by the coming of the white man . . . This book is not the whole story of my people nor is it all that is best in our heritage. Some of our traditions, our hopes and our roots, we will never write down for the world to see. What we will allow the world to see is, in good part, in these pages. Read them my brothers and you white man, you read them too. It is a history of a proud people: a people who believe in the land and themselves. My people were civilized before the white came and we will be civilized and be here after the white man goes away, poisoned by his misuse of the land and eaten up by his own greed and diseases.[9]

In September 2016, at a #NoDAPL protest in Chicago organized by the Native community and groups such as #BlackLivesMatter, I told this family history in front of a crowd of thousands outside the Army Corps headquarters. That city's vibrant Native community was itself a result of federal relocation programs onto traditional Potawatomi territory, an Indigenous nation subjected to genocide and removed from its homelands in the place currently called "Chicago." My ancestors could never have imagined that thousands, perhaps millions, would one day rally to defend the river, our relative Mni Sose. Half a century ago, there were no mass protests against the dams that still wreak havoc on our river, a history I have spent the more than a decade speaking and writing about, with little interest from the outside world.

As we marched, a light rain fell.

"Tell me what the prophecy looks like!" we chanted.

"This is what the prophecy looks like!"

And it *was* prophecy. Prophecy told of Zuzeca Sapa, the Black Snake, extending itself across the land and imperiling all life, beginning with the water. From its heads, or many heads, it would spew death and destruction. Zuzeca Sapa is DAPL—and all oil pipelines trespassing through Indigenous territory. But while the Black Snake prophecy foreshadows doom, it also foreshadows historic resistance and resurgent Indigenous histories not seen for generations, if ever. To protect Unci Maka, Grandmother Earth, Indigenous and non-Indigenous peoples will have to unite to turn back the forces destroying the earth— capitalism and colonialism. But prophets and prophecies do not predict the future, nor are they mystical, ahistorical occurrences. They are simply diagnoses of the times in which we live, and visions of what must be done to get free. In the past, youth followed the guidance of Indigenous elders, the old ones. But in these prophetic times, it is the old ones who are following the leadership of the young, the youth leaders of the #NoDAPL movement—among them, Zaysha Grinnell, Bobbi Jean Three Legs, Jasilyn Charger, and Joseph White Eyes, among others, who brought the message of the Black Snake to the world through thousand-mile relay runs from April to July of 2016.

For the Oceti Sakowin, prophecies like the Black Snake are revolutionary theory, a way to help us think about our relationship to the land, to other humans and other-than-humans, and to history and time. How does one relate to the past? Settler narratives use a linear conception of time to distance themselves from the horrific crimes committed against Indigenous peoples and the land. This includes celebrating bogus origin stories like Thanksgiving. But Indigenous notions of time consider the present to be structured entirely by our past and by our ancestors. There is no separation between past and present, meaning that an alternative future is also determined by our understanding of our past. Our history is the future.

Concepts such as Mni Wiconi (water is life) may be new to some, but like the nation of people the concept belongs to, Mni Wiconi predates and continues to exist in spite of white supremacist empires like the United States.

The protestors called themselves Water Protectors because they weren't simply against a pipeline; they also stood for something greater: the continuation of life on a planet ravaged by capitalism. This reflected the Lakota and Dakota philosophy of Mitakuye Oyasin, meaning "all my relations" or "we are all related." Water Protectors led the movement in a disciplined way, by what Lakotas call Wocekiye, meaning "honoring relations." To the outside world this looks like "praying," the smoking of the Canupa, the sacred pipe, offering tobacco, ceremony, and song to human and other-than-human life. The late Lakota linguist and scholar Albert White Hat Sr. notes that Wocekiye was purposely mistranslated to "praying" by Christian missionaries to describe "bowing and kneeling to a supreme power, which is much different from the original meaning of acknowledging or meeting a relative." There was no equivalent to "praying" in the Lakota language, although the word has taken on that meaning because of Christian influence.[10]

For the Oceti Sakowin, Mni Sose, the Missouri River, is one such nonhuman relative who is alive, and who is also of the Mni Oyate, the Water Nation. Nothing owns her, and therefore she cannot be sold or alienated like a piece of property. (How do you sell a relative?) And protecting one's relatives is part of enacting kinship and being a good relative, or Wotakuye, including from the threat of contamination by pipeline leak—in other words, death. This would also spell death for the Oceti Sakowin and its nonhuman relations. In this way, the rallying cry of Mni Wiconi—"water is life"—is also an affirmation that water is alive. Hunkpapa historian Josephine Waggoner has suggested that the word mni (water) is a combination of the words mi (meaning "I") and ni (meaning "being"), indicating that it also contains life.[11]

Mni Wiconi and these Indigenous ways of relating to human and other-than-human life exist in opposition to capitalism, which transforms both humans and nonhumans into labor and commodities to be bought and sold. These ways of relating also exist in opposition to capitalism's twin, settler colonialism, which calls for the annihilation of Indigenous peoples and their other-than-human kin. This is distinct from the romantic notion of Indigenous people and culture that is popular among non-Natives and has been aided by disciplines such as anthropology—a discipline that has robbed us of a viable future by trapping us in a past that never existed. In the last two centuries, armies of anthropologists, historians, archaeologists, hobbyists, and grave robbers have pillaged and looted Indigenous bodies, knowledges, and histories, in the same way that Indigenous lands and resources were pillaged and looted. Their distorted, misinterpreted Indigenous histories are both irrelevant and unfamiliar to actually existing Indigenous peoples, and they are deeply disempowering.

There exists no better example of Indigenous revolutionary theory, and its purposeful distortion, than the Ghost Dance. In popular history books, the Ghost Dance appears briefly, only to die at the Wounded Knee Massacre in 1890. The Ghost Dance, in the revolutionary sense, was about life, not death; it was about imagining and enacting an anticolonial Indigenous future free from the death world brought on by settler invasion. It originated with Paiute prophet and healer Wovoka. In his vision, the Great Spirit's Red Son transforms the earth. This Red coming of the Messiah wipes away the colonial world, bringing back the animals, plants, and human and other-than-human ancestors destroyed by white men and, in turn, destroying the destroyers. Wovoka did not predict the future. Rather, he profoundly understood the times in which he lived, and his prophecy occurred in response to the hardships brought on by reservation life. Its message of a coming Indigenous future spread like wildfire up the Western Canadian coast, down to the Southwestern United States and Northern Mexico, and onto the Plains. The Ghost Dance unified Indigenous peoples behind a revolutionary movement—one that sought nothing less than the complete departure of the colonial reality. Its visions were powerful and remain so today. Indigenous dancing had itself been outlawed and was therefore a criminal act. Lakota and Dakota Ghost Dancers attempted to shut down the reservation system by refusing to send children to boarding schools or to heed the orders of Indian agents. But the absence of the colonial system was not enough to bring about true freedom; rather, freedom could only find its genuine expression in actions that would create a new Indigenous world to replace the nightmarish present.

The beauty and power of the Ghost Dance moved Oglala prophet Nicholas Black Elk, who saw it as parallel to his own vision: that the people must unite to nourish back to health the tree of life, so that it can bloom once again. The dance brought Black Elk new visions of Wanikiya, the Lakota word for the Red Messiah that literally means "to make live." In 1932, poet John Neihardt published a literary interpretation of Black Elk's vision in *Black Elk Speaks*, an influential book that Standing Rock scholar Vine Deloria Jr. described as "a North American bible of all tribes."[12] After the Seventh Cavalry Regiment massacred more than 300 Lakota Ghost Dancers at Wounded Knee in 1890, the Ghost Dance and Black Elk's vision were thought to be dead or dying, like Native people. Neihardt contributed to this notion by fabricating the most-quoted lines in *Black Elk Speaks*. "A people's dream died there," mourned Black Elk in this made-up version, seeing the carnage at Wounded Knee and his relatives' bodies strewn across the bloody snow. "The nation's hoop is broken and scattered."[13] But Black Elk never believed that, and he knew that collective visions for liberation didn't die at Wound Knee. "The tree that was to bloom just faded away," he said reflecting on the massacre forty years later, "but the roots will stay alive, and we are here to make that tree bloom."[14]

Roots are an apt metaphor to explain how the aspirations for freedom—the tree of life—had stayed alive. Ceremonies, dance, language, warrior and political societies, and spiritual knowledge were forced underground, each of them made illegal by the punitive Civilization Regulations and only fully "legalized" in 1978 with the American Indian Religious Freedom Act. Like many, to protect himself and his family, Black Elk had converted to Catholicism, but he never lost faith in his vision. For him, liberation wasn't a one-off event, a single action, or a moment. If history books do not altogether deny the Wounded Knee Massacre, sympathetic treatments tend to label the Ghost Dance as a "harmless" trend that would have faded into the past, like the Indians practicing it. But if it were *just* dancing that was the threat, then why did the United States deploy nearly half its army against starving, horseless, and unarmed people in order to crush it?

Indigenous resistance draws from a long history, projecting itself backward and forward in time. While traditional historians merely interpret the past, radical Indigenous historians and Indigenous knowledge-keepers aim to change the colonial present, and to imagine a decolonial future by reconnecting to Indigenous places and histories. For this to occur, those suppressed practices must make a crack in history.

Karl Marx explained the nature of revolutions through the figure of the mole, which burrows through history, making elaborate tunnels and preparing to surface again. The most dramatic moments come when the mole breaks the surface: revolution. But revolution is a mere moment within the longer movement of history. The mole is easily defeated on the surface by counterrevolutionary forces if she hasn't adequately prepared her subterranean spaces, which provide shelter and safety; even when pushed back underground, the mole doesn't stop her work. In song and ceremony, Lakotas revere the mole for her hard work collecting medicines from the roots underfoot. During his campaign against US military invasion, to protect himself Crazy Horse collected fresh dirt from mole mounds. Because he knew it to contain medicines, he washed his body with the dirt. Hidden from view to outsiders, this constant tunneling, plotting, planning, harvesting, remembering, and conspiring for freedom—the collective faith that another world is possible—is the most important aspect of revolutionary work. It is from everyday life that the collective confidence to change reality grows, giving rise to extraordinary events.

At Oceti Sakowin Camp, courage manifested through the combination of direct actions and the legal strategy to defeat DAPL in court, which the Standing Rock Sioux Tribe spear-headed. Direct actions drew media attention and thus amplified the messages of #NoDAPL and Mni Wiconi, putting pressure on the federal courts and institutions to weigh in on the issue of Standing Rock's sovereignty. Direct actions also had the immeasurable psychological effect of empowering the powerless to action, by encouraging everyday people to take control of their lives and to shrug off the self-doubt and genuine fear that accompanies centuries of violent occupation. It also formed in everyday camp life.

The camps also performed another critical function: caretaking, or providing nourishment, replenishment, comradery, encouragement, warmth, songs, stories, and love. The ultimate goal for Dakotas, and therefore the Oceti Sakowin, "was quite simple: One must obey kinship rules; one must be a good relative," wrote the Dakota scholar Ella Deloria.[15] This was the underground work of the mole and the foundation of any long term struggle, though it often receives less attention than head-line-grabbing spectacles of mass protest and frontline action. Yet, both are equally important and necessary. As Dakota scholar Kim TallBear argues, caretaking labor is often gendered, and is seen as the work of women. But the fact that many contemporary social movements—in particular #NoDAPL,

Idle No More, and #BlackLivesMatter—were led by women, and Two-Spirit and LGBTQ people, is important.[16]

My friend and relative, Lakota Water Protector Marcella Gilbert, pointed out how these roles have been taken up by generations of Indigenous women. Marcella's mother, Madonna Thunder Hawk, and her aunties, Phyllis Young and Mabel Anne Eagle Hunter, were all leaders and participants of the Red Power Movement during the 1960s and 1970s. They were all pivotal members of the American Indian Movement, helped found the International Indian Treaty Council at Standing Rock in 1974, and formed Women of All Red Nations that same year—movements I will describe later in this book. Their leadership continued at Oceti Sakowin Camp by seeing to it that the next generation carried on the tradition. Phyllis Young was a respected Standing Rock elder and former councilwoman. Madonna and Mabel Anne fell back into leadership roles in their own camps, teaching and mentoring young people. For Marcella, freedom was education. She was a product of the "We Will Remember" Survival School, founded in Rapid City, South Dakota, in 1974. Her mother, Madonna, helped to create the school, where students were taught treaty rights and Native culture and history. We Will Remember was one of many survival schools created to address rampant discrimination against Native students in public schools, and to undo the indoctrination of Christianity and US patriotism at government- and church-run boarding schools. For Marcella, the #NoDAPL camps continued the tradition, providing a radical grassroots education on Indigenous self-determination and political autonomy—what it's like to live and be free—to thousands of young Native people.[17] In other words, moments like #NoDAPL are ones where the Indigenous movement reproduces itself and grows.

Our History Is the Future explores the movement to protect the Missouri River marching under the banner of Mni Wiconi. How did it emerge, and how does settler colonialism, a key element of US history, continue to inform our present? #NoDAPL and Mni Wiconi are part of a longer history of Indigenous resistance against the trespass of settlers, dams, and pipelines across the Mni Sose, the Missouri River. The Oceti Sakowin—our relationship to Mni Sose, and our historic struggle for liberation—are fundamentally tied to our prior history of Indigenous nationhood and political authority. This book is less a story about objects, individuals, and ideas than it is a history of relationships—those between the Oceti Sakowin, Mni Sose, and the United States as an occupying power. By focusing on these relationships, we can see that Indigenous history is not a narrow subfield of US history—or of the history of capitalism or imperialism, for that matter. Rather, Indigenous peoples are central subjects of modern world history.

This is not simply an examination of the past. Like #NoDAPL and Mni Wiconi, what I call *traditions* of Indigenous resistance have far-reaching implications, extending beyond the world that is normally understood as "Indigenous." A tradition is usually defined as a static or unchanging practice. This view often suggests that Indigenous culture or tradition doesn't change over time—that Indigenous people are trapped in the past and thus have no future. But as colonialism changes throughout time, so too does resistance to it. By drawing upon earlier struggles and incorporating elements of them into their own experience, each generation continues to build dynamic and vital traditions of resistance. Such collective experiences build up over time and are grounded in specific Indigenous territories and nations.

For the Oceti Sakowin, the affirmation Mni Wiconi, "water is life," relates to Wotakuye, or "being a good relative." Indigenous resistance to the trespass of settlers, pipelines, and dams is part of being a good relative to the water, land, and animals, not to mention the human world. Contrast this with the actions of Energy Transfer Partners (the financial backers of DAPL)—and of capitalism, more broadly, which seeks above all else to extract profits from the land and all forms of life. This is not to suggest that Indigenous societies possess *the* solution to climate change (and in fact, many Indigenous nations actively participate in resource extraction and capitalist economies in order to strengthen their self-determination). But in its best moments, #NoDAPL showed us a future that becomes possible when everyday Native people take control of their own destinies and lands, while drawing upon their own traditions of resistance. I am interested in the kind of tradition of Indigenous resistance that is a radical consciousness, both anti-capitalist and anti-colonial, and is deeply embedded in history and place—one that expresses the ultimate desire for freedom.

In this book, I move through seven episodes of Oceti Sakowin history and resistance. This history is by no means exhaustive, but I have chosen to focus on these particular cases to show how they inform our present moment, and to chart a historical road map for collective liberation.

Chapter 1 tells the story of the #NoDAPL movement at Standing Rock and its origins in the battle against tar sands extraction and the Keystone XL Pipeline, whose defense of Lakota and Dakota lands are part of a tradition of resistance against US imperialism that began centuries ago. I turn to the beginning of that history in chapter 2, which describes the Oceti Sakowin's emergence as a nation and its first encounters, in the nineteenth century, with the United States as a predator nation.

Before long, those encounters evolved into the Indian Wars of the nineteenth century—the subject of chapter 3—that raged across the Northern Plains, in which the Oceti Sakowin defended against US military invasion and counterinsurgency tactics. By the turn of the twentieth century, Indigenous people had been largely confined to ever-dwindling reservations. The Oceti Sakowin, however, confronted the US military—the

Army Corps of Engineers—again in the mid twentieth century, as US policy turned to the use of large-scale river development to continue the project of Indigenous dispossession—with policymakers attempting, all the while, to relieve themselves of the responsibilities outlined in the treaties.

In chapter 4, I outline these schemes through the story of the mid-century Pick-Sloan Plan, which authorized the Army Corps of Engineers and the Bureau of Reclamation to dam the main stem of the Missouri River. These dams specifically targeted and destroyed Native lives and lands, with 611,642 acres of land condemned through eminent domain, 309,584 acres of which were vital reservation bottomlands. Flooding also forced more than a thousand Native families to relocate, in patent violation of treaties and without prior consent. The memory of this experience was still fresh at the #NoDAPL camps.

Chapter 5 outlines the story of the urban-centered American Indian Movement (AIM) and their 1973 occupation of Wounded Knee in the Pine Ridge Indian Reservation—the culmination of more than a decade of Red Power organizing. This became the catalyst for a mass gathering of thousands at Standing Rock in 1974, which resulted in the founding of the International Indian Treaty Council—a body that would eventually lead international efforts for Indigenous recognition that have had a deep, global significance.

Chapter 6 traces the history of twentieth-century Indigenous internationalism—particularly, the Oceti Sakowin's central role in spearheading the four-decade-long campaign for Indigenous recognition at the United Nations, which was the basis for the 2007 UN Declaration on the Rights of Indigenous Peoples. The global Red Power movement eventually became a catalyst for the contemporary #NoDAPL movement at Standing Rock. Chapter 7 draws out these links, reflecting upon the ways our past and present struggles are connected, as they are to *both* past and present international anti-colonial and anti-capitalist movements around the world.

Two-Spirit Nation leads a march to the police line.
October 2016. Photo by author.

SIEGE

To us, as caretakers of the heart of Mother Earth, falls the special responsibility of turning back the powers of destruction . . . Did you think the Creator would create unnecessary people in a time of such terrible danger?

—Chief Arvol Looking Horse,
Keeper of the Sacred Buffalo Calf Pipe[1]

"We're going to declare war on the Keystone XL Pipeline," announced Oglala Sioux Tribal President Bryan Brewer, before a throng of cameras and microphones.[2] It was late March 2014, at an opening ceremony for a spirit camp on the Rosebud Indian Reservation in South Dakota. A crowd erupted into bursts of akisas and lililis—Lakota war cries and the high-pitched tremolos of assent. Keystone XL (KXL), or any oil pipeline, would not pass through Oceti Sakowin territory without a fight. This is a war story. But it is not always with weapons that warriors wage their struggle.

A dozen tribal national flags fluttered behind Brewer in the prairie wind, a sign of growing unity among Indigenous nations. His speech marked the beginning of a historic resistance that was to coalesce against the Dakota Access Pipeline at Standing Rock in 2016. It was not orchestrated behind closed doors by wealthy think tanks or big environmental NGOs. Rather, like its people, it grew from the earth and this humble landscape, often viewed as flyover country. It also grew from a deep history of struggles over land and water, and a fight for a livable future on a planet so thoroughly devastated by climate change.

Earlier in March, the Rosebud Sioux Tribe, under the direction of its president, Cyril "Whitey" Scott, abruptly ended a lease with a white farmer renting reservation land adjacent to the KXL pipeline's path. The pipeline snaked carefully through a complex checkerboard of private and tribal land ownership, a legacy of the 1887 Dawes General Allotment Act that broke up large chunks of reservation land by selling it off to white settlers. With yellow cornstalks still jutting through the snow from last year's harvest, workers from the Wica Agli men's health initiative, citizens of Rosebud, and supporting Native people erected tipis on reclaimed earth—directly in the path of the pipeline. They called the camp Oyate Wahacanka Woecun, meaning "shield the people." Large, round hay bales were taken from another plot leased by a white rancher and stacked to surround the camp, forming a barrier against harsh winds. The thick straw walls, it was said, may have also stopped bullets fired in the cover of darkness by vengeful white farmers.

It didn't matter if this was private property. It was still treaty territory, territory that generations of Lakotas and Dakotas had died defending and lived to care for. If not stopped, 800,000 barrels of tar sands oil would be transported each day across 1,200 miles of land—from Hardisty, Alberta, to Steele City, Nebraska—traversing 357 streams and rivers (all tributaries of the Missouri River), and crossing the Ogallala Aquifer, North America's largest aquifer. Because everyone depended on the water, whether for drinking or agriculture, Mni Wiconi (Water is life) trumped the sacredness of private property. "It's not an Indian thing, it's not a white thing," Rosebud Sioux Council Representative Wayne Frederick explained. "It's everybody's issue."[3]

White landowners from Nebraska were also at the camp's opening, standing at the edge of the crowd holding signs that read "PIPELINE FIGHTER." They had joined the Cowboy-Indian Alliance, a campaign led by a progressive group of white farmers and ranchers from Bold Nebraska and Dakota

Rural Action. Some of the landowners, however, were liber-
tarians who were more concerned with the sanctity of private
property and the evils of "big government" than with Indian
treaties and climate change. And while they captured much of
the media attention around KXL resistance, they represented
a minority of the affected white landowners from Montana,
South Dakota, and Nebraska.[4] On the plains, solidarity with
Indigenous nations is a hard sell that often comes down to
land and money. By this time, TransCanada, the company
building the KXL, reported at least 92 percent of the 302
South Dakotan landowners in the pipeline's path had agreed
to sell their lands voluntarily.[5] The situation was similar in
Nebraska and Montana. The holdouts had filed lawsuits to
stop eminent domain proceedings, the seizure of private land
for "public use," the definition of which includes privately
owned oil pipelines. But these were a mere handful of individuals, as compared to the many Indigenous nations who,
for the most part, wholly opposed KXL.

This leg of KXL crossed through the permanent reservation boundaries of the Great Sioux Nation and unceded lands
of the 1868 Fort Laramie Treaty, which forbids white settlement without Indigenous consent. The irony, Lakota historian Edward Valandra observed, was that any condemned
private land would be "twice stolen"—land white squatters
first stole from Natives would then be taken by a Canadian
oil company.[6] Settlers and private property have always been
the vanguards of invasion, and the sanctity of private property never applied to Indigenous peoples. But instead of turning their backs, like the first settlers did to them, Native
nations—such as Rosebud, Pine Ridge, Yankton, Cheyenne
River, and Standing Rock—welcomed the potential allies.
After all, "Lakota" (or "Nakota" or "Dakota") translates to
"ally." To turn away, on account of differences, those with
shared enemies or mutual interests goes against the very being
of Lakota culture.

Much as it has been for centuries, this conflict was about the land: who stole it, who owned it, and who claimed it. On the High Plains, land is a matter of race, class, and colonialism. KXL was possible only because Indigenous genocide and removal had cleared the way for private ownership of land. Federal laws such as the Dawes Act and the 1862 Homestead Act, which opened up 270 million acres of Native land, subsidized white settlement to supplant entire Native nations, and eventually concentrated it in the hands of a few. According to a 2002 report by the United States Department of Agriculture (USDA), white settlers own 96 percent of all private agricultural lands in the United States, and 98 percent of private lands overall.[7] According to a 2012 USDA report, in Lakota and Dakota reservations, non-Natives collect 84.5 percent of all agricultural income, controlling nearly 60 percent of the agricultural lands and 65 percent of all reservation-based farms.[8] This includes the white billionaire and media tycoon Ted Turner, who owns more than 2 million acres of ranchland across the globe and more than 200,000 acres of Oceti Sakowin treaty land in western South Dakota.[9] The radical scholar Cedric Robinson identified this system, in which a single white man owns more wealth and land than entire Indigenous nations, as racial capitalism.[10] Capitalism arose under a racist European feudal system. It used "race" as a form of rule—to subordinate, to kill, and to enslave others—and used that difference for profit-making. Racial capitalism was exported globally as imperialism, including to North America in the form of settler colonialism. As a result, the colonized and racialized poor are still burdened with the most harmful effects of capitalism and climate change, and this is why they are at the forefront of resistance. The legacy of racial capitalism and ongoing settler colonialism were why the Oceti Sakowin had gathered to oppose KXL in 2014, and why they would gather again to oppose DAPL.

KXL resistance emerged six years after the US housing market collapsed and the nation's first Black president, Barack Obama, inherited the mantle of a white supremacist empire. As global temperatures continued rising, Obama committed to curbing carbon emissions, but as part of his "all-of-the-above energy strategy," he also embraced the oil industry as it opened new markets and lands to exploit. US domestic crude oil production skyrocketed from 2008 to 2016—an 88 percent increase, thanks to the shale oil boom in the United States and the tar sands boom in Canada. With this acceleration came new oil pipelines and new sites of extraction. As 9.3 million US families—many of them poor, Black, and Latinx—faced home foreclosures, Indigenous lives, lands, waters, and air were once again sacrificed to help pull settler economies out of the gutter.

In response to the economic crisis, revolutionary flowers had blossomed in public squares around the world, offering for a brief moment a vision for a different world. In 2010, young people of the Arab Spring toppled dictators, and tragedy and betrayal soon followed. In 2011, disenchanted millennials of the Occupy Wall Street movement put anti-capitalism back on the agenda to challenge the rule of the 1 percent, the wealthy elite. In response, police bludgeoned, tear gassed, and jailed the 99 percent. Out of this chaos, a mass Indigenous movement reawakened, the seeds of which were planted generations before. While the movements of public squares arose in the cities, the Indigenous uprising mobilized city and country alike, everywhere Indigenous peoples and their allies were found.

During the winter of 2012 to 2013, Indigenous rebellion was afoot on Turtle Island. Its heartbeat was a drum, its voice a song. In what is currently Canada, Indigenous women of Idle No More led a mass movement of round dances (traditional healing and celebratory dancing and singing) in shopping malls and blockades of rail lines transporting oil. They protested Stephen Harper's Conservative government's abuse of Indigenous rights, privatization of Indigenous lands, and rollback of environmental protections to intensify fossil fuel extraction. As Cree Idle No More cofounder Sylvia McAdam noted, it was out of necessity that the movement linked Indigenous and environmental struggles to protest a system that, if not stopped, will continue to "devastate the very things needed to sustain humanity—our lands and waters—for the generations to come."[11] It was more than a battle for the present; it was a battle for the future. The growing alliances resonated across the Medicine Line, the US–Canada divide. In February 2013, one of the largest actions in the history of the US climate movement descended on Washington, DC. More than 40,000 people gathered outside the White House to protest the Keystone XL Pipeline, bringing together Indigenous and non-Indigenous movements committed to halting the extraction and transportation of highly toxic and volatile tar sands.

That summer, Métis and Cree women and elders led hundreds in a two-day journey through the Alberta tar sands during an annual Healing Walk. Jesse Cardinal, a Métis cofounder of the walk, described how "participants [saw] tailings ponds and desert-like areas of 'reclaimed land' that was once the boreal forest and now grows almost nothing."[12] It's a stark and immense landscape, encompassing an area larger than the state of Florida. In Treaty 6 and Treaty 8 territories, tar sands extraction—by companies such as Suncor Energy, ConocoPhillips, ExxonMobil, and Shell Canada—has poisoned water, land, air, plants, animals, and people. Duck and moose—staple foods of many Indigenous communities—have become contaminated with toxins, and harvests of wild berries and plants have been decimated. According to Cardinal, in this modern-day gold rush, "many 'outsiders' are driven here by their own economic desperation."[13]

Like the land itself, the bodies of Indigenous women, girls, trans, and Two-Spirit people are also seen as open for violence and violation. Resource extraction intensifies a murderous heteropatriarchy, meaning that grounding resistance in Indigenous feminist interventions has become all the more urgent. An influx of men has also flooded the region's "man camps," which house migrant oil laborers.[14] Men outnumber women two to one in the tar sands boomtown of Fort McMurray, Alberta. While a movement has existed since the 1970s to honor the lives of the thousands of missing and murdered Indigenous women across Canada, the Two-Spirit Métis activist Sâkihitowin Awâsis has noted the "links between presence of the tar sands industry and heightened rates of missing and murdered Indigenous Two-Spirits, women, and girls."[15] It's no coincidence that Indigenous women led the movement against the tar sands.

Put another way, settler states like Canada and the United States continue to settle the land, raping and killing Native women and Two-Spirit people in order to do so. From the 1970s onward, communities and activists have documented thousands of cases where Indigenous women, girls, trans, and Two-Spirited people who have been murdered, disappeared, and targeted by all forms of violence in Canada. The movement, operating under the hashtag #MMIWG (Missing and Murdered Indigenous Women and Girls), holds rallies around Canada every February 14, honoring the lives of the disappeared and demanding answers—a call that has been partially answered by the creation of the National Inquiry into Murdered and Missing Indigenous Women. Canada's death culture, however, is little different than its southern neighbor. In the United States, May 5 has been declared the National Day of Awareness for Missing and Murdered Native Women and Girls. In a 2016 report, there were 5,712 cases of missing Indigenous women nationwide; experts and activists, however, believe the number to be considerably higher.[16]

And Canadian prosperity is gained not just at the expense of First Nations. More than half the world's mining companies are headquartered in Canada, with properties in more than one hundred countries. Canadian extractive industries target Indigenous and colonized people throughout the world, and some have been linked to egregious human rights abuses, especially against Indigenous peoples. For example, beginning in 2007, Hudbay Minerals, a Canadian company with investments in the Fenix nickel mine, was linked to assassinations, beatings, gang rapes of women and girls, and arsons in Mayan communities in Guatemala.[17]

The links between the extractive industry and violence against Indigenous peoples also turn up in the United States. The Bakken shale oil boom that began in 2007, and would eventually prompt the construction of the Dakota Access pipeline, made North Dakota the second-largest oil producing state, after Texas. Much of this occurred on the Fort Berthold Reservation, the Mandan, Hidatsa, and Arikara (MHA) Nation, which sits atop some of the region's deepest oil reserves. In 2011, Tex Hall, the tribal chairman, adopted the mantra "sovereignty by the barrel," expressing a belief that oil wealth can strengthen economic self-determination and autonomy. Oil revenues, Hall hoped, would bring his nation out of crushing poverty and relieve the enduring devastation caused by the federal government's construction of the Garrison Dam in the heart of the reservation in the 1950s, which forced the reservation's residents from the fertile Missouri River valley onto the open, less productive plains. In short order, the MHA Nation became one of the wealthiest in Indian Country, and with this ascent came political corruption and high rates of violence, especially against women and girls.[18]

"We found a crying, naked, four-year-old girl running down one of the roads right outside of the Man Camp. She had been sexually assaulted," Grace Her Many Horses recalled. It was just one of many horrific incidents of rape, abuse, and sex trafficking during Her Many Horses' time at Fort Berthold in 2013 as a tribal cop. Most of her calls were related to man camps or the oil and gas industry they served.[19] Towns of thousands literally sprang up overnight, made up of mobile homes and

FEMA trailers, as hotels overflowed. Existing towns doubled and quadrupled in population, taxing already overstretched or nonexistent social infrastructure, including reservation emergency services. Nearly all the new arrivals were men, leading to some of the highest concentrations of men, outside of prisons, in North America. While emergency calls and violent assaults were frequent, prosecutions were not. Non-Native oil workers exploited a complex patchwork of federal, state, and tribal jurisdictions in which tribal law enforcement has little or no jurisdiction over non-Natives, allowing perpetrators to escape tribal justice.[20]

Since the Bakken boom, the rolling prairies and lush river valleys that had survived Army Corps flooding in 1953 have been replaced by miles of metal fracking rigs and heavy construction equipment. Clustered constellations of oil flares burning off methane are visible from space at night. "What we're dealing with is a death by a thousand cuts," said Kandi Mossett, an organizer with the Indigenous Environmental Network and citizen of the MHA Nation.[21] She explained that cancer, asthma, and respiratory diseases have increased among the children and elders because of the toxic environment. Mossett herself is a cancer survivor. But this toxic landscape is connected to another. "You would never see this in Houston's most affluent neighborhoods," said Yudith Neito, a resident of Houston's mostly Latinx community Manchester, where the air smells of burnt plastic and diesel from the oil refineries along the Houston Ship Channel next door.[22] These are the refineries that process oil from the Canadian tar sands and the Bakken shale.

Nevertheless, in 2012, despite massive opposition, Obama fast-tracked the construction of KXL's southern leg from Cushing, Oklahoma, to the Gulf Coast. "As long as I'm president," he boasted in 2012, "we're going to keep on encouraging oil development and infrastructure, and we're going to do it in a way that protects the health and safety of American people."[23] But those protections didn't extend to communities like Neito's or Mossett's—nor would they be extended, with the Dakota Access Pipeline, to Standing Rock and the millions who depend on the Missouri River for fresh water.

In response to Obama's order, that same year the Tar Sands Blockade sprang into action, a coalition that reflected the diversity of communities affected: conservative landowners, green anarchists and leftists, Latinx and Mexican-American communities, and Indigenous organizations from Canada and the United States. At an eighty-day sit-in action obstructing KXL construction on its southern route, local authorities and private security crushed the opposition with beatings, Tasers, and pepper spray—a prelude of what was to come.[24] It was also part of what Canadian author and activist Naomi Klein calls "Blockadia," a "roving transnational conflict zone" of grassroots resistance to the fossil fuel developments—whether "open-pit mines, or gas fracking, or tar sands pipelines"—that are not simply causing climate change, but threatening the very livelihoods of communities.[25]

But some communities remained disunited, especially among the Oceti Sakowin. Despite pulling together a historic alliance with non-Natives, one small nation remained an outlier—my own. TransCanada had carefully avoided crossing reservation lands to avoid provoking Indigenous resistance, except at one key location: the Lower Brule Indian Reservation, a place that received little media attention, despite its central role.

TransCanada needed to build a seventy-one-mile electric transmission line that connected hydroelectricity generated at the Big Bend Dam to one of seventeen pipeline pump stations at Witten, South Dakota. Because the power line crossed sixteen acres of Lower Brule land, it required tribal consent. Although a crucial detail, the power line project was easy to miss, buried in the thousand-page technical manuals

TransCanada produced. It was also easy to miss the name of the Lower Brule Sioux tribal chairman, Michael B. Jandreau, listed among the "Consulting Tribes' Points of Contact." Jandreau was the longest-serving tribal chairman in US history, in office for more than three decades before dying in office in 2015. As his health declined during his last term, so too did faith in his administration.

After months of denying negotiating with the company, in March 2014 suspicions surrounding the Lower Brule Tribal Council's collaboration with TransCanada had been confirmed. A November 12, 2013, Lower Brule Sioux Tribal Council resolution had been leaked to the public in which the council spelled out plans to pursue "prospective benefits and working relationships" with TransCanada and to inform President Obama and Vice President Joe Biden of its support for the Canadian oil company.[26] Lower Brule's actions directly violated the spirit of the Mother Earth Accord, which its leaders signed in September 2011 at a historic summit held in Rosebud with Alberta First Nations, Indigenous governments, grassroots treaty councils, human rights NGOs, and the Cheyenne River, Crow Creek, Fort Peck, Pine Ridge, Rosebud, Standing Rock, and Santee Reservations. By signing the accord, the Lower Brule Sioux Tribe committed to end the extraction, transportation, and refinement of Alberta tar sands by asking President Obama to reject the presidential permit required for KXL.[27] Now, Lower Brule had crossed a picket line, betraying not only their relatives in the Oceti Sakowin but also frontline communities around the world being devastated by climate change and extractivism.

The label "sellouts" stung, spurring the small nation into action. The Kul Wicasa, the people of Lower Brule, called an emergency town hall meeting, inviting tribal leaders and organizations from other reservations as well as the entire Lower Brule Tribal Council. Members of Owe Aku (Bring Back the Way), led by renowned Oglala environmentalist

Debra White Plume, facilitated the meeting in a show of solidarity.[28] From Lower Brule, the brother-and-sister twins Loretta and Lewis Grassrope, Kevin Wright, and Marlo Langdeau, among others, organized a town hall meeting calling on their nation to end its relationship with TransCanada, to uphold the Mother Earth Accord, and to join the growing alliance against KXL. More than a hundred attended, including the presidents of Pine Ridge and Rosebud. But the Lower Brule council boycotted the entire gathering.

"I used to be proud to be from here," said Langdeau, with tears in her eyes, after Standing Rock, Cheyenne River, and Rosebud had booted TransCanada officials off the reservation. Now, their leaders refused to face their own people. "It's embarrassing to be called a 'sellout' when you don't even know what's going on."

When there was no response from their elected officials, the organizers took matters into their own hands. Lewis Grassrope and Kevin Wright attempted to occupy land in front of the proposed transmission line, but before they could establish a camp, Bureau of Indian Affairs police (a federal police agency that operates without tribal oversight) stopped them. Undeterred, they set up on Grassrope's mother's homesite, several miles north of Medicine Butte on reservation land. They called the camp "Wiconi Un Tipi," which loosely translates to "the way we live when we live in community." As the name suggests, this was about more than stopping a pipeline. It was about restoring dignity to a little nation of people that had earned the reputation as "the forgotten Sioux."[29]

For Grassrope, a former tribal cop, it was Indigenous people at the grass roots who made the movement. The ikce wicasa, the ikce winyan, (the common men and women, the humble people of the earth), were the ones who changed history, not "great men" or tribal councils. When humble people moved, the earth moved with them. "We don't have a voice. We don't have a standing. We don't have influence. But as you can see here," Grassrope said in November 2016, gesturing to seven tipis embodying the reunification of the Oceti Sakowin Camp at the confluence of the Cannonball and Missouri Rivers, "we are the tip of the spear. We're saying, 'mni wiconi.' We're saying, 'treaty.'"

Wright, a firefighter, was a Water Protector from a different generation and a long-time dissident of his own government. In 1999 Wright joined members of the Lakota Student Alliance in a yearlong occupation of LaFramboise Island, a nature reserve in the middle of the Missouri River and, to the Oceti Sakowin, unceded earth. At the time, he also stood against the Lower Brule council's support of federal legislation known as the "Mitigation Bill," in which South Dakota lawmakers had proposed transferring jurisdiction over more than 200,000 acres of Missouri shoreline from the Army Corps of Engineers to the state of South Dakota. All Missouri River Indigenous nations objected to it except for Cheyenne River and Lower Brule, who chose to support it.[30]

This history of bad faith on the part of both state politicians and their own tribal council was fresh in the minds of the Lower Brule opposition in 2014. To Wright and Grassrope, the primary conflict boiled down to governance. The reservation system and the imposition of the elected tribal councils had all but dissolved traditional governance. In its place, a winner-takes-all electoral system turned relatives against each other, and harsh political divisions broke down the family kinship unit, the tiospaye—an extended network of relatives that was fundamental to decision making and caretaking. The arrangement that replaced it instead fomented division and rivalry over scant resources, catering to outside corporate and state interests; it was a type of neocolonialism.

The divisions were a result of a sordid history of colonial land grabs. In 1889, in advance of North and South Dakota statehood and to encourage white settlement, Congress passed the so-called "Sioux Agreement" that broke up the Great Sioux

Reservation into five separate reservations—Cheyenne River, Standing Rock, Pine Ridge, Rosebud, and Lower Brule. For traditionalists and treaty councils, it was hardly an agreement; the 1889 partition didn't get the required three-fourths approval from adult Native men, as stipulated by the 1868 Fort Laramie Treaty. In their eyes the creation, under the 1934 Indian Reorganization Act (IRA), of modern reservations, which later became separate governments, fractured national unity and undermined customary government and treaty law. This was the primary dispute in 1973 when American Indian Movement members, at the request of Oglala elders, took over Wounded Knee in protest of Pine Ridge's IRA government, which was under the authoritarian leadership of Chairman Dick Wilson, who was criminalizing dissent. In short, AIM and their supporters opposed colonial administration. While AIM promoted traditional governance, it never achieved the reunification of the Oceti Sakowin on the scale realized at Standing Rock in 2016. But AIM's militancy a generation earlier paved the way for the historic movement. While Indigenous nations rallied to support Standing Rock and the Oceti Sakowin, two years earlier Lower Brule was thrown into turmoil as grassroots councils called for overturning the status quo.

The so-called "Lower Brule constitutional crisis" of 2014 to 2016 was not an armed takeover like the one that took place at Wounded Knee in 1973. Nevertheless, it was without hesitation that supporters of the old order called it "an attempted overthrow of the tribal government."[31] And they weren't entirely wrong. In the fall of 2014, a grassroots reform movement had galvanized under the slogan Mni Wiconi, electing three anti-KXL candidates to the six-person council: Sonny Zeigler and Desiree LaRoche as council members, and Kevin Wright as vice-chair. Michael Jandreau defeated Lewis Grassrope for the position of chairman by a slim margin. The new council members quickly set to work pushing for reform and transparency, and they met a strident opposition.

A November council meeting escalated to a shouting match, nearly ending in a fistfight between opposing sides, when Wright called for Jandreau's removal for corruption and financial malfeasance, among other charges. In December, the opposition council members attempted to circumvent Jandreau and his supporters by appointing an entirely new council. This back-and-forth led to a flurry of lawsuits and countersuits, and day-to-day operations ground to a halt. After Jandreau passed away in April 2015, Grassrope was named his successor, but due to opposition from other council members, he never fully assumed the role. In May, in response to the unfolding political chaos, the Kul Wicasa Ospiye, a grassroots treaty organization, gathered signatures from the leadership of the traditional tiospayes of the Kul Wicasa to assert their right to be "self-governing" and that the people, not the federally recognized IRA council, were "the sole source for the Lower Brule Sioux Tribe's existence."[32] The move underscored the gravity of the vicious power struggle that was unfolding, and the profound desire for an accountable government based on Lakota values, including kinship.

In Jandreau's absence, and with the backing of the grassroots movement, Wright called for the removal of TransCanada from 1868 Treaty lands. "We see [TransCanada] as 'bad men' as defined by our treaties with the United States," Wright said in a statement. He cited a treaty clause that allows for the removal of "bad men among the whites" who "commit any wrong upon the person or property of the Indians." It was a bold move: the question of whether or not a corporation, which has personhood under US law, can be removed from treaty lands has yet to be tested in court. But for Wright and his supporters, the existential threat posed by KXL and climate change justified the risk. "This land is all we have," Wright explained, "and we are obligated to preserve it for our future generations."[33] However, the action went nowhere, as the council had failed to form a consensus—or even to convene.

The Lower Brule opposition, even with support from the grassroots community, was unable to dramatically improve conditions on the reservation or to significantly change the structure of the IRA council during their brief two-year tenure. Nevertheless, their advocacy would have a resonating impact. After Obama denied the required presidential permit for KXL's northern leg in December of 2015, the newly elected Lower Brule council changed course. One of its first actions was the passage of a resolution supporting Standing Rock's battle against the Dakota Access Pipeline. And in December 2016, preempting Donald Trump's incoming administration, which was expected to reapprove KXL's northern leg, the council passed a resolution opposing construction of the Big Bend–Witten line that would power KXL, stating that they opposed oil pipeline development and the construction of any infrastructure related to it.[34] Those two major victories would not have occurred without the tumultuous grassroots struggle against KXL, a movement that fed into the DAPL fight.

In November 2016 at Oceti Sakowin Camp, Lewis Grassrope was sitting in his tipi. It was one of seven that were arranged in the shape of a buffalo horn, with a large fire pit in the middle. The entire camp was arranged in a half circle facing Mni Sose and Wiyohiyapata (meaning "where the sun rises"). About half the size of a football field, the camp horn at the confluence of the Missouri and Cannonball rivers was surrounded by Indigenous national camps—such as Ihanktonwan Camp, Oglala Camp, and Kul Wicasa Camp— and organizations' camps—such as Indigenous People's Power Project and Red Warrior Camp. The Seven Council Fires of the seven nations—the Mdewakantonwan, Sissintonwan, Wahpetonwan, Wahpekute, Ihanktonwan, Ihanktonwanna, and Tintonwan—had been lit, and a nation reunited. It was a dream come true. On the horizon, on a hill, shadowy figures of cops in riot gear idled under floodlights and behind tangled razor wire. But the constant drone of the surveillance aircraft circling above was hardly noticeable over the sounds of children playing and the boisterous chuckles around campfires. Young boys and girls sang round dance songs and raced horses along the shoreline. Men and women cleaned and sliced up tripe for menudo. This was Wiconi Un Tipi, Lower Brule's national camp and one of the first camps to set up at Oceti Sakowin after Standing Rock put out the call in August.

"A lot of people didn't believe, they didn't have faith," Grassrope said, reflecting on the adversity he and his small nation faced over the years. He looked outside his tipi to the life, breath, prayer, and song around him. "When KXL happened, the belief came back. When DAPL happened, the belief came back."

The harbingers of the Dakota Access Pipeline arrived on an early fall morning, September 30, 2014, to Fort Yates, the headquarters of the Standing Rock tribe. A special meeting had been scheduled between the Standing Rock Sioux Tribal Council, and representatives of the Dakota Access Pipeline (DAPL) and Energy Transfer Partners (ETP, the Texas-based firm financing the project).

Earlier in 2014, the Army Corps had rerouted the pipeline from upriver of North Dakota's white-dominated capital, Bismarck, to upriver of the poorest county in North Dakota, Sioux County—the Standing Rock Reservation. In its environmental analysis, the Army Corps had concluded that the Bismarck path crossed a "high consequence area," which meant that a spill would have an adverse effect.[35] Not once did it mention Standing Rock, for which a spill half a mile upriver was of no consequence to the Army Corps. The new route also saved on time, constructions costs, and the unwanted headache of contaminating the drinking water of white settlers in the state's capital.

In an audio recording of the September meeting in Fort Yates released by the tribe, Chairman David Archambault II can be heard whispering off mic, "What is the name of the company?" He then asks, "Dakota Access Pipeline, are they here?"[36] No answer. DAPL was late. It seemed fitting. Amid the historic resistance unfolding against tar sands and KXL across the continent, DAPL seemed like an afterthought, arriving late and under the radar. At this time, a year ahead of the pipeline permitting process, hardly anyone had heard of DAPL. But those who saw it coming knew it was dangerous.

When DAPL representatives finally arrived, Archambault made Standing Rock's position clear: "We oppose the pipeline," he stated. Archambault cited a 2012 resolution that forbade any oil pipeline within the boundaries of the Fort Laramie Treaties of 1851 and 1868. Where federal and state governments have historically chosen to ignore them, Standing Rock has recognized and enforced its original treaty boundaries. In their report, DAPL representatives Tammy Ibach, Chuck Frey, and Joe Malucci mentioned that the pipeline crossed less than a mile north of the reservation boundaries, but they never mentioned treaty lands. They also never asked whether Standing Rock wanted the pipeline in the first place. DAPL was looking for "consultation," not consent.

"It's not consultation, because the plan's already done," Councilman Randy White rebuked the representatives. "And to me, that's really wrong."

Wasté Win Young, the Standing Rock Tribal Historic Preservation Officer, agreed. After studying the company's initial reports, what concerned her most was the Army Corps' intention to fast-track the project. (Despite their central role planning DAPL's route, the Army Corps did not attend the September 30 meeting.) Unlike KXL, which crossed an international border and therefore required State Department review and presidential approval, DAPL was a domestic project. This allowed the Army Corps to assess the pipeline according to a Nationwide Permit 12, which only considers individual construction sites, rather than cumulative negative impacts on entire nations of people, ecosystems, or the climate. As Young pointed out, fast-tracking the project under Permit 12 regulations bypassed environmental reviews under the Clean Water Act and the National Environmental Policy Act. It also skirted the type of public scrutiny received by KXL and significantly undermined the ability of impacted communities to mobilize, protect, and defend themselves.

Moreover, DAPL cut through about 380 archeological sites, such as burials, with at least 60 at the confluence of the Cannonball and Missouri Rivers alone. Though not recognized as reservation land, under the National Historic Preservation Act's Section 106, the presence of these culturally sensitive sites made the area "ancestral territory." Any potential disturbance required the Army Corps to consult with Standing Rock in order to proceed, a procedure Young claimed the Army Corps had failed to do in the past. The place where the pipeline crossed the river also held deep historical and cultural significance. Many Horses Heads Bottom, where DAPL crossed the Missouri River, Young explained, was where Dakotas fled generals Sibley and Sully's 1863 "columns of vengeance." After the 1862 Dakota Uprising, the United States punished survivors of that war at the Whitestone Hill Massacre, where they gunned down more than 400 Lakotas and Dakotas on a buffalo hunt. It was a massacre nearly forgotten by settlers, but no less horrific than Sand Creek and Wounded Knee. The soldiers led a manhunt up and down the river, capturing or killing survivors. Mothers plugged their babies' noses to silence their cries as they swam to safety across the river in the cover of darkness.

"I struggled with this last night," said Young at the meeting. "Do we want to tell something so important and sacred to us to a pipeline company?" Descendants of those who survived that genocidal campaign were sitting in the room, face to face with the very people who would two years later bring a whole new wave of chaos and violence.

What concerned Councilwoman Avis Little Eagle was the water. "Every oil pipeline leaks," she said, "and it's going to ruin the water we consume and that future generations are going to consume." Her fears were warranted: from 2010 to 2016, Sunoco Logistics, the operators of DAPL, had more than 200 of their pipelines leak;[37] indeed, DAPL would leak five times within six months of beginning operation.[38] Little Eagle also sat on the Standing Rock water control board, which, having reviewed DAPL's route the previous day, passed a resolution opposing it on the grounds that it threatened the reservation's source of drinking water, the Missouri River. This action fell in line with Standing Rock's Constitution, which was drafted with the water in mind. Article 1 of the Constitution reserves jurisdiction over "all rights-of-way, waterways, watercourses[,] and streams running through any part of the Reservation."[39] A threat to its drinking water was thus a threat to Standing Rock's sovereignty, as well.

"Our water is our single last property that we have for our people, and water is life—Mni Wiconi," remarked Phyllis Young to the DAPL representatives. Young was a councilwoman, a longtime AIM member, and Wasté Win Young's mother. The elder stateswoman described her homelands as a "national sacrifice area." In order to generate hydroelectricity to power homes in far-off cities like Minneapolis and Chicago, the Army Corps had flooded her home in the middle of a cold winter. "I know what it is to be homeless," Young said. "I know what it is to be hungry in this great land of plenty, where we lived in the richest riverbed in the world."

The dams, which I describe in chapter 5, were the reason why the Army Corps had final say over DAPL's route: claiming sole jurisdiction over the river and shoreline, they had inundated the land in the 1950s and 1960s, usurping Indigenous jurisdiction, kicking people out of their homes, destroying the river that nurtured them, and shrinking reservation boundaries in the process. The Army Corps never sought the consent of Missouri River Indigenous nations for these incursions, nor did Congress ever authorize them to extinguish Indigenous jurisdiction over the river.[40] Now, it was also without their consent that the Army Corps sought to route the Dakota Access Pipeline through their homelands.

"We are not stupid people. We are not ignorant people," Young chided the DAPL spokespeople. "Do not underestimate the people of Standing Rock. We know what's going on, and we know what belongs to us, and we know what we have to keep for our children and our grandchildren."

This was a history she had lived through, and it was an intergenerational struggle her children had inherited. In 1974, Phyllis Young and Standing Rock council representatives, including David Archambault Sr. (David Archambault II's father), organized the first International Indian Treaty Council at Standing Rock (detailed in chapter 6). Standing Rock gave AIM the mandate to pursue, at the United Nations, all legal means available to enforce the 1868 Treaty. The historic meeting brought together 5,000 people from ninety-seven Indigenous nations from around the world, and it was the beginning of a movement that culminated in a touchstone document on Indigenous rights: the 2007 UN Declaration on the Rights of Indigenous Peoples. Unlike other federally recognized IRA governments at the time, Standing Rock had maintained amiable relations with treaty councils, grassroots movements, and even militants such as AIM. On occassions when, as in Lower Brule in 2014, the antagonisms between these bodies turned destructive or violent, the Standing Rock's capacity to bridge these divides set it apart from other IRA governments. This history was decisive in the creation of the #NoDAPL movement, which began with the coalescence of tribal councils and Indigenous grassroots movements.

"It's nothing for you to come and say, 'We want to do this [build a pipeline]. We want to be friends with you,'" Young said to DAPL. To her, naming a pipeline, Dakota Access, and a state, North Dakota, after the very people they intended to swindle, and about whom they knew nothing, was an insult. "North Dakota?" she asked. "Miye ma Dakota! I am Dakota! Dakota means 'friend' and 'ally.'" By trespassing, the pipeline company and the state didn't behave as "friends" or "allies." Quite the opposite.

"This is Dakota territory. This is treaty territory. This is where you agreed not to come into my territory," she continued. It was a reminder that treaties are not an "Indian problem"; they are everyone's problem. Signed between settler government and Indigenous nations, they are also the responsibility of non-Natives: an even older document, the US Constitution, regards treaties as "the supreme law of the land."

If DAPL didn't respect Standing Rock's sovereignty or the Oceti Sakowin's ancestral and treaty territory, then, Young warned, "We will put our best warriors in the front. We are the vanguard. We are Hunkpapa Lakota. That means the 'horn of the buffalo.' That's who we are. We are the protectors of our nation, of Oceti Sakowin, the Seven Council Fires. *Know who we are.*" She left them with this final message: "We understand the forked tongue that our grandfathers talked about. We know about talking [out of] both sides of your mouth, smiling with one side of your face. We know all the tricks of the wasicu world [the colonizer's world]. Our young people have mastered it. I have mastered your language. I can speak eloquently in the English language. My grandmother taught me. But I also know the genetic psyche. And I also have the collective memory of the damages that have occurred to my people. And I will never submit to any pipeline to go through my homeland. Mitakuye Oyasin!"

DAPL seemed to have forgotten the lessons imparted that day. "I really wish for the Standing Rock Sioux that they had engaged in discussions way before they did," Kelcy Warren, a billionaire Texas oilman and CEO of ETP, told the *Wall Street Journal* in November 2016. "We could have changed the route. It could have been done, but it's too late."[41] Apparently, Warren didn't consider the initial 2014 meeting a "discussion," nor did he accept Standing Rock's flat-out refusal. In a 2016 statement to a federal judge, however, DAPL Vice-President Joey Mahmoud did confirm his company had received Standing Rock's message loud and clear. He admitted the company was told "to stop the project" and to avoid Oceti Sakowin territory altogether. But Mahmoud found it "an impossible request to accommodate," and he and his employees could hardly hide their contempt.[42] In March 2016, an Army Corps archeologist warned in an email: "Someone needs to tell Joey [Mahmoud] the next RACIST comment will shut down the entire project."[43] The email concerned Mahmoud and his employees' treatment of Native cultural resource workers who had identified culturally sensitive sites, such as graves and sacred sites, along the pipeline route. This wasn't a "clash of cultures" or a lack of "cultural sensitivity" towards those they saw as different; this was full-blown settler colonialism—a struggle over the land and water in which a people were fighting for their lives.

#NoDAPL was also a struggle over the meaning of land. For the Oceti Sakowin, history is the land itself: the earth cradles the bones of the ancestors. As Tasunka Witko, Crazy Horse, once said, "My land is where my dead lie buried." For others, however, the earth had to be tamed and dominated by a plow or drilled for profit. Because Native people remain barriers to capitalist development, their bodies needed to be removed—both from *beneath* and *atop* the soil—therefore eliminating their rightful relationship *with* the land.

Recognizing this, Standing Rock chose a legal route to stop the pipeline, filing a complaint in federal court against the Army Corps on July 27, 2016, the day after the Army Corps approved DAPL's route across the Missouri River and through culturally sensitive sites. In late August 2016, as pipeline construction approached Highway 1806, Standing Rock grew desperate. Legal mechanisms weren't working; more drastic measures had to be taken. Sensing what was coming, on

August 15, DAPL filed a lawsuit seeking an injunction against a number of individuals, including Chairman Archambault, from interfering with pipeline construction (a suit dismissed on September 19). Four days later, the governor, Jack Dalrymple, a legacy Yale man, declared a state of emergency, asking for assistance from the federal government, DAPL, "and any entity we can think of."[44]

"Perhaps only in North Dakota, where oil tycoons wine and dine elected officials, and where the governor, Jack Dalrymple, serves as an adviser to the Trump campaign, would state and county governments act as the armed enforcement for corporate interests," penned Archambault in a *New York Times* op-ed, days before police arrested him. "In recent weeks, the state has militarized my reservation, with road blocks and license-plate checks, low-flying aircraft and racial profiling of Indians."[45]

Standing Rock, the nation of the great Tatanka Iyotake, Sitting Bull, was facing down county, state, federal, and corporate powers. His people—some of the poorest in North America, and armed only with sage, prayer bundles, Canupas (sacred pipes), and the spirit of their ancestors—were facing down a mounting legion of police and private security backed by some of the most powerful people in the world.

On Friday, August 26, Chairman Dave Archambault II gave tribal employees the day off. He joined a prayer action at the location where DAPL crossed the highway and was arrested trying to break through a police line, along with eighteen others, during a two-day blockade of a construction site. Tribal cultural resource management experts, among them Tim Mentz Sr., an elder and citizen of Standing Rock, had identified at least twenty-seven burials west of the highway—on private land, and directly in the pipeline's path. The immense historical importance of the discoveries, in other circumstances, would have given pause to tribal historians and scholars. Mentz characterized one finding—a rock structure arranged in the shape of the Dakota constellation Iyokaptan Tanka (the "Big Dipper")—as "one of the most significant archeological finds in North Dakota in many years."[46] He notified a federal court of the discovery on Friday, September 2, and requested immediate action to protect the site. What happened the next day, Mentz and others believed, was no accident.

In the early morning hours of Saturday, September 3, 2016, blood was spilled in the struggle over hallowed ground. Caterpillar earthmovers came barreling across the prairie. A small army of attack dogs and their handlers, private security hired by DAPL, guarded the site, followed closely by a spotter helicopter whirling above; all of them were ready for a fight. It was Saturday of Labor Day weekend, a holiday celebrating the working poor who had picketed and protested (and were beaten and shot) to win an eight-hour workday. But this holiday weekend, it was unionized pipeline workers who clocked in while Indigenous people formed a picket line. The Indigenous marchers who showed up that day were *working* to protect their lands and waters—they were Land Defenders and Water Protectors.[47] Workers who cross picket lines, on the other hand, are called "scabs" because they undermine working-class solidarity. The pipeline workers met a march of Water Protectors coming down Highway 1806, which had begun with the Canupa, a pipe ceremony (as had nearly all actions), to grant strength and protection for the ancestors who might be unearthed. When the Water Protectors saw the heavy machinery that morning turning soil, it was human remains—their relatives—that were unearthed. Native people quickly formed a blockade. The Water Protectors pushed down fences, throwing themselves in front of bulldozers. A white man jumped from a truck, spraying a line of women and children with CS gas, a chemical that burns skin, eyes, and throats and can cause blindness. The handlers—the people who train animals to hunt human beings: manhunters—sicced attack dogs on the picket line. Blood dripped from the dogs' maws.

"In that moment, everything changed," recalled LaDonna BraveBull Allard, Tamakawastewin, Her Good Earth Woman. That morning *Democracy Now!*'s Amy Goodman was interviewing BraveBull Allard when the phone rang. "The bulldozers are here!" They rushed to film the scene. BraveBull Allard had been in the middle of telling the story of Nape Hota Winyan, her great-grandmother, a survivor of the Whitestone Hill Massacre, which occurred September 3, 1863; the same day 155 years later, Caterpillar earthmovers desecrated her ancestors' graves. At Whitestone Hill, women tied their babies to dogs in hopes that they would escape the soldiers. As soldiers finished off the wounded, the order came to shoot the dogs. These terrible histories, separated by time, were eerily similar.

"They took our footprint out of the ground," said BraveBull Allard of the havoc wreaked upon the land. "And who has the right to do that?" Before DAPL, Ladonna BraveBull Allard considered herself a tribal historian, but never an activist. That changed when DAPL released its plans showing the proposed pipeline crossing near the confluence of Mni Sose (the Missouri River) and Inyan Wakanagapi Wakpa (the Cannonball River), threatening the land and water. Once, shallow waters made it a place of passage, trade, and commerce. Large villages of the Mandan, Arikara, and Dakota peoples hugged the lush riverfront, and the Cheyennes and Pawnees were known to frequent the area, too. Many came to fast and hold ceremony; and because of its deep spiritual significance, the landscape was also considered neutral territory where, out of reverence, warring factions laid down their arms and camped within sight of each other without incident. Lewis and Clark misnamed it "Cannonball"—to their minds, the spherical sandstones resembled tools of war—but for the Dakota people, it was a place of life. They called it "Inyan Wakangapi Wakpa" (River that Makes the Sacred Stones). BraveBull Allard's grandfather, Tatanka Ohitika (Brave Bull) held sun dances here, continuing to maintain relations with the land-scape by putting medicine and prayer into the earth while also harvesting food from it.

It was here that water shaped earth—making sacred stones. It was also here that state institutions used water and earth to shape and destroy a people's history. After the Army Corps dredged the mouth of the Cannonball River, the swirling waters stopped creating the sacred stones. In the 1950s, the Army Corps built the Oahe Dam, flooding the sun dance grounds and the most fertile, arable land. When land and water are taken and destroyed, so too is the possibility of a livable future.

"Our people are in that water," recalled BraveBull Allard who, as a little girl, saw the floodwaters take her land. "This river holds the story of my entire life." To honor this history, "Inyan Wakanagapi Oti," the name for the Cannon Ball area, became the name for the prayer camp that BraveBull Allard helped found in April 2016. She was in Long Soldier District at a meeting on the KXL fight with Joye Braun, Jasilyn Charger, and Joseph White Eyes from Cheyenne River, and Wiyaka Eagleman from Standing Rock. Together they decided to start a #NoDAPL camp. BraveBull Allard approached Braun afterward and offered up her land.

On April 1, they attended a meeting with the Army Corps to give testimony against DAPL. The Oceti Sakowin, Lakota, Dakota, and Nakota nations arrived in caravans by horse, motorcycle, and car to show support. Indigenous youth organized a run. Elders came to offer their Canupas and prayers, and tipis went up; they called it "Sacred Stone."

BraveBull Allard remembers one day coming down to camp after work: "They were roasting deer meat on the grill. The women were cutting meat on the side to dry it. Kids were running and screaming. All of these people sitting around the fire were telling stories and what it was like to live on the river. Here was the catch: nobody was speaking English. They were all speaking Dakota. I looked at them and I thought, 'This is how we're supposed to live. This makes sense to me.' Every day I came down to the camp and saw such blessings. I saw our culture and our way of life come alive. Nobody can take that away from me."

Between the first meeting with DAPL in 2014 and the founding of Sacred Stone in 2016, Standing Rock ran grassroots awareness campaigns about Mni Wiconi and #NoDAPL. Chairman Dave Archambault II traveled tirelessly from district to district, informing the reservation that DAPL was coming. The youth organized a water campaign called "Rezpect Our Water," crafting the media message to the outside world and demonstrating this was a youth-led movement. But as construction began in April 2016, a sense of urgency grew. Given that Obama denied the permit for KXL, would he do the same for DAPL? Did he care about Native sovereignty and lives?

Archambault once had a connection to, and admiration for, President Obama. His sister, Jodi Archambault Gillette, had served as the president's special assistant for Native American affairs from 2009 to 2015. On June 13, 2014, Obama gave the opening remarks at Cannon Ball's annual Flag Day Powwow, accompanied by Archambault and his family. Obama's visit was historic. Only eight sitting US presidents had ever visited Indian reservations, the last being Bill Clinton.

During his speech, Obama focused on Native youth and played off the oft-quoted line by Sitting Bull: "Let's put our minds together to see what life we can build for our children." "Let's put our minds together to advance justice—because like every American, you deserve to be safe in your communities and treated equally under the law," Obama told a crowd of thousands of cheering Lakotas and Dakotas.

Shortly after Obama's visit, Archambault issued a statement assuring Native youth across the nation "that the President and First Lady are truly listening to them."[48] But were they really? Beginning in July 2016, thirty-eight Indigenous youth ran a grueling 2,000 mile relay from their homes in North Dakota to Washington, DC and hand-delivered to the White House and the Army Corps a petition with 160,000 signatures opposing DAPL's construction. Tariq Brownotter, a sixteen-year-old Standing Rock youth runner and organizer with Rezpect Our Water, wrote to Obama: "After your visit to Standing Rock you said you felt we were like your own children. Mr. President and First Lady we have no doubt you meant every word you said and we know you have not forgotten us."[49] There was no public response from Obama to the youth's demands to stop DAPL.

Not until November 2—months after DAPL began construction, and hundreds of arrests later— did Obama speak publicly about the pipeline, simply saying he wanted to respect Native sacred lands, was open to a possible reroute (by then the pipeline was less than a half mile from the river), and would take cues from the Army Corps of Engineers. He would "let it play out for several more weeks."[50] This stance angered both North Dakota politicians like governor Jack Dalrymple, who demanded federal intervention to crush the protests, and Indigenous people, who were being mercilessly brutalized by cops. Obama's statement came five days after live video showed a militarized police force, acting on orders from the state of North Dakota, violently evict the short-lived 1851 Treaty Camp that blockaded DAPL construction crews on Highway 1806. Cops in riot gear conducted tipi-by-tipi raids, slashing tents and tipi canvases. They dragged half-naked elders from ceremonial sweat lodges, tasered a man in the face, doused people with CS gas and tear gas, and blasted adults and youth with deafening LRAD sound cannons. The 142 arrested were marked with a number in black permanent marker on their forearm, led onto buses, and kept overnight in dog kennels. To add insult to injury, personal belongings—including ceremonial items like pipes and eagle feathers, as well as jackets and tents—confiscated by the police during the raid were returned soaked in urine.

When asked what Obama thought about this level of brutality and dehumanization, the Nobel laureate admonished "both sides," the unarmed protestors defending Indigenous land and the heavily-militarized, small army of police who ritualistically beat the Water Protectors, all the while extolling the virtues of civility: "There's an obligation for protestors to be peaceful and there's and obligation for authorities to show restraint."[51]

Three days before the 1851 Treaty Camp raid, Archambault wrote to US Attorney General Lorretta Lynch, urgently requesting a civil rights investigation into the escalating police violence. After declaring a state of emergency, Governor Dalrymple immediately went to work soliciting aid and personnel under the Emergency Management Assistance Compact. It was the largest mobilization of cops and military in the state's history since 1890, when nearly half the standing military was deployed to crush the horseless and starving Ghost Dancers in Standing Rock. Seventy-six law enforcement jurisdictions responded to Dalrymple's call and were deployed alongside the National Guard and private security firms hired by DAPL such as TigerSwan. The agencies that arrived were among the largest recipients of the Department of Defense's 1033 Program that ships surplus military equipment to law enforcement agencies nationwide. For example, between 2006 and 2015 the South Dakota Highway Patrol, which sent troopers to police Water Protectors, obtained $2 million worth of military equipment, including dozens of assault rifles and five armored vehicles. The Lake County Sheriff's Office in northwestern Indiana, which sent four deputies, had collected $1.5 million in military gear, including one hundred assault rifles and two armored trucks. (Demonstrating incompetence with this military-grade weaponry, one deputy shot himself in the foot with one of the assault rifles while deployed at the protests.)

The fifteen-ton, tank-like MRAP vehicles, which were visible at nearly all the major police actions, were also Department of Defense military surplus placed at the disposal of county sheriff's offices.[52] Because of the large influx of equipment and personnel, police saw it "as a sort of law enforcement laboratory." Tom Butler, a colonel with Montana Highway Patrol, called the multi-agency police response "enlightening and educational," encouraging police agencies in western states like Montana to attend on account that they share "all those same issues" with states like North Dakota. To Butler, those "same issues" were the large, land-based Indigenous nations protesting extractive industries.[53] In other words, these states had a lot to learn from North Dakota about how better to police their own "Indian problem."

Despite the intimidating display of force, it was the standard-issue weapons of police—chemical weapons like tear gas and pepper spray—that inflicted the most pain and violence. As Paiute anthropologist Kristen Simmons points out, because these weapons were the dominant means of crowd control, rather than military combat gear, they inflicted more injuries upon Water Protectors. While the Geneva Protocol prohibits such chemical weapons in warfare, they are, paradoxically, permitted for domestic policing. For example, on November 20, a day known as "Backwater Sunday," police sprayed Water Protectors with water laced with pepper spray from a water cannon mounted to an MRAP and shot with tear gas canisters, used as projectile weapons. Temperatures dropped below freezing. Police also used beanbag rounds, rubber bullets, and flashbang grenades to pummel the young, the old, the unarmed. More than 200 people suffered injuries—one Navajo woman lost an eye, becoming permanently disabled, and one white woman had her arm nearly blown off by an exploding crowd-control agent lobbed at her by police. Most, however, suffered from hypothermia and chemical exposure. Camp medics saved many lives that night by treating hypothermia with heat blankets and by applying an antacid mixture to chemical burns in the eyes, nose, and mouth to prevent suffocation.[54]

In a *Democracy Now!* interview, Archambault also pointed out how police humiliated Water Protectors by strip-searching them upon arrest (he was also strip-searched in late August).[55] According to Laguna Pueblo journalist Jenni Monet, strip searches were common and primarily reserved for Native people and people of color, while white inmates were often exempt. Monet also reported that some Native transgender people were separated from the general population and placed in solitary confinement as a "policy."[56] The police also targeted journalists covering the protests, arresting Amy Goodman in September 2016, Monet in January 2017, and several reporters from the media collective *Unicorn Riot.*

In his letter to Lynch, Archambault compared the policing tactics used against Water Protectors as "reminiscent of the tactics used against protesters during the civil rights movement some 50 years ago." In an 2018 Netflix interview, Obama spoke of being inspired by the courage of Black civil rights activists and freedom riders, who faced dog attacks, fire hoses, and police brutality, and "who risked everything to advance democracy."[57] Yet under his watch, private security working on behalf of DAPL unleashed attack dogs on unarmed Water Protectors who were attempting to stop bulldozers from destroying a burial ground; Morton County sheriff's deputies sprayed Water Protectors with water cannons in freezing temperatures, injuring hundreds; and police officers and private security guards brutalized hundreds of unarmed protesters. All of this violence was part of an effort to put a pipeline through Indigenous lands. In the twilight of his presidency, on December 4, 2016, the Army Corps denied the permit for DAPL to cross the Missouri River. But the move was too little, too late, and it was quickly reversed by President Trump within two weeks of taking office. (Trump also reversed KXL's presidential permit, bringing back to life the all-but-dead pipeline project.)

Even though Obama had thus far turned his back on Indigenous youth and written off the violence inflicted upon them by police, their courage, demonstrated in the thousand-mile relay across the country, had won the hearts and minds of conscientious people, regardless of political affiliation. Following the historic run, the ranks of Sacred Stone swelled. By late August there were more than 90 Indigenous nations present, as well as allies from across the globe; by November that number had grown to nearly 400. Oceti Sakowin Camp was created partially to capture the growing influx of people, who came pouring in from all corners of the globe.

The media also arrived in droves, often covering the violent clashes between Water Protectors and the police that, while frequent, also gave a distorted view of both everyday camp life and the actions themselves. From August to October, marches and rallies occurred almost daily, and without incident. At first, they started from Oceti Sakowin Camp and headed several miles north, where the pipeline crossed Highway 1806. The keeper of the White Buffalo Calf Pipe, Chief Arvol Looking Horse, frequently led these early marches, beginning with a pipe ceremony. Later on, marches branched out to target construction sites or to provide a distraction for those brave enough to chain themselves to heavy machinery.

"Men have come up to me, young men who said they were ready to lay down their lives," Archambault said to a crowd in late August. From the beginning, he had feared someone would be killed (fortunately, no one was), and his message was one of life: "But I told them, no! We do not want that! We want you to live and prosper and be good fathers and grandfathers."

Indeed, Mni Wiconi and the spirit of #NoDAPL, enacted daily in camp life, embodied a brief vision of what Native life could be.

"I think it's a rebirth of a nation," Faith Spotted Eagle said. "And I think that all of these young people here dreamed that one day they would live in a camp like this, because they heard the old people tell them stories of living along the river. They heard them talking about the campfires and the Horse Nation, and they're actually living it. They're living the dream."[58]

All one had to do was walk through camp to witness that dream. Flag Row—a half-mile procession of more than 300 Indigenous national flags that lined each side of the road—cut through the heart of camp. Starting at the north gate, where new arrivals checked in with camp security, it was the "main drag" of the "Indian city"—the tenth-largest city in North Dakota at its peak. Alcohol and drugs were strictly prohibited. Media were required to report to the media tent. No photographs of children, or of anyone, were permitted without consent. Nor was the recording of prayers or ceremonies. Facebook Hill rose beyond the main camp kitchen; a grassy knoll with the only decent cellphone reception in the entire camp, it was where people reconnected with loved ones. (Someone jokingly called it "little Brooklyn," for all the white filmmakers from Brooklyn who congregated there.)

The main camp was a fully functioning city. There was no running water, but the Cannon Ball Community Center opened its doors for showers. There was no electricity, but Prairie Knights Casino, the tribal casino two miles up the road, had Wi-Fi. And there were no flushable toilets, but Standing Rock paid for porta potties. Where physical infrastructure lacked, an infrastructure of Indigenous resistance and caretaking of relations proliferated—of living and being in community according to Indigenous values—which for the most part kept people safe and warm.

If you brought donations, you checked in at the main council fire. Supervised by Standing Rock elders, the council fire remained lit twenty-four hours a day. A steady rotation of young Native men, the firekeepers, fed logs to the fire at all hours, a humble but important duty. An Eyapaha (a town crier or emcee) handled the mic, announcing grand entries of visiting delegations, mealtimes, activities for children, missing or lost items, and guest speakers. At sunup and sundown, elders of Standing Rock and the Oceti Sakowin sang grandmother's lullabies for the children and gave words of encouragement to Water Protectors. Next to the PA system stood several large fire pits with industrial-grade cooking pots, always boiling corn and soup. The main kitchen served three hot meals a day. (At its height, there were about thirteen free camp kitchens and a half dozen medic tents.) Elders and children ate first, following a meal prayer. If there were guests (and there were often delegations from around the world), they ate first. The donations tent was well stocked with sleeping bags, blankets, tents, socks, gloves, hats, boots, and so forth. Native families frequently arrived by the carload, sometimes wearing only T-shirts and gym shorts. Everyone was fed and clothed. Everyone had a place. At camp check-in, bodies were needed to cook, dig compost holes, chop wood, take care of children, give rides to Walmart, among other tasks. Many quit their jobs, instead making it their full-time work to cook and to keep others warm and safe. After all, one ceases to be Lakota if relatives or travelers from afar are not nurtured and welcomed. Generosity, Wowacantognake, is a fundamental Lakota virtue. And it was this Indigenous generosity—so often exploited as a weakness— that held the camp together.

It was an all-ages affair in which youth played a major role, and there was a fully functioning day school. The camp was an unprecedented concentration of Indigenous knowledge keepers. Standing Rock Lakota language specialist Alayna Eagle Shield saw this. She went to every camp asking if they could share their knowledge with the children families brought with them. "From there," Eagle Shield recalled, "I was told that we need a school and a place for children to be."[59] So she founded the Mní Wič̓hóni Nakíc̓ižin Owáyawa, the Defenders of the Water School, a name chosen by the students. Education centered treaties, language, culture, and land and water defense. The curriculum of Indigenous song, dance, math, history, and science was less about indoctrinating youth to be good citizens of settler society. As Indigenous educator Sandy Grande points out, the Defenders of the Water School provided anticolonial education for liberation—how to live and be free and in good relation with others and the land and water.[60]

If one was willing and able, there were nonviolent direct action trainings hosted daily. Mark Tilsen, an Oglala poet and teacher from Pine Ridge, led most of the direct action trainings. He possessed a biting but magnetic humor that added a playfulness to otherwise-serious trainings on nonviolent resistance. Dallas Goldtooth, comedian and organizer with Indigenous Environmental Network, lightheartedly referred to Tilsen as the camp's "spirit animal" because nearly everyone knew him and turned to him for advice on actions. Almost every day, Tilsen read aloud and explained the Oceti Sakowin Camp principles to new arrivals, whose numbers typically ranged from a handful to several dozen. The rules, which applied to everyone, were scrawled on whiteboards and hand-painted signs:

> We are protectors.
> We are peaceful and prayerful.
> "Isms" have no place here.
> Here we all stand together.
> We are non-violent. We are proud to stand, no masks.
> Respect locals.
> No weapons or what could be construed as a weapon.
> Property damage does not get us closer to our goal.
> All campers must get an orientation.
> Direct action training is required for everyone taking action.
> We keep each other accountable to these principles.
> This is a ceremony—act accordingly.

Campers were also directed to the legal tent, where they wrote a phone number in permanent marker on their forearms to call in case they were arrested. Volunteer lawyers from the National Lawyers Guild and elsewhere provided free legal aid and kept in touch with arrestees.

Prayer actions generally started with the call "Kikta po! Kikta po! Wake up! Wake up!"—a voice blaring over a megaphone as the sun rose. When there was an action planned for the day, an Eyapaha rode through the camp on a bicycle, a horse, or in the back of a pickup rousing people from slumber. "You didn't come here to sleep. This ain't a vacation. We came here to stop a pipeline!"

At one action in mid October, the Two-Spirit Nation led the prayer and march. Police intercepted the caravan of cars and barred vehicle travel on a gravel road. Only foot traffic, they said. By the time the march arrived at the construction site, more than a hundred police officers with riot gear and sniper rifles, a dozen SUVs, and an armored personnel carrier had formed a police line. The Two-Spirit Nation offered tobacco and water to the land and marched toward the police line. The officers rebuffed them, telling the entire crowd to disperse over a megaphone. But where? It was surreal, but soon it became a normal experience. Unlike protest marches in the cities where there are bystanders, buildings, and plenty of media, the majority of #NoDAPL marches happened on backcountry roads where there was no CNN, just independent media like *Democracy Now!*, *Unicorn Riot*, and *Indian Country Today*. Sometimes the police outnumbered protestors—in the middle of nowhere! Because it was private property, Water Protectors couldn't go as far as the ditch on the road; the fields were off limits. And there were certainly no bathrooms or water fountains to be found in the midday heat. That day, the march was a grueling eight miles, and an elder fainted from exhaustion.

"What you're doing here is wrong," Brandon Sazue, the Crow Creek tribal chairman, approached the line of masked police as Water Protectors retreated once the action ended. "What we're doing here is right, because we are not the ones [who are] trespassing. You are trespassing for big money. But we pray for you, we pray for your children."

Sazue was a man of his people. In 2009, the IRS attempted to seize 7,100 acres of Crow Creek land—in Buffalo County, the poorest in the United States—for purported back payroll taxes. During the brutal South Dakota winter of 2009 to 2010, Sazue camped out on a portion of the land in protest of the sale. He joined the DAPL protests in August, providing tribal resources to the Crow Creek Riders, a group of youth horse riders. On October 27, Sazue was arrested during the police raid of the 1851 Treaty Camp.

While the media foregrounded images of the camp's leadership, often donning headdresses, and frequently men, it was common for Two-Spirited people and women to hold leadership roles in all aspects of camp life—from sitting on the general camp council (composed of elders and traditional leadership), to leading direct actions. Candi Brings Plenty, an Oglala trans and queer healthcare specialist, was the leader of Two-Spirit Nation at Oceti Sakowin camp. For Brings Plenty, "Two-Spirit" is "an umbrella term for Indigenous people who identify as LGBTQAI+." Colonization imposed a gender binary that largely destroyed historically plural Indigenous gender formations and fluid Indigenous sexualities, which are much more dynamic and expansive than those of the hetero-nuclear family introduced by white Christian society. Prior to colonization, Two-Spirited people also held social and cultural significance among Indigenous societies, from performing naming ceremonies to adopting the roles and responsibilities of male-, female-, or nonbinary-gendered people. Two-Spirit Nation played a central role in camp life, and one that went far beyond merely calling out heteropatriarchy. "We have Two-Spirit folk in security, at the school, at the medics, at the kitchen, and I sit on the Council," Brings Plenty explained. In other words, Two-Spirit

Nation was represented in all aspects of everyday life at camp.[61]

The vision of an anticolonial Indigenous world coexisting with non-Indigenous people has been overshadowed by violent police crackdowns. There were important political victories, but they were short lived, too late, and not enough to stop DAPL. On November 25, 2016, the Army Corps issued an evacuation order for Oceti Sakowin Camp, setting December 5 as the deadline. On December 4, the Army Corps announced that they would not grant DAPL the easement to cross the Missouri River, pending a more thorough environmental assessment. This temporary win coincided with the arrival of more than 4,000 veterans, who braved a whiteout blizzard to march to the barricade where police were mercilessly dousing Water Protectors with chemical weapons and water in freezing temperatures. Veterans also staged a forgiveness ceremony, asking Indigenous elders—Arvol Looking Horse, Faith Spotted Eagle, Phyllis Young, Paula Horne, Jon Eagle Sr., and Leonard Crow Dog—for forgiveness for the horrors the US military inflicted upon Indigenous peoples that continued with the police and military violence against unarmed protesters. It was vindication for the months of brutality. But it didn't last long.

While the punishment was collective, it proved effective at fomenting divisions. For months police blockaded Highway 1806, cutting off Standing Rock from the state of North Dakota and creating a strain between the camps and local community. Chairman Archambault asked Water Protectors to go home in December, in hopes of relieving the burden of the police checkpoints and constant influx of outsiders to the reservation. When Trump took office in January 2017, he expedited the environmental review process, giving the go-ahead for DAPL to drill under the Missouri River. With the camps largely evacuated, Standing Rock activist Chase Iron Eyes led a group called "Last Child Camp" to reclaim treaty land in response to Trump's decision. Police quickly raided the camp, which was on private land, and arrested seventy-six, including Iron Eyes.

In February, the Cannon Ball District and the Standing Rock Council passed resolutions calling for the evacuation of remaining campers at Sacred Stone and the defunct Oceti Sakowin Camp. It was a controversial move that pitted factions against each other at a critical juncture when unity was needed most.

On February 22, 2017, the Army Corps, Morton County deputies, and North Dakota Highway Patrol forcefully evicted the remaining campers at Oceti Sakowin. The same day, the Bureau of Indian Affairs raided and evicted campers at Sacred Stone—the only police action to take place on reservation land, and one that contributed to mounting divisions between grassroots organizers and Standing Rock. Those divisions came to a head at a March 10 Native Nations Rise march in Washington, DC, when Water Protectors booed Archambault during his speech and confronted him as he left the rally. The march garnered 5,000 attendees and arrived on the heels of the larger Women's March. Despite the smaller turnout, it was a unified showing of support for Standing Rock, even if some didn't agree with its political leadership. There was also mounting disillusionment with the established political order, both Democrat and Republican, for selling out the movement under Obama, and now under Trump.

"There's only one resolution," said Lewis Grassrope reflecting on the camp eviction and the march in Washington, DC. "Let us be who we are. Let us live. Let us be free."

By the time that the last Water Protector was led off the land in handcuffs, 832 had been arrested. Four Water Protectors face years in prison. Red Fawn Fallis faced charges for discharging a firearm (later dropped) when she was arrested during the October 27, 2016, Treaty Camp raid. The gun belonged to Heath Harmon, an FBI informant, who had infiltrated the camp and had a relationship with Fallis. As it has for all political struggles, the state created a new generation of political prisoners to discourage other potential movements. Fallis's family was active in AIM and had been also surveilled by the

FBI. In their day, Dakota political prisoner Leonard Peltier, who is currently serving two life sentences, represented the suppression of the Red Power movement. During the #NoDAPL movement, Obama once again turned his back on Indigenous peoples. Because he had already issued so many pardons (including, for example, Puerto Rican political prisoner Oscar López Rivera), and with so much pressure mounting from the horrific police violence against Water Protectors, many through Indian Country thought Obama would grant clemency to Peltier. But Obama denied his clemency application. And after #NoDAPL, there are even more Native political prisoners, more Leonard Peltiers: Redfawn Fallis was sentenced to 57 months in federal prison; Michael "Little Feather" Giron was sentenced to 36 months in federal prison; and Michael "Rattler" Markus and Dion Ortiz face years in federal prison.[62]

Though not without its faults, the reunification of the Oceti Sakowin reawakened an Indigenous movement intent on making, and remaking, a world premised on Indigenous values, rather than on private ownership and heteropatriarchy. While Indigenous peoples committed themselves to caretaking relations, the police had also taken up their familiar role as caretakers of violence, attempting to snuff out the fires of resistance before they burned too hot or spread too far. But the fire of the prophesied Seventh Generation had been lit, and although the Oceti Sakowin campfire was ceremonially extinguished to mark the end of one form of resistance (and the beginning of another), its warm coals went on to rekindle the fires of Water Protectors' home communities.

For Lakotas, fire is also a gateway to the past, because it is around fires that histories are shared and ceremonies held. Now, the long tradition of Indigenous resistance also includes the story of #NoDAPL. But to understand it, we have to look further into the past: to the history of the land, the water, and its people, the Oceti Sakowin.

The first pictograph of the 1880 Battiste Good (Brown Hat)
winter count documents the arrival of Pte Ska Win, the
White Buffalo Calf Woman, the most significant historical
figure of the Oceti Sakowin, who formalized the first treaty
with the human and other-than-human worlds.
Manuscript 2372: Box 12: F6, National Anthropological Archives,
Smithsonian Institution, National Anthropological Archives,
Smithsonian Museum Support Center, Suitland, Maryland.

2

ORIGINS

There are no two sides to the history of the United States and
its relationship to people who have lived here for thousands of
years. There are no two sides to that story. You have no right to
displace people, to steal their resources, and steal their lives . . .
What America has done is criminal. And they're still doing it.

—Elizabeth Cook-Lynn[1]

There is one essential reason why Indigenous peoples resist,
refuse, and contest US rule: land. In fact, US history is all
about land and the transformation of space, fundamentally
driven by territorial expansion, the elimination of Indigenous
peoples, and white settlement. From its original 1784 boundaries of the first thirteen colonies, the US rapidly expanded
westward from the Atlantic Seaboard to the Pacific coast,
annexing nearly 2 billion acres of Indigenous territory in less
than a century. Most was west of the Mississippi River.

This includes the Missouri basin, a massive circulatory
system of streams, rivers, creeks, and tributaries that empties
into its main artery, Mni Sose (the Missouri River). In Oceti
Sakowin cosmology, Mni Sose begins everywhere the water
falls from the sky to touch the earth and trickle into one of
these waterways. The river is 2,466 miles long, with a drain-
age basin encompassing a massive 529,000 square miles, a
landmass one-sixth the size of the continental United States.
The Oceti Sakowin and the Indigenous nations with which it
has shared territory, and has sometimes fought, are as much
defined by Mni Sose as they are by their own political,
cultural, and social relationship to its life-giving waters.

In this world, water is life, and so too is the buffalo nation, the Pte Oyate. Vast buffalo herds once migrated according to the river's seasonal ebbs and flows, followed by the hunting nations of the Northern Plains. At the center of this world is He Sapa, the Black Hills, *the heart of everything that is.* If He Sapa is the heart of the earth, then Mni Sose is its aorta. It is from this country that the Oceti Sakowin emerged as a nation, a people, and gained its humanity.

Much has been written about the history of the Missouri River. Yet, few histories have focused on the river's role in the colonial project. Book titles such as *Unruly River, River of Promise, River of Peril,* and *The Dark Missouri,* as well as the settler nickname for the Missouri—"Old Misery," for its frequent flooding and the property damage that ensued— depict the river as a deadly, treacherous, and inhospitable landscape.[2] Early settlers often described the Missouri basin as an irrational and violent country, plagued by endless inter-Indigenous warfare; settlers saw Indigenous peoples as equally irrational and violent. "This is a delightful country," wrote British trader Alexander Henry about the Northern Plains in 1800, "and were it not for perpetual wars, the natives might be the happiest people on earth."[3]

European and US explorers, traders, and settlers dubbed the many nations here "the Sioux," mythologizing them as the most hated, the most feared, and the most violent North American Indigenous people. Viewed as a noble warrior society, they have come to symbolize the violent hypermasculinity of the frontier and are the basis of the standard image of Indigenous culture as equestrians who lived in tipis, wore headdresses, and aimlessly wandered the land like the wild game they called kin. The University of North Dakota's racist "Fighting Sioux" mascot (retired in 2012), a disembodied head of a Native male warrior, represented such views. (Among the tribes in the state, the Standing Rock Sioux Tribe stood alone in opposing it).[4] The "Sioux warrior" myth is portrayed in the award-winning film *Dances with Wolves* (1990). Such stereo types, however, are not confined to the realm of popular culture. Prominent US historians such as Richard White portray the Sioux as a pillaging band of expansionists who violently expelled their Indigenous neighbors, and who never crossed west of the Missouri River—with no small irony— until the signing of the Declaration of Independence in 1776.[5] In fact, these attempts to classify the Sioux as imperialist newcomers—a label that more accurately describes the United States—marked the Sioux as nomadic, rootless, unsettled, and malicious, which made their removal, genocide, and coloniza-tion more palatable.[6] Oral histories and careful Indigenous record keeping, including Dakota and Lakota winter counts, show otherwise. Winter counts marked each year or winter by recording a significant event with a pictograph on hide (or sometimes on paper), accompanied by an oral recounting of the event, and constitute a meticulous record of family, indi-vidual, and larger national histories.[7] US historians, however, have misinterpreted winter counts to support their claims that the Lakotas crossed the Missouri River and subsequently "discovered" the Black Hills sometime around 1776.[8]

The Dakota, Nakota, and Lakota nations never called them-selves "Sioux"—that term derives from an abbreviation of "Nadouessioux," a French adoption of the Ojibwe word for "little snakes," denoting the Ojibwe's enemies to its west. Instead, they simply called themselves the "Oyate," the "Nation," or the "People," and sometimes the "Oyate Luta" (the Red Nation); as a political confederacy, they called themselves the "Oceti Sakowin Oyate" (the Nation of the Seven Council Fires). Their geographical span was vast. The oldest Dakota-speaking nations were located mostly in the western Great Lakes forests, glacial lakes, and rivers. They are the Mdewakantonwan (the Sacred Nation that Lives by the Water); the Sissintonwan (the Medicine Nation that Lives by the Water); the Wahpetonwan (the Nation that Lives in the Forest); and the Wahpekute (the Nation that

Shoots Among the Leaves).[9] The Nakota-speaking nations are the caretakers of the middle territory that began on the eastern banks of the Missouri River. Their names came from their location in the camp horn: Ihanktonwan (the Nation that Camps at the End) and Ihanktonwanna (the Little Nation that Camps at the End). And the youngest and largest, the Lakota-speaking nations, covered the vast expanse of the Northern Plains west of the Missouri River, called Tintonwan (the Nation of the Plains). Among the Tintonwans, there are also seven divisions: the Oglala (the Nation that Scatters Their Own); the Sicangu (the Nation of the Burnt Thighs, also known as the Brulé); the Hunkpapa (the Nation at the Head of the Circle); the Mniconjou (the Nation that Plants by the Water); Itazipco (the Nation without Bows, or the Sans Arc); the Sihasapa (the Blackfeet Nation); and the Oohenupa (the Nation of Two Kettles).[10]

Like most human societies, the origin stories of the Oceti Sakowin are as diverse as its people and the lands they continue to live with and protect. To name but a few examples, their origin histories include emergence from the earth—from the Wase (red clay); emergence from He Sapa; emergence from Bde Wakan (Spirit Lake or Mille Lacs); descent from the Wicahpi Oyate (the Star Nation); descent from the Pte Oyate (the Buffalo Nation); and westward and southern migrations from the Atlantic Seaboard or Central America. None of these origin stories are more or less true than others. What they have in common, however, is their collective significance in defining both a historical experience within a specific geography, and the moral universe of how one relates to others and the land. The origin stories contradict settler narratives that describe the Oceti Sakowin as "late arrivals" west of the Missouri River, at best; or as expansionists, at worst—driven, like their US counterpart, by purely economic motives to control river trade by violently displacing other Indigenous nations.

In the absence of written law, according to Lakota author Luther Standing Bear, "a great tribal consciousness" reigned at

the individual level in Oceti Sakowin societies. No human institution employed force or violence to compel behavior. Social
conduct was based on mutual solidarity and kinship, in what
Standing Bear calls Woucage, "our way of doing things." The
ultimate punishment for breaking group solidarity was exile,
which "meant to lose identity or die." An individual's responsibility was first and foremost to ensure the survival of the collective. Decisions—concerning anything from hunting to travel to
warfare—were made at the community level in the open council, a decentralized political authority that frequently rotated
leadership, affording equal say, that is, to separate societies of
men and of women and, in some cases, places of honor to Wintke
societies, those who did not conform to the binary gender roles.
An Oyate Okizu, or the assembly of the entire Oceti Sakowin,
was called only for matters of great importance such as sun
dances, or, in the late nineteenth century, the negotiation of treaties and repulsion of US invasion. In contrast to their own
customary laws, Lakotas created the word Woope Wasicu to
describe the white man's law. Woope Wasicu described "the
cruel equipment" of law—from armed soldiers and cops, to
guns, cannons, balls and chains, and prisons. According to
Luther Standing Bear, this kind of law "designated not order but
force and disorder."[11] Next to the maintenance of good relations
within the nation, an individual's second duty was the protection of communal territory. In the east, the vast wild rice patties
and seasonal farms that grew corn, beans, and squash demar-
cated Dakota territory. In the west, Lakota territory extended as
far as the buffalo herds that traveled in the fertile Powder River
country. For Dakotas, Lakotas, and Nakotas, territory was
defined as any place where they cultivated relations with plant
and animal life; this often overlaid, and was sometimes in
conflict, with other Indigenous nations.

For example, the Lakotas were by no means the only
Indigenous nation with connections to the Black Hills. When
different peoples combined through alliance (whether through

the formation of kinship relations, or purely for survival), they often incorporated aspects of one another's histories. Among the more than fifty Indigenous nations who possessed similar, often overlapping, relationships and claims to the Black Hills were the Arikara, Osage, Shoshone, Assiniboine, Gros Ventre, Pawnee, Mandan, Hidatsa, Kiowa, Ponca, Crow, Omaha, Winnebago, Cheyenne, Arapaho, and Blackfeet.[12]

Like the countries that constitute the United Nations, the political authority of the Oceti Sakowin didn't prevent them from sometimes warring with other Indigenous nations. Luther Standing Bear, commenting on Lakota warfare in 1931, admits as much. He notes how the United States criminalized the assertion of Indigenous political authority to make war and defend territory. "We kept our lands to ourselves," he writes, "by making all other tribes stay away from us." When whites began to fear the Oceti Sakowin's political power, Standing Bear observed, "they called us Sioux."[13] In settler vernacular, "Sioux" became equivalent to "criminal" and was used to justify invasion and endless war. But, as Indigenous scholars and intellectuals have contended for the last two centuries, war, diplomacy, and sovereignty are just a few of the Oceti Sakowin's many characteristics. Nonetheless, "Sioux" warfare, diplomacy, and sovereignty dominate settler histories of nineteenth-century Indigenous life on the Missouri River and in the Northern Plains. This is not because Indigenous nations are inherently militaristic, but because they had come to know the United States—which the Lakotas called "Milahanskan" (the nation of the long knives)—best through its army.

The first Indigenous–US interactions on the Missouri River were military encounters. In 1803 President Thomas Jefferson finalized the Louisiana Purchase from the French Republic: an annexation of 827 million acres. Louisiana Territory encompassed the entire Missouri River basin and more than doubled the territory of the fledgling United States. Shortly thereafter, Jefferson sent Meriwether Lewis and William Clark to lead a military expedition up the Missouri River, bearing arms, flags, and "gifts," to claim the "new" land and its people. Their goal was to proclaim US sovereignty over the region and its nations, and to bring the Indigenous people into trade relations with the United States. And of all the Indigenous nations, Jefferson mentioned only "the Sioux" by name. "On that nation," Jefferson ordered Lewis, "we wish most particularly to make a friendly impression, because of their immense power, and because we learn they are very desirous of being on the most friendly terms with us."[14]

The Corps of Discovery (a unit of the US Army) met several divisions of the Oceti Sakowin as they traveled upriver. After navigating the Big Bend of the Missouri (present-day Crow Creek and Lower Brule Reservations) in late September of 1804, the expedition was intercepted by a camp of Sicangus, a political subdivision of the Lakotas.[15] As per custom, the Lakotas hailed the corps with a plume of smoke that rose in the northwest, signaling the expedition had been spotted. The Lakotas sought council and some form of payment to pass through their territory, but Lewis and Clark rebuffed the Lakotas' assertion to determine who shall pass and at what cost—clearly disobeying Jefferson's instructions "to make a friendly impression."

After eight days of failing to negotiate their passage without paying a toll, Lewis and Clark resorted to violence. According to John Ordway, an expedition volunteer, Clark informed the intransigent Lakota headman, Black Buffalo, that they were sent by Thomas Jefferson, who could "have them all distroyed [sic]."[16] But, obviously surrounded and overwhelmed, Lewis and Clark's threats were worthless. Because he led the negotiations between the Corps of Discovery and the Sicangus and he refused to let the expedition pass, Lewis and Clark took Buffalo Medicine (and possibly other leaders like him) hostage and to secure their passage north. (Buffalo Medicine was later released once the expedition was free from Lakota country.) Taking

Indigenous hostages was common practice; Jefferson had earlier advised Lewis that "taking influential chiefs" or their children "would give some security to your party."[17] Reflecting on the encounter, Clark later wrote that the Lakotas were "the vilest miscreants of the savage race, and must ever remain the pirates of the Missouri." "Unless these people are reduced to order, by coercive measures, I am ready to pronounce that the citizens of the United States can never enjoy but partially the advantages which the Missouri presents," he continued. "[The Sioux] view with contempt the merchants of the Missouri, whom they never fail to plunder, when in their power."[18]

Historians have uncritically taken Lewis and Clark's testimony of that first encounter at face value: they were waylaid by a band of river pirates straight from the pages of a Robinson Crusoe fantasy novel. This was most recently retold in popular accounts like US historian Stephen Ambrose's 1997 best-selling book *Undaunted Courage* and documentarian Ken Burns's 2001 PBS film *Lewis and Clark*.[19] But in their estimation, the Lakotas didn't make much of the encounter. Lewis and Clark came and left, and the Lakotas continued living as before. This was a fairly routine engagement: merely a different flavor of whites traveling through their territory bearing flags and guns. According to Clark, even the downriver and more "peaceful" Ihanktonwan "invariably arrested the progress" of all traders traversing the river by exacting tolls and demanding more accommodating trade prices.[20] However, for the United States this first interaction held great significance, and it profoundly shaped their feelings toward a nation they viewed as criminal "pirates of the Missouri." As Oglala historian Craig Howe observes, this exchange "gave rise to storm clouds of deceit that have in some sense darkened two centuries" of Lakota–US relations.[21]

But for the historian Jeffrey Ostler, the foundation for genocide in US Indian policy had in fact been laid decades earlier, in the 1787 Northwest Ordinance.[22] The ordinance opened up the area north of the Ohio River and in the Great Lakes region for settlement, creating territories that became the states of Ohio, Indiana, Illinois, Michigan, and Wisconsin. Additionally, Article 3 stated (of the "Indians") that "in their property, rights, and liberty, *they shall never be invaded or disturbed, unless in just and lawful wars authorized by Congress.*" While, as Ostler observes, this "did not call for genocide in the first instance," it legalized genocidal war in the event that land cessions could not be achieved through "peaceful" means and Indigenous people were unwilling to submit to US authority."[23]

The 1823 Supreme Court decision *Johnson v. M'Intosh*, in which Chief Justice John Marshall spelled out the rights of the United States to Indigenous lands, also drew upon a centuries-old doctrine. Indigenous peoples, he ruled, only possessed "occupancy" rights, meaning their lands could be taken by powers that "discovered" them: the "Doctrine of Discovery." The origin of this notion was a fifteenth-century papal bull known as the "Doctrine of Christian Discovery" that distinguished Christian from non-Christian nations. The latter were regarded as little more than "savage" peoples awaiting the gift of European civilization, and according to Lenape scholar Steven Newcomb, the United States interpreted the doctrine as describing Indigenous peoples as "politically non-existent, partially or entirely."[24] Therefore, Indigenous title to the land could not be extinguished where it did not exist. Commenting on the *Johnson* decision, Onondaga international jurist Tonya Gonnella Frichner observes, "The newly formed United States needed to manufacture an American Indian political identity and concept of Indian land that would open the way for the United States in its westward colonial expansion."[25] This founding myth eventually became known as "Manifest Destiny."

In 1807, following the expedition, Jefferson appointed Clark brigadier general and Indian agent for Louisiana Territory, and he served as an Indian Affairs agent under the War Department until his death in 1838. The expedition and the annexation of land west of the Mississippi was a part of a rapid push westward, and the Louisiana Purchase was a landmark achievement. For one, it provided the means by which southern plantation capitalists could expand their "cotton kingdom" to new markets—hence the importance of imposing trade relations with the Indigenous nations. Without expansion, the plantation system was doomed to fail.[26] Jefferson envisioned an "Empire of Liberty" for the lands west of the Mississippi; one that required the expansion of Black slavery and the transformation of Indigenous land into private property for advancing a yeoman farming empire. In this way, the expansion of the plantation system coincided with Indigenous dispossession and removal.

Jefferson saw the Louisiana Territory as a partial solution to the "Indian problem"—the problem being that the "Indian tribes" still resided on lands coveted by the United States. His primary targets were the so-called "Five Civilized Tribes"— the Cherokee, Choctaw, Chickasaw, Muscogee, and Seminole—and his intention was to break up and ultimately dissolve these eastern nations. Because these nations had become slaveowners with farms and plantations, like their white neighbors, their system of land tenure resembled a claim to permanence. Thus, they had to be departed. And new lands in the West offered a new opportunity for eastern Indigenous removal. For example, Section 15 of the 1804 Louisiana Territorial Act afforded that "the President of the United States is hereby authorized to stipulate with any Indian tribes owning lands on the east side of the Mississippi, and residing thereon, for an exchange of lands, the property of the United States, on the west side of the Mississippi, in case the said tribes shall remove and settle thereon." Jefferson wanted to further concentrate eastern Indigenous nations into ever-diminishing territories. By making their wild game, land, and resources scarce, he could force them to either "incorporate" or "remove beyond the Mississippi."[27]

Dakotas, Nakotas, and Lakotas had been trading with the French and British for decades by the time the Lewis and Clark expedition arrived. By the early 1800s, the fur trade had enveloped Northern Plains life (the Europeans also brought the Bible, the gun, and disease), and the Lakotas had a vested interest in maintaining a foothold in the river trade; they certainly didn't consent to the US claim over the land and waterway.[28] But the Lakotas never saw themselves as owning the river; on the contrary, it was to the river that they belonged. The many centuries they spent living in relationship to the land and water reinforced this understanding. And by 1804 they also belonged to the river trade, both economically and politically, making the river a different source of their livelihood and survival.

Early settlers and traders heavily relied on Indigenous labor and patronage for trapping and hunting, while Indigenous societies in turn relied on trade goods such as cloth, guns, ammunition, knives, iron cooking utensils, and food items.[29] From the early colonial times through the end of the nineteenth century, the fur trade was dominated by rival trading firms (and rival European colonizers), who encouraged sporadic inter-Indigenous trade wars. From 1806 to 1835, US Indian policy introduced a factory system of trade houses to curb the criminal behavior of these white traders, but the policy had little effect, because the US government and traders themselves participated in the same criminal enterprise of trespass and theft.[30] All of these companies were in the business of trading beaver pelts, to be sold on the European and US markets; however, by the 1830s beaver populations had been all but exterminated.

Historians and archeologists largely view Indigenous peoples as responsible for the decline of fur-bearing animals in the Northern Plains, and the adoption of horse culture increased the ability of Indigenous peoples to hunt buffalo.[31] But their capabilities never compared to the killing efficiency of white trappers and hunters. For example, the killing efficiency of the "Rocky Mountain system" of trapping, dominant in the early nineteenth century, rapidly depleted fur-bearing animals. Made up of heavily armed company employees, these units knowingly trespassed into Lakota and Arikara territories, fortifying their positions and trade routes as they advanced.[32] According to Indigenous custom, no one was barred from hunting for subsistence and survival. But they did place restrictions on whites who hunted for profit; thus, these highly romanticized frontiersmen were in fact little more than poachers. As beaver populations declined and demand for their pelts decreased, buffalo robes were quick to fill their place. Yet when US companies began to bypass Indigenous peoples and dominate the trade, buffalo herds, like the beaver, were all but exterminated, from the 1870s to the 1880s. This expropriation went hand in hand with military-sponsored extermination campaigns, which began in 1865.[33] Taking only the hides, white hunters not only left buffalo carcasses to rot on the plains, but also poisoned them with strychnine to kill off coyotes, wolves, and other scavengers—and sometimes starving Native people.[34] Estimates place the precontact North American buffalo population at 25 to 30 million. It took settlers nearly a century to exterminate the herds in the east, forcing the survivors of the holocaust, much like their human kin, west of the Mississippi River. Annihilating the remaining 10 to 15 million in the Great Plains took just two decades.[35]

These were acts of genocide. For genocide encompasses much more than merely acts committed during war, as most US historians believe. The 1948 UN Convention on the Prevention and Punishment of the Crime of Genocide defines the intent of genocide as "to destroy, in whole or in part, a national, ethnical, racial or religious group." Examples include, but are not limited to, murder, torture, or the deliberate deprivation of resources needed for physical survival, like clean water, food (e.g., buffalo), clothing, shelter or medical services. This definition also includes actions targeting women specifically, like involuntary sterilization, forced abortion, prohibition of marriage, and long-term separation of men and women, all of which threaten the ability to produce future generations. (Another tactic is the forcible transfer of children.) United States policy has subjected Indigenous peoples to all of these genocidal acts. Some of which are historical, others are ongoing. "Settler colonialism is inherently genocidal in terms of the genocide convention," writes historian Roxanne Dunbar-Ortiz.[36] Although the genocide convention is not retroactive (it only became applicable in the United States in 1988, the year the US Senate ratified it), it is a useful lens for studying Indigenous history.

The fur trading forts were rampant with sexual violence. White traders, low-level laborers, and soldiers often stopped by for a drunken "frolic," which involved demanding the sexual services of Indigenous women's bodies—with or without their consent. Access to whiskey, treaty annuities, and trade goods sometimes came with the expectation that Indigenous men should forfeit their daughters', sisters', and wives' bodies to white men (as if Indigenous women's bodies were theirs to give), and soldiers also frequently raped Indigenous women whom they had taken prisoner. "To celebrate victory, troopers often rounded up the prettiest girls to be passed around among the officers, leaving the enlisted men with the less attractive, older women," wrote Sicangu scholar Virginia Driving Hawk Sneve in her account, based on family oral histories of the well-known abuses against Lakota women at Fort Platte (in operation from 1840 to 1846).[37] Many Indigenous activists today have identified "man camps," the transient all-men communities of oil and gas workers, as hubs for the exploitation of Indigenous women through trafficking and sex work.[38] In some ways, trading forts were the first man camps—the vanguards of capital that extracted wealth not only from the land, but also through the conquest of Indigenous women's bodies. Later, these trade forts also became border towns, the white-dominated settlements that today ring Indigenous reservations.

The fur trade also violently transformed gender relations. As Driving Hawk Sneve recounts, Lakota society didn't adhere to monogamous sexual values, possessed nothing on par with the puritanical Christian views of sexual conduct or marriage, and considered property in the home to be owned by the women.[39] But Lakota women who married white traders were placed under the protection and control of a patriarch (a practice known as "coverture"). Descending from a society where women owned all the property in the home, losing control of their property, their bodies, and their children, and being placed under the dominion of a white patriarch was a harrowing, alien experience.[40] Maybe this should come as no surprise. In white society women and children held little or no political authority and were little more than domestic servants. Diplomacy, trade, and war—the public sphere—were the sole privilege of men. This included the sale and trade of hides at European or US forts along the Missouri River, unlike the Indigenous systems they had replaced, in which trade, exchange, and the sharing of material wealth was intended to strengthen kinship relations, rather than a market economy and private ownership. During the fur trade, Indigenous women labored to prepare the buffalo hides, but they didn't "own" the hides sold to whites because the hunting and sale of those hides was a male-dominated business. And white traders often owned or "married" multiple Indigenous women to increase their access to the women's relatives—and their trade markets—or to sell her off to others. In this sense, the subordination of Indigenous women was lucrative for a trader and increased his social standing.[41]

One of these men was the French Canadian trader Toussaint Charbonneau, who is famous for joining Lewis and Clark in November 1804, when the expedition camped among the Mandans at Fort Mandan. He offered up his services and those of his "wife," a Shoshone woman by the name of Sacagawea, as interlocutors and interpreters for Indigenous peoples they would encounter upriver. Although Sacagawea has surpassed Charbonneau in fame for her aid to the expedition, little is known about her other than her services to white men. Captured by Hidatsas at the age of thirteen, Sacagawea was one of many women Charbonneau purchased throughout his life.[42] Although she bore him children, Sacagawea was little more than chattel to Charbonneau—a piece of property he sometimes resented, and at others physically abused.[43] And it wasn't only Sacagawea whom he subjected to violence. In May 1795, while working for the Montreal-based North West Company, Charbonneau was sent to pick up supplies at a trading post near Lake Manitou. According to the journal of John Macdonell, a North West Company clerk, an elder Ojibwe woman caught Charbonneau "in the act of committing Rape upon her Daughter." Furious, the woman stabbed Charbonneau with a canoe awl, "a fate he highly deserved for his brutality."[44]

Like Charbonneau, white traders, explorers, soldiers, and settlers believed they possessed the right to trespass freely across Indigenous territory, and they also believed they possessed unrestricted access to Indigenous women's bodies and their children. Muscogee jurist Sarah Deer argues that rape "can be employed as a metaphor for the entire concept of colonialism" because it is not only experienced individually but is also part of an ongoing structure of domination—one with a beginning, but no end.[45] More so than Indigenous men, the subordination of Indigenous women was about realizing profits in the fur trade. Violence against Native women undermined their customary political authority and used their bodies to create profit. As noted above, unlike their white counterparts, whose bodies were used for sexual reproduction, Indigenous women's bodies increased white traders' access to new markets through their kin—and by extension, land, capital, and political and economic influence. Thus, while Indigenous women did bear children for white men, their main use was for securing the future of white settlement. As Athabascan scholar Dian Million puts it, "Gender violence marks . . . the evisceration of Indigenous nations."[46] White traders and trappers appropriated Indigenous women's bodies as much as they had appropriated the wealth of the land by harvesting and selling the skins of animals. The two practices went hand in hand.

But this was only one component of settler society's attack on Indigenous women's political authority. With women already shut out of the fur trade, the treaties, which barred Indigenous women from participation in this specific realm of diplomacy, offered an externally imposed means to recognize Indigenous men's political authority.[47] From 1805 to 1873, the United States made thirty-five treaties and agreements with various political divisions of the Oceti Sakowin—or, as they became known in treaty parlance, "the Sioux Nation of Indians." Not one woman was allowed to "touch-the-pen," place an "x-mark," or formally consent to any land cessions, peace agreements, or political relationships with the United States.[48] By the time the Oceti Sakowin had been forcefully confined to reservations in the 1890s, Indigenous women had been completely confined to the domestic sphere, while Indigenous men occupied the primary roles in the reservation political economy, including as reservation police, political leaders, and traders.[49] Gender divisions were sometimes enforced by military rule, and the boarding school system, which was controlled by the military like the reservations, further entrenched these divisions, ripping children from their families and educating young girls and boys on their proper places in a "civilized Christian society": homemaking for the girls, and wage labor for the boys.[50] Finally, in 1924—after Indigenous peoples had achieved a relative degree of "civilization"—the United States granted them citizenship, annexing both Indigenous lands and lives into the US nation-state. It was not only within the home that Indigenous women's political authority been domesticated, but also in the settler nation as a whole.

This upheaval of gender relations significantly undermined the political traditions of the Oceti Sakowin. After all, it was a woman who formalized the first compact—or treaty—with the human and other-than-human world. Pte Ska Win, White Buffalo Calf Woman—the most significant historical figure in Oceti Sakowin history—established not only the basis of customary and ceremonial laws of humans, but also how humans would exist in correct relations to the Pte Oyate and the nonhuman world. In his earliest entry on his winter count, the Sicangu historian Brown Hat depicts White Buffalo Calf Woman as a white buffalo arriving in the center of a camp circle in the first decade of the tenth century. Above her are the Calf Pipe, a yucca plant, and a cornstalk. To the right, in English, Brown Hat lists the various animal nations the White Buffalo Calf Woman brought into formal relations with the Oceti Sakowin: elk, deer, antelope, buffalo, beaver, and wolves. Corn kernels fall from her udders into water, making the connection between humans, plants, animals, the earth, and water.[51] Therefore, no one had the right to cede these rela tions to the land, water, plants, and animals—because those relations were grounded in the first compact, the first treaty with Pte Ska Win. (This is why Arvol Looking Horse, the nineteenth-generation keeper of this Calf Pipe, led the prayer marches at #NoDAPL to honor those original instruction and the Oceti Sakowin's first commitments.)

To gain access to Indigenous lands, white men had used Indigenous men to break communal land practices and under-mine Indigenous women's political authority. As a result, Indigenous women are largely absent from early historical narratives.[52] Yet their power posed an obstacle to US annexa-tion of Indigenous lands.[53] It should come as no surprise that #NoDAPL was led primarily by Indigenous women, from youth leaders, such as Bobbi Jean Three Legs, Zaysha Grinnell,

Tokata Iron Eyes, and Jasilyn Charger; to women like LaDonna BraveBull Allard, Phyllis Young, and Faith Spotted Eagle.

Zaysha Grinnell, a fifteen-year-old citizen of the Mandan Hidatsa Arikara Nation, the descendants of Sacagawea, successfully petitioned her tribal council in March 2016 to oppose DAPL. She described the scene faced by her nation during the oil boom as similar to the one confronted by her ancestors during the fur trade, two centuries ago:

> When these oil companies come in, they bring in the men . . . These men bring with them the man camps, and with that comes violence and sex trafficking. Indigenous women and girls near the camps are really affected by this and we are not going to put up with it. Making more girls into leaders, because we witness it firsthand, is so important.[54]

As the first entry of capitalism in the Upper Missouri, the fur trade, spreading through existing Indigenous networks, brought with it apocalypse in the form of smallpox. By the time Lewis and Clark arrived, the European disease had already devastated the Missouri River Indigenous peoples several times, most likely being introduced by French and British traders. The advent of steamboats greatly increased the spread of smallpox. In 1824 Congress authorized the Army Corps of Engineers, a construction branch of the military, to regulate the navigation of rivers and harbors. By 1838 Congress had assigned the Army Corps to pull snags and clear the river for steamboat traffic coming from St. Louis. The federal government assumed its authority over navigable waterways under the Constitution's commerce clause—the same clause that also regulated trade with Indigenous nations. Indian affairs, under the supervision of the War Department, was tasked with the creation and management of federally subsidized trading posts to undercut British, Spanish, and French trade and bolster US influence over Indigenous nations.[55] The increase in steamboat traffic intensified the fur trade; and the fur trade in turn intensified commerce and, therefore, US authority over the river. As R. G. Robertson points out, the fur trade "was the primary means by which smallpox reached the Indians in the interior."[56] In other words, the spread of smallpox and other diseases coincided with an intensification of colonial invasion.

Steamships transporting treaty annuities, ammunition, Indian agents, traders and soldiers to Missouri River forts and trading posts also brought disease and death. The consequences of their passage brought pure horror to Indigenous nations. In the summer of 1837, an American Fur Company steamboat, the *St. Peters*, traveled from St. Louis transporting trade goods and Indigenous treaty annuities; it was, in turn, to collect Indigenous-harvested buffalo hides. It also knowingly carried, in its human cargo, the smallpox virus.

At Fort Clark, where the Mandans lived, along the Missouri River, the deadly virus arrived on June 19, 1837, via the *St. Peters*. As early as April, the crew had seen signs of the disease among themselves, but they nevertheless unloaded treaty annuities and loaded buffalo robes onto the ship that day. Smallpox, too, was unloaded, as the infected crew embarked on a drunken "frolic" with the Mandans. Within twenty-five days, the Mandans showed the first signs of infections. The only ones spared were elders who had built up an immunity, and who were already scarred from previous outbreaks. Children and adults writhed and stung from intense fevers. Putrid, hideous sores filled with pus, scarring them for life—if they survived. Francis A. Chardon, a fur trader at the fort, stopped counting the dead "as they die so fast it is impossible." To end the suffering, parents killed their children; friends, relatives, and lovers killed each other; and some committed suicide. The smell of decaying corpses was discernable from miles away.[57]

Many have speculated that Indigenous peoples were incapable of understanding infection and the spread of disease. What is clear from Chardon's journals is that Indigenous peoples knew the source of their affliction—the fur trade and the trading forts—and sought retribution against the traders and the fur trade itself. "We are badly situated," wrote Chardon, "as we are threatened to be Murdered by the Indians every instant." Indigenous peoples knew traders and explorers sometimes carried smallpox or cowpox with them in vials for inoculations. George Catlin, a white painter and traveler of the American West, recounted a story he heard among the Pawnees that a trader threatened unleashing smallpox upon them if they didn't submit to his will: "He would let the smallpox out of a bottle and destroy the whole [lot] of them."[58] "The Sioux had it in contemplation . . . to murder us in the spring," Lewis wrote while he and Clark wintered with the Mandans in 1805 and 1805, "but were prevented from making the attack, by our threatening to spread the *smallpox*, with all its horrors among them."[59]

Accurate Indigenous population data does not exist, but some studies suggest that Indigenous nations with closer contact to the whites had increased exposure to diseases. These nations, such as the Mandans at Fort Clark, had positioned themselves as brokers in the fur trade, often settling near trading forts or allowing trade posts in or near their villages. Diseases were quick to spread in these intimate river communities, making quarantine or flight nearly impossible. Some calculations estimate that from 1780 to 1877, Indigenous river nations lost around 80 percent of their populations, with the Mandan, Caddo, Wichita, and Pawnee experiencing almost 90 percent population loss. Buffalo-hunting nations on the Northern Plains from 1780 to 1877 experienced a 40 percent population decline overall; among them, this figure approached 80 percent for the Assiniboine, Atsina, and Comanche. While smallpox epidemics arrived again and again to the Plains nations—1778, 1781, 1801—the 1837 outbreak was the most devastating for those along the Missouri River, nearly wiping out the Mandans and forcing them to join together with the Hidatsas and Arikaras.

(The Lakotas and Dakotas, however, largely escaped the outbreak because of prior inoculation and by avoiding trading posts after learning of the epidemic.)[60] In 1849 cholera killed about one-fourth of the Pawnees, along with many Lakotas. The last major smallpox epidemic in the region occurred in 1871, killing thousands of Assiniboines and Blackfeet.[61]

Turning the river into profit required little capital investment in Indigenous lives, as long as the trade goods and annuities continued to flow. But it did require the continual extraction of furs. The employment of Indigenous societies as trappers, hunters, and patrons was the first effort at turning the river into a source of wealth. But the Missouri River wasn't a "middle ground" scenario where all parties were equals, even when the British and French dominated trade. A popular convention in US history, the "middle ground" thesis posits that in some cases, such as the fur trade, Indigenous and white people found common ground in forms of trade where one group was not allowed to assert too much control or influence over the other.[62] Lost in these imaginary and ahistorical situations, however, is the simple fact that early European and US colonization, in all its forms, was fundamentally extractive and imperial. Lakotas and Dakotas *did* actively compete with other Indigenous nations for control over the river trade, but such conflict never approached the holocaust brought by disease and the calculated violence of the US military and traders.

The Oceti Sakowin had good reason to despise the imposition of white traders and US forts. As the fur trade peaked, the Oceti Sakowin east and west of the Missouri began to wage defensive wars to expel the invaders whom they rightfully blamed for the disappearing buffalo and other animal kin. Foremost among their grievances was the devastation inflicted by white traders, emigrants traversing the land, and the increasing US military presence. Each was a foreboding sign of white encroachment. Instead of justice, however, what they got was a "peace" through the permanence of war.

Rochelle Bullhead wears a penny dress during the October
27, 2016 police raid on the 1851 Treaty Camp.
Photo by Linsey Norton.

3

WAR

The whole world is coming.
A Nation is coming,
A Nation is coming.
The Eagle has brought the message to the Nation . . .
Over the whole earth they are coming.
The Buffalo are coming,
The Buffalo are coming.

—"Maka Sitomaniya Olowan,"
Lakota Ghost Dance Song, 1890[1]

The history of the United States is a history of settler colonialism—the specific form of colonialism whereby an imperial power seizes Native territory, eliminates the original people by force, and resettles the land with a foreign, invading population. Unlike other forms of colonialism in which the colonizers rule from afar and sometimes leave, settler colonialism attempts to permanently and completely replace Natives with a settler population. The process is never complete, and the colonial state's methods for gaining access to new territories change over time, evolving from a program of outright extermination to one of making Indigenous peoples "racial minorities" and "domestic dependent nations" within their own lands, and of sacrificing Indigenous lands for resource extraction. But even if elimination strategies evolve to appear more humane or ethical, "the question of genocide," writes anthropologist Patrick Wolfe, "is never far from discussions of settler colonialism."[2]

Indigenous elimination, in all its orientations, is *the* organizing principle of settler society. Unlike the European

Holocaust, which had a beginning and an end, and targeted humans alone, Indigenous elimination, as a practice and formal policy, continues today, entailing the wholesale destruction of nonhuman relations. Today's state violence and surveillance against Water Protectors is a continuation of the Indian Wars of the nineteenth century. It is no coincidence that the law enforcement agency that led the siege against the #NoDAPL camps in order to protect DAPL construction, the Morton County Sheriff's Department, inherited the legacy of the infamous Indian fighter and Seventh Cavalry general George Armstrong Custer. Present-day Mandan, North Dakota, a white-dominated border town to Standing Rock and the county seat of Morton County, is seven miles north of Fort Abraham Lincoln, where Custer was stationed to secure the passage of the Northern Pacific Railroad across the Missouri River and through Oceti Sakowin territory.

Bloody wars of conquest defined the period following the United States' assertion of control over the river trade, lasting for nearly half of the nineteenth century. Its goal was to control the river, and then the entire Missouri River basin (especially the fertile buffalo hunting grounds in the western Powder River country). Following the Civil War, the Oceti Sakowin's relationship with the Missouri River was increasingly defined by avoidance, because the river had since been enflamed by invasion: violence, death, and disease. The escalation of the river trade brought unwanted changes, such as an increased US presence through the construction of military and trade forts, and an intensifying assault on rapidly thinning buffalo herds.

Initially, Indigenous subsistence hunting, gathering, and agriculture had provided the means to effectively resist settler encroachment. But by separating Indigenous producers from the land and attempting to make them dependent on treaty annuities or cash economies, the colonizers waged total war on Indigenous life. The Oceti Sakowin were not the first to confront US total war. Haudenosaunees, for instance, call every US commander in chief "town destroyer"—a title bestowed on the first US president, George Washington, who ordered a bloody, punitive campaign that burned forty Haudenosaunee towns in New York during the Revolutionary War. Haudenosaunee cornfields were also burned to thwart the reclamation of the land and impose starvation. To consummate possession by mixing blood and soil, the troops responsible for razing the Haudenosaunee towns were afterward rewarded with title to Indigenous lands.[3]

In a very real sense, the founding of the United States was a declaration of war against Indigenous peoples. But to formally declare war would have been to acknowledge Indigenous peoples' status among the "civilized" or "Christian" nations. On the other hand, an undeclared war was a "savage war," in which the rules of "civilized war" were suspended. US army historian Andrew Birtle reports that the military academy at West Point studies US Indian Wars only in its course on the law, and in "the same manner as it did the treatment of guerrillas and actively hostile civilian populations in civilized warfare." The implication was "that soldiers were free to employ the harshest measures necessary to subdue them."[4]

In other words, the US Indian Wars developed the tactics and strategies that would inform US counterinsurgency operations abroad. As Chickasaw scholar Jodi Byrd argues, "the United States propagates empire not through frontiers but through the production of a paradigmatic Indianness."[5] As the US military became professionalized following the Civil War, these lessons were passed down informally, though most never became written doctrine. And as anthropologist Laleh Khalili argues, they "became the necessary, if unwritten, manual for subsequent overseas asymmetric warfare, in the Philippines, the Caribbean, and Latin America."[6] These included techniques like the use of native scouts, the establishment of reservations to control and monitor native fighters and civilians, and attacks on villages to undermine native economies.

But because Indigenous peoples are not seen as full sovereigns under US or international law, Indigenous resistance to colonialism—even if for self-defense—is considered criminal, much as it was in places throughout the Americas, Africa, and more recently in Palestine.[7] Libraries have been filled with volumes written by armchair historians, colonial apologists, and scholars of all stripes—too many to name here—on Northern Plains Indigenous warfare. Very few researchers, however, have actually questioned the premises of waging just wars on the part of Indigenous nations *against US empire*. A question that many historians have entertained—did the Oceti Sakowin have a right to defend itself with armed force?—is not posed here. The simple truth is that Indigenous nations, like all nations, possess the right to defend themselves, and how a people choose to defend themselves cannot be placed neatly into categories of "right" and "wrong." Survival by any means necessary is an act of resistance.

It was through war and self-defense that the Oceti Sakowin made their most historic agreements with the United States: the 1851 and 1868 treaties of peace. In 1849 Congress transferred the Bureau of Indian Affairs from the Department of War to the Department of Interior, a newly created federal bureaucracy dedicated to the management of wildlife, public lands, and the conservation of natural resources. Indian affairs have remained there ever since. The shift marked a new direction in Indian policy that emphasized "peace" while explicitly promoting the "civilizing mission." "Peace and friendship" treaties had already placed the various divisions of the Oceti Sakowin exclusively "under the protection of the United States of America, and of no other nation, power, or sovereign" (in 1805, 1815 and 1825), but they never ceded large amounts of territory or drastically diminished Oceti Sakowin political authority.[8]

The Oceti Sakowiŋ possessed significant military and political power, so it is unlikely this Indigenous nation viewed treaties with the United States as acquiescing to a superior sovereign power. This began to change after decades of the fur trade and diseases exacted their toll on the Northern Plains ecology and Indigenous nations. By the time of the peace policy, thousands of Lakotas had already withdrawn west of the Missouri into the Powder River country to avoid the unfolding apocalypse brought on by the river trade. In the east traders had swindled the Dakotas out of land and treaty annuities, reducing them to starvation and creating the conditions for an Indigenous uprising. In some areas, the once-numerous buffalo nations that blackened the Missouri River valley had been all but wiped out, and elsewhere they had been totally exterminated. Infectious disease—cholera, measles, and smallpox outbreaks—arrived with the white invasion of the West, which swept through Pawnee, Crow, Cheyenne, Lakota, and Arapaho hunting grounds and into Oregon Territory.

In 1847 Brigham Young led an exodus of tens of thousands of Mormons to settle Indigenous lands in Utah, while the discovery of gold in California in 1849 and later in Montana in 1853 added to the westward white flood. In 1846 a group of Sicangus and Oglalas in Powder River country demanded payment for the damages that the increased overland travel had inflicted on the land: the depletion of game, the clearing of scarce timber, and the spreading of disease.[9] They got escalated military occupation instead. The US military found it impossible to control the waves of white settlers and mounting Indigenous indignation. The year the peace policy was declared, the United States established a fort at the confluence of the North Platte and Laramie rivers to address the problem. Fort Laramie thus became the site for them to pursue "peace" by means of increased military occupation in Powder River country. Strategically positioned at the point where the overland trail trespassed through the territory of the last remaining large buffalo herds, the fort was a symbol of increasing US presence and authority.

The vision for the military outpost came from the Upper Platte Indian agent Thomas Fitzpatrick, a leading advocate of peace by military occupation.[10] As part of his vision for peace, Fitzpatrick hoped to advance US interests by securing a wide-ranging inter-Indigenous peace treaty to definitively establish Indigenous territory, guarantee safe passage for overland travelers, and secure land cessions. The Plains nations called a mass council. For three weeks in September 1851, tens of thousands from the Arikara, Mandan, Hidatsa, Crow, Gros Ventre, Blackfeet, Assiniboine, Shoshone, Arapaho, Cheyenne, Lakota, and Dakota nations met with US treaty commissioners at Horse Creek, thirty-six miles downriver of Fort Laramie. The first Fort Laramie Treaty of 1851 was signed by all parties, ensuring the right of the United States to build wagon roads and railroads, and payment of $50,000 for fifty years for damages caused by the overland emigrations.[11] Perhaps demonstrating the commitment of the United States to this "peace" policy, the Senate limited the period of treaty annuities to ten years, with the possibility of a five-year renewal. The amendment was sent back to the Plains nations for approval, and then back to the Senate, where it was never ratified. Regardless, the United States paid the $50,000 in annuities for the next fifteen years.[12] The spirit of peace, however, was short-lived and the treaty was deeply flawed.

Six headmen of the Oceti Sakowin signed the treaty, presumably with the understanding that the emigrant depredations would cease and that the United States would live up to its commitments. The Oceti Sakowin representatives, however, protested over having to select a single "head chief" to represent all the nations in the treaty negotiations because it contradicted the decentralized political structure more familiar to them, which allowed each division to select its own representatives. This configuration offended the autonomy previously possessed by each political division. Mato Wayuhi (Conquering Bear), a Sicangu, was arbitrarily chosen by the Oceti Sakowin councils as a representative of the 1851 Fort Laramie Treaty, but he protested his appointment because of his own young age—he was fifty years old, not yet an elder—and lack of experience.[13] The selection of "treaty chiefs" to represent entire Indigenous nations was an age-old settler tactic to exert influence and concentrate leadership, while cleaving political factions. Most Indigenous leaders were more committed to diplomacy than to armed resistance, though the two strategies sometimes worked in tandem. Some wanted to give up the Powder River country and remove to reservations to start a new life. "The hostiles," as the Indian agents called them, wished to end treaty making altogether and keep their lands free of reservations and restrictions. Although the two divisions both agreed with the premises of the 1851 Treaty, the western divisions demanded that the reservation groups cease accepting annuities and remove themselves from the negative influence of the trading forts, where the annuities were distributed.[14]

In 1853 Fitzpatrick criticized the outcome of the 1851 Treaty, calling it a temporary fix to coming war. "Either an inducement must be offered to them greater than the gains of plunder, or a force must be at hand able to restrain them and check their depredations. Any compromise between the systems will only be liable to all the miseries of failure," he argued.[15] Neither was agreeable to the Oceti Sakowin. Annuities meant submission and land cessions, while an increased military presence meant violence. To the Oceti Sakowin, treaty making became more and more a zero-sum game, in which all roads led to diminishing independence and increasing relations with the United States.

Three years after the treaty signing, in August, a lame calf belonging to an emigrant Mormon wandered into a camp of near-starving Sicangus. Believing the calf was abandoned, it was killed, butchered, and almost immediately consumed. The Mormon owner called for retribution, and John L. Grattan, a young West Point graduate stationed at the nearby Fort Laramie, answered. Although Indigenous peoples at first allowed the overland emigrants to travel through and hunt freely within their territories, under US law the killing or theft of a domestic animal, such as a lame calf, was considered a property crime. Private property held more sanctity than the Indigenous treaties or lives. Grattan descended on the camp, demanding that Conquering Bear relinquish the guilty party. As the "treaty chief" of the 1851 Treaty that was committed to maintaining peace, Conquering Bear offered restitution to the Mormon and pled for a peaceful resolution. Grattan's men responded by shooting Conquering Bear. The Sicangus descended on Grattan and his soldiers, killing him and all twenty-eight of his men. Six days later, Conquering Bear died, and with him the spirit of the 1851 peace treaty. The Sicangus, quick to seek revenge, robbed a mail coach near Fort Laramie, making off with a large amount of money and killing three white men.[16]

Tensions remained high. While treaty annuities continued to arrive on time, white traders preyed on the Lakotas and Dakotas collecting their annuities at Missouri River trading posts. In the winter of 1853 to 1854, Sihasapas and Hunkpapas refused treaty annuities and began to wage war on white traders. Traders (and even contemporary historians) have mistakenly called treaty annuities "gifts." Annuities were not gifts, but contractual treaty obligations. Although their intended purpose was to guarantee peace, they were often withheld to pay trade "debts" or used to coerce "hostile" groups into submitting to a trader's will. White traders were welcomed for their seemingly endless supply of highly prized commodities such as guns and cloth, for which the Oceti Sakowin called them "Wasichun," or "people who possess a mysterious power." Now, it was clear that this power also brought evil, earning them a second name, which played on the first: "Wasicu"—the "fat taker," the settler, the colonizer, the capitalist. To be called "Wasicu" was the highest insult. It meant that a person behaved selfishly, individualistically, with no accountability, as if they had no relatives. Such behavior was normally punished by alienation or banishment. "Wasicu" became synonymous with the United States, a nation that behaved as if it had no relatives.[17]

For this reason, Little Bear, a leader of the Hunkpapa, waged a bitter campaign against the white traders on the Upper Missouri. According to American Fur Company employee Edwin Thompson Denig, in 1853 when the fur company attempted to construct a trade fort in Hunkpapa territory without their consent, Little Bear's akicitas (soldiers) "cut up the carts, killed the horses, and flogged the traders and sent them home." Little Bear first earned his status as a leader when he killed a despised white trader from the American Fur Company in the trader's own home, for which Denig assumed he sought the "destruction of all traders in the country." According to Denig, the Sihasapas and Hunkpapas under Little Bear's command

> cut off every white man they meet and pillage or destroy all property outside the forts at the Yellowstone. They declare war to the knife with the Government of the United States and all whites in the country, threaten to burn up the forts, make no buffalo robes except what they want for their own use and wish to return to their primitive mode of life.[18]

Some Missouri River Lakotas and Dakotas revolted against the fur trade and the profit motive by eschewing alcohol, boycotting the fur and river trade, and actively sabotaging the trading forts—the primary source of their affliction. These efforts, along with the return to subsistence buffalo hunting, allowed Indigenous nations to resist the encroachment of capitalism.

Later that year Indian agent Alfred J. Vaughn traveled the Missouri River, meeting with various divisions of the Oceti Sakowin to distribute annuities and gather reports on the recent hostilities against traders. When he arrived at the Sihasapas and Hunkpapas' camp, they firmly refused Vaughn's annuities. And in an encounter with the Ihanktonwannas, the headman, Red Leaf, cut open all the bags of the Indian agent's provisions, scattering the contents across the prairie. The akicitas then threw the remaining gunpowder keg in the river, shooting it until it exploded.[19] The more militant divisions among the Oceti Sakowin resented what the trading posts and the treaty annuities symbolized: nonconsensual occupation and an attack on the land. The frequency of these acts of resistance should put to rest any claims that the Oceti Sakowin had become helplessly dependent and devastatingly transformed by the fur trade, thus leading to their inevitable defeat and collapse. However, this strident refusal depended upon maintaining access to a crucial resource: the buffalo herds. Like a good relative, the Pte Oyate initially provided the means to confront invasion; however, this dependency would soon be exploited as a weakness when the military targeted the buffalo nations for extermination. An attack on the land and the buffalo was an attack on Indigenous subsistence practices and the ability to resist encroachment.

The military and traders were quick to claim victimhood following Grattan's defeat and the war on the Missouri River trade.[20] In response the War Department sent 600 soldiers under the command of General William S. Harney up the Platte River. On September 5, 1855, Harney engaged 250 Sicangus camped at Blue Water Creek. The leaders, Tukiha Maza (Iron Shell), and Wakinyan Cikala (Little Thunder), asked for peace, telling Harney their camp was peaceful and mostly made up of women and children. Harney ordered his men to raze the camp, killing eighty-six—half of them women and children. They took another seventy women and children as prisoners, holding them at Fort Laramie. According to one account, the soldiers seized an infant from her wounded mother and used the child as target practice.[21] At Fort Laramie, the officers raped the Sicangu women, who, according to the testimony of Susan Bettelyoun Bordeaux, "became the property of their captors." In a letter accompanying Bordeaux's testimony, Hunkpapa historian Josephine Waggoner writes, "There were many war babies born after Harney left Laramie."[22] That day Harney earned his Lakota name—"Woman Killer."[23]

Woman Killer intended to terrorize the Lakotas into submission, but this had the opposite effect. A young man, who would later earn the name "Tasunka Witko" (Crazy Horse), returned from a hunting trip to find his relatives' mutilated bodies scattered across the prairie. That day Crazy Horse committed his life to fighting the Woman Killer's nation. Crazy Horse's uncle Sinte Gleska (Spotted Tail) had attempted to stop the massacre. Although unarmed and surrounded by soldiers, Spotted Tail grabbed a soldier's knife and killed ten of Woman Killer's men before being taken down, wounded but not killed, by two bullets.[24] Crazy Horse and Spotted Tail came to represent two traditions of Indigenous resistance; one would follow a path of armed struggle, the other the path of diplomacy. Despite these divergences, the two remained good relatives to each other in the trying years to come, a testament to the strong bonds of kinship that held the nation together as their world was taken from them. While Crazy Horse and Spotted Tail were accomplished warriors and leaders, their highest virtue was their commitment to the defense of their human and nonhuman relations. The events of that day forever shaped their resolve for self-defense and survival; this did not always mean picking up the gun, but sometimes it did. At that moment, however, for both Crazy Horse and Spotted Tail, preserving a grounded authority in the land was the theory, and the gun was the practice. Both were necessary for the survival of human and nonhuman relations. It was from settler colonialism's nightmarish scenario of fight, flight, or accommodate that Indigenous heroes were made and immortalized—some known, and many more unknown. Heroes of Indigenous resistance didn't just make history. History made them.

While in the west the Lakotas confronted the punitive campaigns of the US peace policy, in the east the Dakotas faced increased settler encroachment. White settlements depleted nearly all the game, and the treaty annuities were meager and slow to arrive—when they arrived at all. Starvation set in. To make matters worse, Minnesota Territory organized in 1849 and began its path toward statehood, which meant the expulsion of Indigenous peoples. In 1857 Inkpaduta, a Wahpekute leader, led a retaliatory campaign against white settlers at Spirit Lake and Springfield after settlers wantonly murdered his brother and forcefully exiled the Wahpekutes from their homelands in 1856. In total the Wahpekutes killed twenty-eight settlers and sustained minimal casualties. Inkpaduta, whose body was badly scarred from the 1837 smallpox scourge, which he survived as a child, became a veteran of many major engagements with the US military and died in exile Canada in the 1880s. His attacks on settlements earned him the reputation as a frontier bogeyman. He was so hated and feared by whites that his name was never translated into English unlike his more celebrated and well-known contemporaries.[25] Nevertheless, Inkpaduta's legacy is now widely revered for his evasion of capture and death, refusal to surrender, and rejection of reservation life.

The Wahpekute's attacks were also partly in response to the Treaty of Traverse des Sioux and the Treaty of Mendota. Together these treaties, signed in 1851 by all four Dakota nations, ceded all Dakota land claims except for a narrow twenty-mile strip. There is no doubt that the Dakota leaders were coerced into making such disastrous concessions. To force signatures, treaty commissioners threatened military force and the withholding of rations. White traders got first access to any treaty moneys, which they used to pay outstanding debts allegedly accrued by the Dakotas. When the treaties went through the Senate for approval, amendments were attached that left the Dakotas without any legal title to the land, essentially making them homeless or trespassers in their own homelands.[26]

In August 1862, when Taoyateduta (He Loves His Red Nation), also known as Kangi Cistinna (Little Crow), and his warriors began to expel white settlers from their Dakota homelands, most of the Dakota communities were starving, horseless, unarmed, and living on reservations. With the outbreak of the Civil War, treaty annuities arrived late or not at all—and were sometimes intentionally withheld by traders. Andrew Myrick, a notorious white trader responsible for distributing treaty annuities and rations at the Lower Sioux Agency, put it bluntly: "So far as I'm concerned, if they are hungry, let them eat grass or dung." The Dakotas, facing the real possibility of starving to death, came to the Lower Agency, and, some stories say, killed Myrick while he was running away; according to these accounts, his body was found with grass stuffed in his mouth.[27] The criminal acts of the traders and agency officials had led to the uprising. But the United States' theft, mass killing, starvation, and punishment of all Dakotas remained "lawful."

The Dakotas waged deadly battles, killing more than 800 white settlers, traders, and soldiers. By late September most Dakotas had surrendered, ending the brief thirty seven-day war. The captured Dakotas were not treated as prisoners of war but instead faced a military tribunal created by Henry Sibley, Minnesota's first governor, and colonel of the state militia. Military officers who had just fought Dakotas were appointed to oversee the trials. By November the military tribunal tried 392 Dakotas for "murder and outrages," convicting 323 of them, 303 of whom they condemned to death. More than 2,000 Dakotas were also imprisoned at Fort Snelling in a large concentration camp, where many died. Whether or not they participated in the war mattered little; all Dakotas became targets for collective punishment. President Lincoln, though he commuted most of the Dakota death sentences, maintained an iron fist to crush Indigenous resistance—one he wielded not only against the Dakotas, but others too. In 1864 in the Southwest, a similar policy of collective punishment and removal targeted Navajo and Apache resistance, resulting in the Hwéeldi, or the Long Walk. The removal, forced march, and imprisonment at Bosque Redondo in New Mexico killed more than 2,000 Navajos.[28]

On December 26, 1862, a week before signing the Emancipation Proclamation, Lincoln ordered the hanging of the thirty-eight Dakota men at Maka To (or "Blue Earth"—present-day Mankato, Minnesota) as retribution for the 1862 US-Dakota War. The execution of the Dakota thirty-eight remains the largest mass execution in US history. Minnesota Governor Alexander Ramsey, who helped negotiate the 1851 Treaty with the Dakotas, then ordered the extermination or complete banishment of remaining Dakotas from the state. Settlers were encouraged and rewarded to take their own revenge with government-issued $25 scalp bounties, which later increased to $200. When the Civil War came to an end, very few confederate officials and soldiers were sent to prison, and only one was hanged for war crimes. After surrender, many confederates went back to holding public office. General Sibley ordered that the Dakotas were to be treated as criminals, and not as prisoners of war.[29] The aftermath of the war to maintain slavery, which cost half a million lives, was profoundly different from the aftermath of the Dakota uprising—and rarely are the two stories told side by side.

In punishment for his part in the uprising, in 1863 Minnesotan settlers murdered Little Crow, collecting $500 for his scalp and decapitated head. Little Crow's scalp, severed head, and the rest of his body were collected and put on public display by the Minnesota Historical Society until 1915, a grim trophy to remind settlers exactly how they "won" the land. Little Crow's remains were only returned to his family in 1971. Nearly a thousand Dakotas fled to Canada, and 2,500 remained at large, fleeing into Dakota Territory to join their relatives on the Missouri River. In 1863 in Minnesota, General John Pope organized "columns of vengeance" to punish and capture fugitive Dakotas.[30] Instead of recognizing their own criminality for outright land theft and state-imposed starvation, they would force Dakotas to pay with their lives. Facing scalp bounties and the harsh imprisonment of their relatives, surrender usually meant death and was simply not an option. To survive—to resist—meant to flee.

Pope sent two columns, led by brigadier generals Henry Sibley and Alfred Sully, to halt the fleeing Dakotas from crossing the Missouri River and joining their western relatives. The campaign had three goals: crush the fleeing Dakotas, secure the Missouri River for steamboat travel, and eliminate remaining Indigenous opposition to the settlement of eastern Dakota Territory. By 1863, overland travel on the Oregon Trail had greatly subsided. But the 1862 Montana gold rush drew throngs of miners and settlers who traveled overland on the Bozeman Trail, which cut through 1851 Treaty territory and up the Missouri River via steamship. Sibley's mounted cavalry headed south, then traveled north up the eastern shoreline of the Missouri, encountering little opposition. Sully commanded more than 2,000 soldiers, and the skirmishes they engaged in were minor and inflicted minimal casualties—all except for one.

On September 3, 1863, Sibley's men attacked 4,000 peaceful Dakotas and Lakotas in a summer camp after a buffalo hunt at Inyan Ska (Whitestone Hill). Standing Rock historian and Sacred Stone Camp founder LaDonna Bravebull Allard recounts the events of that day through the oral history of her ancestor Mary Big Moccasin:

> It was a time of celebration and ceremony—a time to pray for the coming year, meet relatives, arrange marriages, and make plans for winter camps. Many refugees from the 1862 uprising in Minnesota, mostly women and children, had been taken in as family. Mary's father, Oyate Tawa, was one of the 38 Dah'kotah hanged in Mankato, Minnesota, less than a year earlier, in the largest mass execution in the country's history ... As my great-great-grandmother Mary Big Moccasin told the story, the attack came the day after the big hunt, when spirits were high. The sun was setting and everyone was sharing an evening meal when Sully's soldiers surrounded the camp on Whitestone Hill. In the chaos that ensued, people tied their children to their horses and dogs and fled. Mary was 9 years old. As she ran, she was shot in the hip and went down. She laid there until morning, when a soldier found her. As he loaded her into the wagon, she heard her relatives moaning and crying on the battlefield. She was taken to a prisoner of war camp in Crow Creek where she stayed until her release in 1870.[31]

The dogs returned to camp with babies still tied to them, where they were shot by the soldiers. In all, the soldiers slaughtered more than 400 Lakotas and Dakotas, most of them women and children. They destroyed half a million pounds of dried buffalo meat and razed more than 300 lodges. Thirty-two men and 124 women were taken prisoner and transported to Fort Pierre to be shipped to Crow Creek, where the remaining survivors of the US-Dakota War were held.[32]

The massacre had a profound psychological impact on the Dakotas and Lakotas. The scorched-earth campaign against the Dakotas and the "columns of vengeance" were intended to deter a military alliance among the Oceti Sakowin; and indeed, the tactic may have worked on some. On the other hand, it also encouraged many to risk everything to repel the invaders. The success of armed resistance, in fact, would be measured not in the annihilation of the United States as an enemy nation, but in the resilience of the political alliances that formed.

Immediately following the punitive campaigns waged against the Dakotas, in November 1863 Colonel John M. Chivington and his soldiers massacred more than 200 peaceful Cheyennes at Sand Creek in Colorado Territory, taking scalps and severed genitals as souvenirs. Enraged at the growing brutality, the Cheyennes, Lakotas, Arapahos, and some Dakotas formed a political alliance under the leadership of Mahpiya Luta (Red Cloud). Believing the United States had violated the spirit of the 1851 Fort Laramie Treaty with the construction of the Bozeman Trail, the historic alliance vowed to expel them from the buffalo hunting grounds.[33] The alliance successfully defeated the US military in hit-and-run battles from 1866 to 1868. In December 1866, most famously, Crazy Horse, a rising military leader, drew one hundred soldiers under the command of Colonel William J. Fetterman from Fort Kearney into a trap, killing Fetterman and all his men. The fort had been established along the Bozeman Trail to protect white miners heading to the Montana goldmines.[34] Facing an undefeatable, highly mobile guerrilla force, in 1868 the United States once again sought peace.

In the summer of 1868, a mass council was called at Mato Paha (Bear Butte) to discuss a treaty of peace, and Red Cloud was selected to lead any negotiations with the United States. Since 1857 most of the Oceti Sakowin had been gathering annually at Mato Paha, at the northeast fringes of the Black Hills, to discuss the peace treaties and mounting resistance. Some historians and scholars have challenged the idea that the "Sioux Nation," or the Oceti Sakowin, ever existed, or that such gatherings took place in the Black Hills prior to US invasion. What is known is that all seven political divisions met at these annual summer councils, and that all were represented in the most famous battles. But it is true the Oceti Sakowin had not gathered in quite this way since 1857, when they were joined by allied nations such as the Arapaho and Cheyenne in considering "taking the fight to the *wasicu*" (in other words, to US imperialism)—by marching all the way down to St. Louis and wiping out every white settlement—as Sicangu historian Edward Valandra has asserted.[35]

Previously, the Oceti Sakowin more often gathered at Mato Paha for peace, including for the Wiwang Wacipi, the sun dance. The Oceti Sakowin war councils, however, have drawn more scrutiny and attention than the ceremonial celebrations of life.[36] In fact, most political divisions chose to avoid armed resistance altogether and, as the buffalo became scarce, slowly began to accustom themselves to living near the agencies. Soldiers and fellow Indigenous peoples pejoratively termed these people "loafer bands" for hanging around the forts.[37] Others who were willing to break policy and sell land, which they were not authorized to do, were called Maka Utacipi, or "earth eaters."[38] Many Oceti Sakowin disapproved of these individuals' behavior, but they were still considered relatives, though pitied for "eating" the land for the annuities and food rations they received for selling it. Political custom dictated that families and larger political divisions were allowed to disagree with or decline to follow a course of action set out by others. If the disagreement was serious, individuals or entire nations were allowed to leave. Just as easily as they could leave, they could also rejoin their relatives. Force or coercion never compelled others to action, or to stay.[39] But when the entire Oceti Sakowin was confined to the reservation, this harmony was disturbed because differing factions could not depart each other's company. In other instances, "agency chiefs" were selected to represent an entire Indigenous nation, breaking down internal democratic processes. Whatever these competing views, the war on the Bozeman Trail drew the United States to the negotiation table once again.

By 1865, the 1851 Treaty had expired with little consequence, having failed to bring about the peace it promised. Another costly military campaign in the Northern Plains was not an option. Most of the US military was stationed in the South to oversee Reconstruction, following the conclusion of the Civil War. As an effort to make freed Blacks into citizens, W. E. B. Du Bois called Reconstruction "a splendid failure"—one that offered only a temporary vision of a free society, because absolute equality demanded too much of a departure from the white supremacist status quo.[40] The same could also be said of its contemporaneous US–Indigenous treaties. Allowing Indigenous peoples to live in peace and respecting their political autonomy proved too much to ask of a settler state. So why did it make Indigenous treaties in the first place?

Treaties are the central agreements among sovereigns and the primary instruments of international relations. After all, a sovereign nation does not enter into international relations with internal or domestic peoples. But despite the 1831 Supreme Court decision that found Indigenous nations to be "domestic dependent nations," the United States entered into international relations with the Oceti Sakowin.[41] This is the fundamental paradox of federal Indian law: it takes international agreements and attempts to determine their validity in the realm of domestic federal law—that is, in the courts of the colonizers.

Patrick Wolfe argues that "domestic dependent nations" was less a legal redefinition than a "manifesto" for settler colonialism.[42] The intention behind the treaties was not to recognize the inherent political sovereignty or self-determining authority of Indigenous nations, but to facilitate land cessions and eventual incorporation. Justifying what would otherwise be a criminal act—invasion—the treaties were really an instrument for affirming US design over all lands, and especially lands that could not be taken by force. And to carry out the land cessions, the US government needed settlers to hold private property in perpetuity. Private ownership (or "fee simple") is seen, under US law, as the highest possible form of ownership, while Indigenous occupancy is seen as temporary; thus, collective Indigenous ownership and use could be dissolved for private ownership, but not the other way around. But because private property is exclusive, the two systems of land tenure fundamentally could not overlap. The confinement and removal of Indigenous peoples to reservations was racial segregation, and Indigenous peoples were the original "Red Scare."

It was from this belief of political superiority that the United States sued the Oceti Sakowin for peace. As a token of good will, the United States abandoned several forts along the Bozeman Trail, and Red Cloud and his followers set fire to the deserted buildings. The forts on the Missouri River, however, remained untouched and became the new bases of operations for corralling the Oceti Sakowin closer to the influence of the United States, and away from the Powder River country which more and more represented freedom.[43] The 1868 Fort Laramie Treaty established a 32-million-acre "permanent reservation," which encompassed the entirety of the present-day West River region of South Dakota. To appease those who refused agency life, a vast expanse of hunting grounds was set aside at nearly the same acreage of the permanent reservation, making the total territory more than 70 million acres, or about the size of the present-day state of Nevada. Article 11 of the treaty, however, stipulated that the Lakotas surrendered "all right to occupy permanently the territory outside their reservation as herein defined," but retained the right to hunt in the Powder River country "so long as the buffalo may range thereon in such numbers to justify the chase."[44] General William Tecumseh Sherman, a member of the peace commission, at first opposed this provision, fearing that sustained resistance through buffalo hunting over a vast region would make it impossible to reign in the militant divisions. Fellow peace commissioners, however, assured him the treaty's clause was "merely temporary" because once the buffalo were vanquished so too would the millions of acres of hunting territory.[45]

In 1903 Red Cloud recalled what Lakotas said to treaty commissioners regarding the hunting lands: "We told them that the country of the buffalo was the country of the Lakotas. We told them that the buffalo must have their country and the Lakotas must have their buffalo."[46] The Lakotas didn't believe the United States had the authority to simply "give" them back land that already rightfully belonged to them and their buffalo kin. Red Cloud made clear that the 1868 Treaty was not just an agreement between two human nations, but also an agreement among the nonhuman ones as well—including the buffalo nations. His interpretation, that Lakota territory began and ended with the buffalo nations' territory, was not a "mystical" reading, but a simple fact of Lakota life—and, at the time, a fact linked to pure survival.

For example, the most significant figure in Oceti Sakowin history descended from the Pte Oyate. It was a woman, Pte Ska Win (the White Calf Buffalo Woman), who made the first treaty with the human and nonhuman worlds. To be a good relative is to honor that original instruction. Lakotas often viewed treaties with the United States and other nations as commitments not just to human relations, but also to nonhuman ones. And such agreements were not the sole domain of men, as was the tradition of white society. Most important, pte means "female buffalo," and the Pte Oyate was alternatively known as "her nation."[47] When Red Cloud spoke of the Pte Oyate, he spoke of their true leaders—of the women, not the bulls (men), and of the original covenant with the White Buffalo Calf Woman. The future of the Oceti Sakowin was bound to the future of the Pte Oyate.

For its part, the military began to take seriously this vital connection with the buffalo as sustaining continued Indigenous resistance. The frontier army's operations turned toward exterminating Oceti Sakowin kin—the Pte Oyate— as defeating highly mobile Plains nations in conventional battles was near impossible. From 1865 to 1883, the frontier army sanctioned the mass slaughter of buffalo to shatter the will to resist by eliminating a primary food supply and a close relative. Russia's Grand Duke Alexie Alexandrovich even joined a buffalo hunt in 1872 near Denver with the frontier army, under the command of Lieutenant Colonel George Armstrong Custer and General Philip Sheridan. As they descended upon a herd, the hunters and soldiers acted as if the buffalo slaughter was also a massacre of Indigenous peoples, with a guide, Chalkley M. Beeson, recounting that they even called the buffalo "redskins."[48]

The extermination of the buffalo was incredibly effective and efficient. In two decades, soldiers and hunters had eradicated the remaining 10 to 15 million buffalo, leaving only several hundred survivors. The "Indian problem" was also a "buffalo problem," and both faced similar extermination processes, as much connected in death as they were in life. The destruction of one required the destruction of the other. The treaty clause "so long as the buffalo may range" was effectively a warrant to kill millions of buffalo, which translated literally into the killing of Indians and the seizure of millions of acres of 1868 Treaty territory—a direct attack on Indigenous sovereignty.

Another contentious aspect of the 1868 Treaty was the granting of the right to construct railroads through Oceti Sakowin territory. By the time the Northern Pacific Railroad began building its line through the Yellowstone Valley connecting Duluth, Minnesota, to the Puget Sound,

Red Cloud, Spotted Tail, and their followers had accepted the terms of the peace treaty. Most took it to mean that if they refrained from attacking the railroads, stage coaches, and overland emigrants, they would in turn be free from the threat of attack if they stayed within the reservation boundaries. The hunting grounds remained open, and so they thought that they could go on living as they always had, with little change. But railroads threatened that precarious peace and the provisional space of the hunting grounds that came with it. They provoked another fight and hardened the resolve of the remaining militants to stay off the reservations. Tatanka Iyotake (Sitting Bull), a powerful political leader of the Hunkpapas, refused the conditions of peace specifically over the question of rail lines and began making war on the railroad surveyors as they trespassed into Yellowstone territory. The military sent two expeditions of thousands of men in 1871 and 1873 to secure the passage of railroad engineers. But Sitting Bull and his followers halted construction of the Northern Pacific across the Missouri River at Bismarck, and the 1873 economic crisis further imperiled the Northern Pacific's progress westward. Nevertheless, the military now had a sizeable standing army at Fort Rice downriver, under the command of Custer, a less well-known veteran officer of the Civil War who history would only remember because he was killed by the Lakota, Cheyenne, and Arapaho alliance in 1876 at the Battle of Greasy Grass (Battle of the Little Bighorn). Custer and his men were stationed at the northern border of the "Great Sioux Reservation" to prevent the Hunkpapas and Sihasapas from leaving the reservation, waging war on the railroad surveys, and joining their off-reservation relatives in the west.[49]

Soon, those living off the reservation were considered outlaws, renegades, hostiles, and criminals to be hunted down, summarily shot, hanged, or imprisoned. Those on the reservation were considered "peaceful," and as "friendlies" who were not to be disturbed. Either way, soldiers and settlers could hardly distinguish between the two; when it came to collective punishment, all were at fault.

Since 1865, transcontinental railroads began lurching from east to west. With the Panic of 1873, US capitalists and politicians sought a new form of currency and a new national project that would pull the country out of recession. Relief would come in the form of gold, more railroads, and continuous westward expansion—in other words, through the acquisition of more Indigenous land, and more Indian Wars. The discovery of gold in the Black Hills in 1874 triggered a massive push to quickly end the Indian problem on the Northern Plains. From the military's perspective, reformers had failed to secure peace with the 1868 Treaty. Prior military campaigns in the West and the South were also coming to a close. The wars of conquests against the Apaches, Arapahos, Cheyennes, Comanches, Kiowas, and Modocs from 1869 to 1873 had largely ended. Meanwhile, in the South, Radical Reconstruction had lost political backing from a growing conservatism in the North, and as the United States began withdrawing federal troops, freed Blacks were left to fend for themselves against the white Southern elites who sought to violently recapture political and economic power. Facing the squeeze of economic recession, labor in the industrial east also began agitating. As historian Richard Slotkin argues, depictions of Black lawlessness in the South, relentless Indigenous criminality in the West, and growing labor militancy in the east provided the moral justification for the seizure of the Black Hills as a way to prioritize national economic development.[50] To contain the "threat" on its western frontier, in an 1871 Indian appropriations bill the United States abolished treaty making with Indigenous nations (although the treaties themselves were never abolished). Meanwhile, the nationalistic military campaign to seize the Black Hills and continue westward expansion was a much-needed pressure valve for anxieties of social unrest and economic uncertainty. An order to the US military went out to notify all the Lakotas and Dakotas to return to the reservation by January 31, 1876, or face military action. Because it was issued during winter, both the US military and the Oceti Sakowin largely ignored the impractical command.

By spring 1876, the majority of the Lakotas lived on reservations and were horseless, unarmed, and starving. Nevertheless, several groups had refused reservation life, and the Lakota, Cheyenne, and Arapaho alliance had evaded army capture for several years. Crazy Horse, no longer a military leader at this point, led several small groups into the Black Hills, killing numerous white miners. But the imposition of reservation borders combined with the cutting off of British-Canadian and US traders made ammunition scarce and sustained armed resistance increasingly impossible.[51] General Sheridan and Brigadier General George Crook had decided to stop evicting gold miners, in hopes of making real what could only be imagined at this point: the takeover of the Black Hills, the settlement of treaty lands, and the final surrender of the Oceti Sakowin. Allowing the trespass of settlers and miners was a clear violation of the 1868 Treaty, which forbade whites from entering the permanent reservation encompassing the entirety of the Black Hills. A violation of the treaty, as an international agreement, would have meant conditions reverted to pre-treaty terms. Therefore, the Oceti Sakowin, at this point, could have suspended their obligations—such as allowing the passage of settlers, roads, or railways, or the cession of certain lands. However, instead of curbing the criminal behavior of the white trespassers and living up to their treaty obligations, the army mobilized to the enforce the "peace" of the 1868 Treaty by making war against the Cheyennes, Lakotas, and Arapahos who refused to stay on the reservation.

On June 25, 1876, Custer and Brigadier General Marcus Reno led a group of 650 men against a camp of thousands of Lakotas, Cheyennes, and Arapahos. Among them were Sitting Bull, Pizi (or Gall), Inkpaduta, Crazy Horse, Pretty Nose, Left Hand, Two Moons, Wooden Leg, and many more who would be remembered as among the heroic armed resisters of the Cheyennes, Arapahos, Dakotas, and Lakotas. Custer led the first assault on the large camp, which was supposed to be a surprise attack. Custer's men were quickly halted and forced to retreat uphill. Despite popular myths, Custer and his men never mounted a brave last stand but were instead taken down as they ran away from the Indigenous warrior men and warrior women. For his courage, Custer was promoted to the rank of general after his death.

Hunkpapa warrior woman Moving Robe Woman, who fought against cavalrymen, later remembered that historic day. A young woman at the time, Moving Robe Woman was harvesting tinpsila, or prairie turnips, when the cavalry stormed the camp. After hearing her brother was killed in the initial attack, she recalled, "I ran to a nearby thicket and got my black horse. I painted my face with crimson and braided my black hair. I was mourning. I was a woman, but I was not afraid."[52] Among Plains nations, it was common for warriors to be women. In fact, according to Northern Cheyenne histories, Buffalo Calf Trail Woman is credited for knocking Custer from his horse before he was killed.[53] Indigenous women also knew what defeat meant—if they were not killed, their bodies would be forced over to the desires of their captors. They fought back not because they wanted to, but because they had to.

The defeat of Custer's Seventh Calvary and the killing of 268 of his men was a major victory. But according to Moving Robe Woman, no one "staged a victory dance that night. They were mourning for their own dead."[54] About four dozen Indigenous warriors were killed during the fight. Many popular accounts of the Battle of Greasy Grass and histories of the West over-romanticize the extreme violence and wanton slaughter of what became known as "the Great Sioux Wars." Each victory against the invaders also resulted in immeasurable casualties in later battles, and armed resistance was a calculated risk that was not undertaken carelessly. Either way, the Oceti Sakowin was in constant mourning over the theft of their lives, their world, and so many countless relatives—ancestors both present and future. Armed Indigenous resistance has always been a future-oriented and life-oriented project, and it is because of this fearless struggle that we survived and that we can remember.

After Greasy Grass, the military sought retribution. Unable to sustain long, drawn-out resistance, the Plains alliance dispersed and Sitting Bull and his followers, including Inkpaduta, fled to Canada. In May 1877, Crazy Horse surrendered himself and his followers at the Red Cloud Agency near Fort Robinson in Nebraska, and he was imprisoned there by the reservation authorities. On September 5, 1877, Crazy Horse was led to Fort Robinson to be formally arrested on the charge he was planning an uprising. While attempting to flee, one of the guards stabbed Crazy Horse in the back with a bayonet, killing him. He was thirty-seven. In 1881 Sitting Bull finally surrendered himself and his followers and was taken to Fort Yates on the Missouri River at present-day Standing Rock. The battleground had shifted: Christian missionaries, boarding schools, and military discipline and punishment were the new vanguards of white civilization.

The design and development of the carceral reservation world was well under way by the time Cheyennes, Lakotas, and Arapahos made Custer and his Seventh Cavalry famous. In 1876 Indian Commissioner John Q. Smith envisioned US Indian policy as having three central goals: to concentrate remaining Indigenous peoples onto fewer reservations, to allot remaining lands, and to expand US laws and courts' jurisdiction over reservations.[55] Although the number of reservations didn't decline, the latter two goals were achieved through the disintegration of political and social structures, and the carving up of the remaining communally held lands. The fur trade may have introduced the capitalist market, but it never made the Oceti Sakowin truly individualistic, and communal land practices and social customs still prevailed. This was the final frontier.

First came the assertion of US law. In 1881 an ongoing dispute between Spotted Tail and Kangi Sunka (Crow Dog) on the Rosebud Reservation led to Crow Dog murdering Spotted Tail, a reservation leader and "agency chief." Crow Dog made amends with Spotted Tail's surviving family, paying restitution for the slain relative according to customary law. Internal harmony was quickly and effectively restored. Nevertheless, federal and territorial officials demanded Crow Dog's arrest and prosecution. With little legal authority to do so, the case wound up at the Supreme Court, where it was ruled federal courts had no jurisdiction on reservation lands. As a result, Congress passed the 1885 Major Crimes Act, authorizing federal jurisdiction over certain crimes committed in Indian Country—including murder, larceny, rape, arson, and burglary. Congress used Crow Dog's case as an opportunity to extend plenary power—or complete or absolute power—over Indigenous nations and assert criminal jurisdiction, further eroding and defining the parameters of Indigenous sovereignty.[56]

The creation of the modern-day reservation system had a significant impact on both Indigenous and settler societies. Military and trading forts grew into either white settlements or reservation agency towns. As a new spatial arrangement of apartheid, the confinement of Native people to diminishing reservation lands made it simpler for settlers to assume ownership over "unused" land. Among the most highly prized possessions were the gold-rich Black Hills. To secure title to the land, Congress passed the 1877 Black Hills Act, which stole the Black Hills from the Oceti Sakowin and opened it to white settlement. A clause of the 1868 Treaty stipulated that any future land cessions, including the Black Hills, must "be signed by three-fourths of all the adult male" members. Its passage was thus a clear case of fraud and theft, as the United States was able to obtain only 10 percent of the needed signatures.[57]

Agency towns, which were often located at military forts or near them, were established to control and surveil the movements and the behaviors of Indigenous peoples, both on and off reservation. Reservations thus became sites where social engineering was used to break communal organization. In 1878, to administer law and order, the first reservation police forces were formed, drawing from Indigenous ranks to enforce the new social order dictated by federal agents and church officials. In 1883 the Bureau of Indian Affairs created the Court of Indian Offenses to compel "civilization." Punishable offenses included sun dancing, ceremonial dancing, customary giveaways, owning guns or weapons, owning ponies, men wearing long hair, polygamy, large feasts not organized by the church, Indigenous funerary rites, leaving the reservation, and honoring ceremonies. A violation brought punishment through starvation by withholding rations or imprisonment. These "offenses," also known as "the civilization regulations," were enforced until their repeal in 1935.[58] The use of coercive force by an armed body of the state, such as the police or the courts, to control behavior was relatively unknown to the Oceti Sakowin. "No Lakota chief," writes Luther Standing Bear, "ever dreamed of using the power of a judge in court, or a policeman on a street corner, for it was not a tenet of his society that one individual should account to another for his conduct."[59]

As punishment for the defiant political leadership, their children were taken from them and sent to far-off boarding schools, where many died. Although leaders such as Red Cloud and Spotted Tail voluntarily sent their children to boarding schools, they protested the military-like discipline and corporal punishment. The system, however, was as much about taking the children hostage as it was using them as leverage to coerce the behavior of reservation leadership. Richard Pratt, a former Indian fighter who marched under Custer against the Oceti Sakowin, was the main architect for the modern off-reservation boarding school system. The idea first came to him when in charge of Indigenous prisoners of war at Fort Marion in Florida. Assigned to oversee the confinement of Kiowa, Comanche, and Cheyenne inmates, Pratt experimented with assimilation through education. To his military mind, the Indian War would no longer be waged on the battlefield but in the classroom. Pratt's vision won him the backing of Indian reformers, and in 1879 he founded the Carlisle Boarding School in Pennsylvania.

The success of the Fort Marion experiment, however, could only be reproduced in similar prison-like and militarized conditions because it was impossible to "recruit" and "retain" students without the use of force. Complete removal from their parents, it was believed, was the only way to prevent relapse to Indigenous ways. Taken and then returned to their communities, the children were sometimes alienated from their parents and relatives because they could not speak their languages or had no bonds to their kin. At Carlisle, Indigenous students were subjected to a highly regimented routine. Although founded on military principles of discipline and order, the boarding schools didn't train Indigenous students to fight; rather, they taught them docility, compliance, and submission—the necessary ingredients for indoctrinating US patriotism and citizenship. "The Indians are destined to become absorbed into the national life," one Indian commissioner advised in an 1889 memo entitled "Inculcation of Patriotism in Indian

Schools," "not as Indians, but as Americans."[60]

To many the US flag, which flew above the soldiers as they killed, raped, and pillaged Indigenous peoples and lands, was a detested symbol of growing US authority. It was one of the first means used to signify US supremacy at reservation headquarters. When soldiers attempted to build the first flagpole to fly the "Stars and Stripes" at the Red Cloud Agency in 1874, outraged Oglalas took hatchets and chopped it down. The troopers rebuilt the flagpole and proceeded to take the population count of the reservation agency—wielding two highly symbolic instruments of growing colonial rule: a flag and a census.[61] With armed struggle mostly abandoned, Indigenous resistance changed from military resistance to a strategy of challenging the reservation system by continuing to refuse to sell land or to cooperate with reservation officials.

On the heels of a five-year recession, from 1878 to 1887 the desire for cheap or "free" Indigenous land in Dakota Territory infected white settlers like a fever. The decade, during which the white population in the region nearly doubled, was known as the "Great Dakota Boom." In 1887, under increasing pressure to open more of the remaining 1868 Treaty lands, Congress passed the Dawes Severalty Act, signaling a new assault on Lakota and Dakota lands. Dawes sought to disintegrate collective Native identities and communal land practices by allotting private plots to Native families and opening millions of acres of "excess" land for white settlement. The Plains nations began organizing against the Dawes Bill as soon as they learned of its dire consequences, and the Lakotas and Dakotas came to a consensus that they would refuse unconditionally to sell the land or to accept the terms of allotment. Achieving mass consensus and the consent of all divisions of the western Lakotas and Dakotas—under the ever-watchful eye of agency and church officials, and in conditions where most were half-starved—was a significant feat of political mobilization and discipline. In 1888 Pratt led a commission to convince the Lakotas to accept the terms of the Dawes Bill. While the United States had not followed 1868 Treaty protocol for the Black Hills Act, this time the Pratt Commission, as it was known, attempted to obtain the three-fourths male consent required to fractionate remaining reservation lands and open up millions of acres for eventual settlement.

In one instance the Pratt Commission came to the Standing Rock Reservation. All the commissioners needed were votes of either "yes" or "no" to accept allotment or not. Twenty-two million acres remained of the 1868 Treaty lands. If half were sold, the United States would sell land at 50 cents an acre, which would create a permanent fund of $1 million. Earning 5 percent interest per year, half would go toward education and agriculture, while the other half would be payed to those who accepted allotments. Under the leadership of Hunkpapa John Grass, the entire Standing Rock Reservation held council to discuss the conditions of the Dawes Bill. In all-night meetings, the Standing Rock council calculated the total distribution of money, which would amount to an insulting payment of $1 per year to each individual on the reservations. Grass had signed the 1877 Black Hills Act, which ceded the Black Hills, without understanding the terms. For him, the Dawes Bill was most likely another elaborate scheme to swindle lands. On the basis of the earlier act's outright fraud and failure to address either past wrongs or ongoing depredations, Grass led Standing Rock's opposition to allotment. In a speech enunciating his refusal to sign any paper—either the red for "no," or the black for "yes"—Grass remarked,

> The whole nation here that are located on this reservation
> have come to the conclusion that we will not sign that black
> paper. We say also that we will not sign the red paper. You
> know exactly how many there are of us. I do not see what

further evidence you would want. Here is the whole nation, and we say: "We decline."[62]

The Pratt Commission, unable to acquire minimal consent to even vote on the Dawes Bill at Standing Rock, went to the remaining reservations and faced similar unified refusal. An utter failure, the bill received a mere 120 signatures.

The initial defeat of the Dawes Bill was but a momentary victory. In 1889 General George Crook, a veteran Indian fighter who was responsible for coaxing Crazy Horse to surrender, led another commission to secure "consent." This time Crook lied about the bill, saying it would alleviate restrictions on dancing and generally improve reservation life without affecting prior treaty agreements. At first, when lies didn't work, threats of violence and of the outright taking of the land, with or without Indigenous consent, pressured many to sign. When met with resistance, the Indian agent at Rosebud warned the opposition that their refusal to sign would jeopardize not just their standing with the United States, but also their entire legacy: "After you are dead and gone, and somebody reads . . . the names of the people who signed this treaty, I think you will want your names to be read out."[63] At Pine Ridge Agency, when Oglalas under the leadership of Red Cloud refused to sign, an Indian agent "read the riot act" to Red Cloud and his followers to criminalize those who refused to sign away land.[64] Oglala leader Wasicu Tasunka (American Horse) had signed but regretted his decision later when beef rations were drastically cut, further imperiling an already famished people. The commissioners previously stated that the bill would not affect rations or annuities. Cutting rations, combined with a whole host of other grievances that went unaddressed, according to American Horse, was like "cutting our heads off."[65] Among the unfulfilled promises were the failure to improve the poor quality of annuity goods such as clothing and farming equipment, and continued unexplained deaths of children at off-reservation boarding schools such as Carlisle.

Indeed, the new reservation political order had attempted to sever the heads of the Oceti Sakowin by taking children, usurping land, exterminating the buffalo nations, and diminishing Indigenous political authority. Having gained the necessary signatures to enforce allotment, the "permanent reservation" guaranteed under the 1868 Treaty was now open for white settlement. Crook's commission had left the western divisions of the Oceti Sakowin deeply divided and in disarray after it destroyed the unified effort to resist the sale and further dissolution of remaining reservation lands. Now the Black Hills had been taken and 9 million acres of land opened for white settlement. What became known as the 1889 Sioux Agreement created the six modern reservation boundaries for the Pine Ridge, Rosebud, Cheyenne River, Standing Rock, Lower Brule, and Crow Creek Reservations.

During the late 1880s—disarmed, hungry, horseless, confined to concentration camps, the buffalo nearly exterminated, their land broken up and taken, and their children stolen from them—a new political movement spread like prairie fire across the West, promising Indigenous rebirth. Wovoka, a Paiute holy man, had a vision that assured the restoration of Indigenous peoples to their rightful place in a world taken from them. According to him, dead relatives and the buffalo nations would once again walk the earth. The Ghost Dance prophecy envisioned the end of the present world through the settlers' erasure from the earth, and the return of human and nonhuman relations that had been vanquished by colonialism. It was foretold that, at some unspecified time in the near future, a cataclysmic event—such as an earthquake or whirlwind—would wipe the United States off the surface of the earth. Once the land was cleansed, life would be free of disease and colonialism, and correct relations among human and nonhuman worlds would be restored. Dakota anthropologist Ella Deloria recorded the following description of the Ghost Dance from the viewpoint of an unnamed Lakota man who participated in the dance at the Pine Ridge Agency as a young runaway from boarding school:

The rumor got about: "The dead are to return. The buffalo are to return. The Dakota people will get back their own way of life. The white people will soon go away, and that will mean happier times for us once more!" That part about the dead returning was what appealed to me . . .

Soon fifty of us, little boys about eight to ten, started out across country over hills and valleys, running all night . . . There on Porcupine Creek thousands of Dakota people were in camp, all hurrying about very purposefully . . . A woman quickly spied us and came weeping toward us. "These [children] also shall take part," she was saying of us. So a man called out, "You runaway boys, come here." They stripped our ugly clothes from us and sent us inside [a purification lodge]. When we were well purified, they sent us out the other end and placed sacred shirts on us . . . Everyone wore one magpie and one eagle feather in his hair, but in our case there was nothing to tie them to. The school had promptly ruined us by shaving off our long hair till our scalps showed lighter than our faces!

The people, wearing the sacred shirts and feathers, now formed a ring . . . All walked cautiously and in awe, feeling their dead were close at hand . . . The leaders beat time and sang as the people danced going round to the left in a sidewise step. They danced without rest, on and on, and they got out of breath but still they kept going as long as possible. Occasionally someone thoroughly exhausted and dizzy fell unconscious into the center and lay there "dead" . . . After a while, many lay about in that condition. They were now "dead" and seeing their dear ones. As each one came to, she, or he, slowly sat up and looked about, bewildered, and then began wailing inconsolably . . .

The visions varied at the start, but they ended the same way, like a chorus describing a great encampment of all the Dakotas who had ever died, where the buffalo came eagerly to feed them, and there was no sorrow but only joy, where relatives thronged out with happy laughter to greet the newcomer. That was the best of all!

Waking up to the drab and wretched present after such a glowing vision, it was little wonder that they walked as if their poor hearts would break in two with disillusionment. But at least they had seen! . . . They preferred that to rest or food or sleep. And so I suppose the authorities did think they were crazy—but they weren't. They were only terribly unhappy.[66]

The visions were not escapist, but rather part of a growing anticolonial theory and movement. Participants were transported to a forthcoming world where the old ways and dead relatives lived. It was a utopian dream that briefly suspended the nightmare of the "wretched present" by folding the remembered experience of a precolonial freedom into an anticolonial future. Upon awakening, dancers were forced to relive the horrors of their current reality. Above all, the visions were a reminder that life need not always be this way, and the Ghost Dance anticipated nothing less than the utter destruction of the colonial relation with the United States. But this was no cultural revitalization movement—anyway, the Ghost Dance did not derive from Oceti Sakowin culture. Also, the Ghost Dance was fundamentally oppositional in spirit. Lakota Ghost Dancers, historian Jeffrey Ostler observes, "hoped to see the present world destroyed and a new one come into being."[67] Indigenous life could not be remade inside reservations, nor within a colonial system, but only through the complete destruction of both.

Nineteenth- and twentieth-century anthropologists and historians have often downplayed (or misconstrued) the revolutionary premises of the Ghost Dance. The most widely used text on the movement, *The Ghost-Dance Religion and Wounded Knee*, written in 1896 by armchair ethnographer

James Mooney, for instance, distorted the meaning of the Ghost Dance. Pandering to the sympathies of a US public in an attempt to make the Ghost Dance more palatable, Mooney used cultural relativism to justify its existence. In his mind, because Ghost Dancers followed a Christ-like messianic figure, Wovoka, the movement had largely embraced elements of Christianity and thus resembled modern Judeo-Christian religions. Further, he claimed, Lakota Ghost Dancers failed to properly adhere to Wovoka's message of nonviolence and pacifism, warping it into a "hostile expression" and confirming the US military's later characterization of the Lakota Ghost Dancers as "militants."[68] But in reality, Wovoka taught peace—not through perpetual harmony with white settlers, and certainly not through submission to Christian morality or dogmatic pacifism. Rather, his call for peace was pragmatic: under present conditions, armed Indigenous resistance was futile. Thus, the Ghost Dance's mass appeal had less in common with Christianity than it did with earlier prophet-inspired pan-Indigenous movements. These include the 1760s Lenni Lenape prophet Neolin and his Odawa follower Pontiac (who fought British military occupation in the Great Lakes region); the 1800s Shawnee prophet Tenskwatawa and his brother Tecumseh, who together fought US occupation of the Ohio River valley; the 1860s Wanapum prophet Smohalla and his follower, the Nez Perce leader Chief Joseph; and the 1870s Pauite prophet Wodziwob, Wovoka's predecessor and the first practitioner of the Ghost Dance.[69] Each of these successive prophets built upon the messages and doctrines of the others by calling for pan-Indigenous resistance—sometimes through armed struggle—to reject colonial occupation. Each drew upon an accumulation of historical experience, and all were united by a common desire for Indigenous liberation.

Public debate at the time over Lakotas' adherence to the Ghost Dance's alleged pacifism served only to divide people fighting for survival into two camps: "legitimate" nonviolent pacifists and "illegitimate" violent militants. Indeed, these divisions cater to the feelings of settler society more than they accurately portray the lived experiences of real Indigenous peoples. The categories of "good Indians" and "bad Indians" purposefully create criminal elements within Indigenous nations and movements, in order to obscure or hide the United States' own criminal enterprise. But the Ghost Dance was not meant for the US colonizers, nor did its followers seek its recognition as a "legitimate" religion equivalent to Christianity. It was the US state's criminalization of not only the dancers themselves, but all things defying the civilizing mission, that led the military to conclude that the dance was a "hostile expression." All dancing—and practicing Indigenous lifeways, in general—was a criminal act punishable by imprisonment or the withholding of rations. To reservation officials, it didn't matter if the dancers were militant or nonviolent: Ghost Dancing was inherently an oppositional, political act.

Nearly a third of all Lakotas—between four and five thousand—along with many Dakotas, participated in the Ghost Dance, a figure that demonstrates its mass influence. As a resistance movement, its tactics included complete withdrawal from reservation life; opposition to reservation authorities; the creation of resistance camps in remote areas far removed the influence of the agency; the pilfering of annuity distribution centers (and sometimes white settlers' cattle and crops); the destruction of agricultural equipment; and the refusal to send children to school, to speak English, to participate in censuses, and to attend work, church, or agency and council meetings; their tactics also included the refusal to live on assigned allotments, to obey "agency chiefs," to cut one's hair, to quit dancing, to wear white clothing and attire, or to use metal tools. In short, the movement posed a comprehensive challenge to the colonial order of things. At first Indian police were sent to suppress the dances, which were illegal, but their resolve was shaken when they were met by armed guards willing to defend the dancers with violence if necessary. Upon meeting a strident refusal to quit dancing, some Indian police simply resigned, rather than face the prospect of killing their relatives or imprisoning them.[70]

The widespread appeal of the Ghost Dance as an anti-colonial movement was in large part due to historical experience of its primary promoters and interlocutors: boarding school–educated Indigenous students. Two of its primary Lakota visionaries, Mato Wanahtake (Kicking Bear) and Tatanka Ptecela (Short Bull), used trains and writing to diffuse the message of the Ghost Dance to the Oceti Sakowin. Boarding school students who could read and write, often in both English and Lakota, transcribed Kicking Bear's and Short Bull's reports after the two men traveled by train to meet with Wovoka in Nevada. Ghost Dance prophesies, prayers, and songs were also transcribed and mailed to the various reservations, where boarding school students would read them aloud to fellow Ghost Dancers. Without this means of dissemination, the Ghost Dance would not have been so widespread—a fact Mooney admits in his ethnography. Letters conveying Ghost Dance songs and doctrines poured into Oceti Sakowin reservations from Indigenous nations in Utah, Wyoming, Montana, and Oklahoma.[71]

When Ghost Dancing began among the Lakotas, it was reported in the press as troubling and unrelenting. The largest deployment of the military since the Civil War arrived on the Northern Plains to crush the movement, and National Guard units from the surrounding states were brought in as backup for the federal troops. The first target was Sitting Bull, the last remaining powerful leader who had never signed a treaty and who still resisted the imposition of reservation life. The Standing Rock Indian agent, James McLaughlin, feared Sitting Bull and his Ghost Dancers would leave the reservation. On December 15, 1890, under heavy surveillance for his role in spreading the Ghost Dance, Indian police attempted to arrest

Sitting Bull. Roused from bed early that morning, Indian police dragged Sitting Bull from his log cabin and shot him in the head. A brief firefight ensued, in which Sitting Bull's followers killed six Indian police and the Indian police killed seven of his followers. After Sitting Bull's assassination, military arrest warrants were issued for other Ghost Dance leaders such as Mniconjou chief Unphan Gleska (Spotted Elk). In an effort to diminish Spotted Elk's standing among his own people, white soldiers derisively called him "Si Tanka," or "Big Foot," because he wore US government–issued shoes that were too small for his feet. Fearing further reprisals, Sitting Bull's followers joined with Spotted Elk's people at the Cheyenne River Reservation. The Ghost Dancers then fled to turn themselves in at Red Cloud's agency in Pine Ridge, where they were detained at Wounded Knee Creek and surrounded by soldiers. The Seventh Cavalry, Custer's old regiment, took command of the camp and began by demanding the group turn over all weapons and surrender. They conducted tipi-by-tipi raids, confiscating anything that could be construed as a weapon, such as hatchets and knives.

On the morning of December 29, 1890, Spotted Elk and all the camp leaders were called to council with soldiers to turn in the last remaining guns. Hotchkiss guns (mobile light artillery) were strategically placed on the hillsides and trained at the starving, surrendering, and mostly unarmed Ghost Dancers. A scuffle broke out and a shot was fired. The Seventh Cavalry massacred between 270 and 300 Lakotas that day, including Spotted Elk. More than two-thirds among the slain were women and children. The Ghost Dancers fought back against the soldiers, inflicting casualties; if not for their struggle, there is no doubt more would have been killed, and that others would not have been able to escape. In the course of several hours, the cavalry chased down and killed the fleeing Lakotas. When the soldiers administered the killing blows, often by point-blank execution, they were heard muttering, "Remember Custer."[72]

The military still refers to the massacre of half-starved and surrendering people as a battle against armed militants. Congress awarded twenty medals of honor to the soldiers involved in the massacre. In retaliation for the unprovoked slaughter, Ghost Dancers sought revenge. The story of a young Sicangu Carlisle boarding school graduate who returned to the reservation and joined the Ghost Dance movement is significant in this regard. Tasunka (Plenty Horses) was stripped of his language and culture at a crucial moment in his childhood, returning to his family and community with nothing to offer. "I found that the education I had received," Plenty Horses recalled, "was of no benefit to me. There was no chance to get employment, nothing for me to do whereby I could earn my board and clothes, no opportunity to learn more and remain with the whites. It disheartened me and I went back to live as I had before going to school."[73]

His experience was not exceptional. The civilization experiment failed. Growing his hair long and donning pre–boarding school Lakota clothing, Plenty Horses joined armed resisters in the aftermath of the Wounded Knee Massacre. Lieutenant Edward Casey went to meet with the resistance camp that had holed up in the Badlands. Angry at what he had experienced in boarding school, the starving conditions to which he returned on the reservation, and witnessing his people killed with impunity at Wounded Knee, Plenty Horses positioned himself behind Casey as he approached and shot him in the back of the head. Army officials charged Plenty Horses with murder, but he was later acquitted. Had he been guilty of murder, then so too were the soldiers who massacred his people at Wounded Knee, the court reasoned. At trial, the court concluded that a state of war existed, although not formally declared, and therefore that Plenty Horses was not at fault, and neither were the soldiers involved in the Wounded Knee massacre—thus suspending the criminal act of genocidal murder.[74]

In the aftermath of the October 27, 2016, raid on the 1851 Treaty Camp blockading the Dakota Access Pipeline, a rancid smell permeated the camps. Police and private security had heaped the camp's remnants—ceremonial items, such as eagle feathers, pipes, medicine bundles, and staffs, along with mangled tents, sleeping bags, clothing, and tipis—into a large pile near the entrance of Oceti Sakowin Camp. Cops and private security had urinated on the items before returning them.

One night, after it was decided to ceremonially burn the urine-soaked remnants, an Ihanktonwan elder gathered young Water Protectors around a fire. She was dressed in the regalia she wore the day of the raid. Hundreds of copper pennies hung by red ribbons from her dark blue trade cloth dress. She told of her ancestors who were killed during the 1862 US-Dakota War. Evicted from their homelands, they fled to present-day Standing Rock, crossing the Missouri River not far from the location of Oceti Sakowin Camp, after US cavalrymen massacred Dakotas and Lakotas in the Whitestone Hill buffalo hunt camp. This was, to the day, exactly 150 years before DAPL private security unleashed attack dogs on unarmed Water Protectors at a nearby pipeline construction site.

The day after Christmas in 1862, soldiers gathered up thirty-eight Dakota men and boys at Mankato, Minnesota. Their medicine bundles were confiscated, heaped in a large pile, and burned as they were led to the gallows, singing their death songs. Their crime? Defending their nation and homelands. The same week that President Abraham Lincoln signed the Emancipation Proclamation freeing Black slaves, he also signed the death sentences of the thirty-eight Dakota patriots. The copper pennies hanging from the elder's regalia had holes drilled into Lincoln's ears with red ribbon threaded through. "He didn't listen," she said of the Great Emancipator, "so we opened his ears."

After the 1876 Battle of Greasy Grass, Lakota women used awls to carve holes in Custer's ears so he would hear better in the afterlife. Now, it was President Barack Obama, North Dakota Governor Jack Dalrymple, and Morton County Sheriff Kyle Kirchmeier who refused to listen. As singers began a prayer song, the elder reminded the younger ones that the tears flowing from their eyes were their "ancestors speaking through them," and that they were not tears of trauma but of liberation. "We survived genocide after genocide."

Then she danced, and the pennies swayed with the flickering fire and billowing smoke. Behind her, armed police were perched on a hill half a mile away, and their bright floodlights glared down on us. Our history is the future.

What continues to sustain Indigenous peoples through the horrors of settler colonialism are the recent memories of freedom, the visions enacting it, and the daring conspiracies to recapture it. The Ghost Dance was not a monolithic movement, but an accumulation of prior anti-colonial experiences, sentiments, and struggles that informed #NoDAPL. Each struggle had adopted essential features of previous traditions of Indigenous resistance, while creating new tactics and visions to address the present reality, and, consequently, projected Indigenous liberation into the future. Trauma played a major role. But if we oversimplify Indigenous peoples as perpetually wounded, we cannot possibly understand how they formed kinship bonds and constantly recreated and kept intact families, communities, and governance structures while surviving as fugitives and prisoners of a settler state and as conspirators against empire; how they loved, cried, laughed, imagined, dreamed, and defended themselves; or how they remain, to this day, the first sovereigns of this land and the oldest political authority.

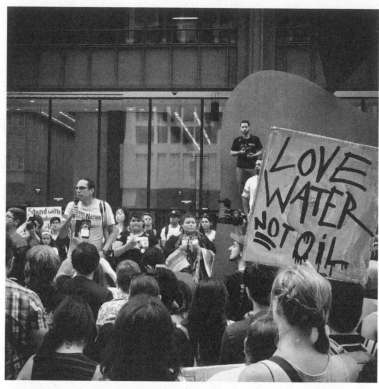

Water Protectors protest against the Dakota Access Pipeline outside the US Army Corps of Engineers headquarters in downtown Chicago. September 2016. Photo by Kristen Simmons.

4

FLOOD

When our land is gone, our way of life is gone, our tribes are destroyed. The bottom lands the Corps of Engineers want to take are the very best on the reservations. They are our heart lands. They can never be replaced. No similar lands are for sale. We depend on land for our livelihood, it furnishes us our income. To take our land is to take our homes and income, and a part of our history and heritage.

—J. W. "Jiggs" Thompson, US Senate Subcommittee
on Public Works, Washington, DC, 1959[1]

After Wounded Knee, spectacular armed struggle would not come again until the 1970s. In the meantime, nevertheless, the fight for land, life, and self-determination continued. Over the course of the mid twentieth century, the United States increasingly used its powers of eminent domain to seize Indigenous lands for large public works projects, especially for Army Corps of Engineers dams. For the Oceti Sakowin along the Missouri River, dispossession through eminent domain emerged in the form of floods and dams. The Pick-Sloan Plan, a joint water-development project designed by the Army Corps of Engineers and the Bureau of Reclamation in 1944 with the input of Missouri River states, called for the construction of large multipurpose earthen-rolled dams for flood control, reclamation, and irrigation that, as its promoters claimed, promised to make otherwise-arid grasslands bloom. Four of the five Pick-Sloan dams flooded seven Missouri River Lakota and Dakota reservations—Santee, Yankton, Rosebud, Lower Brule, Crow Creek, Cheyenne River, and Standing Rock. But unlike during the previous century, when Indigenous land was coveted for its endless bounty, for the Pick-Sloan Plan in the twentieth century, Indigenous land was desired merely so that it could be wasted—covered with water. All of the risks, and none of the rewards, of cheap hydroelectricity and irrigation, were imposed on generations of Indigenous people who depended upon their relations to the land and water for life. And floodwaters provided the physical means to terminate Indigenous nations and relocate people—a violent severing of those relations—to end the "Indian problem" once and for all.

The Pick-Sloan dams were a twentieth-century Indigenous apocalypse, inflicting an immeasurable amount of loss that is still experienced today. When the river trade increased violence in the nineteenth century, the Oceti Sakowin escaped invasion by following the buffalo onto the plains. When the US Army annihilated the buffalo, the survivors were forced onto reservations, where they found refuge once again in the lush river bottomlands where food and game abounded, subsistence agriculture flourished, and fresh water was plenty. When the reservation cattle boom came in the early twentieth century, river bottomlands provided shelter for livestock and prime ranchland for small-scale, Native-owned cattle enterprises. A mixed economy consisted of subsistence hunting and gathering, along with small-scale agriculture and small-scale reservation cattle enterprises. Virtually all reservation timber was concentrated along shoreland, providing the necessary materials for home construction, shelter, and fuel for heating and cooking. What could not be produced by the sale of livestock was replaced with the harvest of wild game, fruits, and vegetables that flourished in the river valley. Those less fortunate avoided starvation in winter months, when employment was scarce, through total dependence on "the free goods of nature" that the river provided.

All of this was destroyed by the Pick-Sloan Plan, setting the stage for the #NoDAPL movement half a century later. The

Army Corps' discretion to plot the path of the Dakota Access Pipeline in 2014 rested on power they assumed under the Pick-Sloan Plan, following which the Army Corps have continually asserted—but never been officially granted—jurisdiction over the Missouri River flowing through Oceti Sakowin reservations. This was a direct violation of the 1868 Fort Laramie Treaty, which delineated treaty territory as encompassing the entire channel of the river flowing through it, including the eastern shoreline. According to US law, only Congress had the power to alter treaty boundaries or extinguish Indigenous jurisdiction, and the Pick-Sloan Plan authorized the Army Corps to do neither; it merely authorized them to build dams on the reservations. However, the assertion of jurisdiction didn't just happen with the stroke of a pen. Rather, it arrived as a wall of water brought on by the dams—extinguishing life and Indigenous jurisdiction along with it. And because reservation life had imposed starvation conditions on the Oceti Sakowin in the earlier half of the twentieth century, by the mid twentieth century when the Pick-Sloan dams were built, it was hard to assemble a formidable resistance against the Army Corps and its allied federal agencies. The results were nothing short of genocide: by destroying the land—and with it the plants, animals, and water—the dams targeted and destroyed the very nations of people who reproduced themselves upon the soil. In this way, taking land and water also took away the possibility of a viable future.

Pick-Sloan also dovetailed with federal policies of termination and relocation, which liquidated federally recognized Indigenous nations and removed people from the reservation to far-off urban centers. In 1953, Congress passed House Concurrent Resolution 108, which called for the immediate termination of the Flathead, Klamath, Menominee, Potawatomi, and Turtle Mountain Chippewa tribes—opening millions of acres of Indigenous lands for privatization. The bill adopted a perverse logic: only through the destruction of Indigenous nations could they "be freed from Federal supervision and control from all disabilities and limitations."² That same year, Public Law 280 authorized states to assume criminal and civil jurisdiction over Native lands. Together, the bills promised to end federal trust protections and transfer payments guaranteed by treaties and agreements, extinguishing what little Indigenous political authority remained after close to a century of genocidal policies. In tandem with this termination legislation, the Bureau of Indian Affairs began busing Natives off reservations to cities like San Francisco, Denver, Chicago, Los Angeles, and Cleveland as part of the federal relocation program. Between the 1950s and 1960s, an estimated 750,000 Native people moved off reservation. Termination, in the words of Edward Valandra, "made legal the overthrow of Native governments, the stealing of their lands, and the extermination of Native Peoples and cultures."³

Termination marked a dramatic shift in policy from the gains made during the Indian New Deal, which, despite its flaws, had ushered in a new era of tribal self-determination under the 1935 Indian Reorganization Act (IRA). The dramatic reforms overhauled years of collective punishment that the Indian Bureau had inflicted on whole nations held captive on reservations. The year of the Wounded Knee Massacre, the US Census concluded that the western frontier was officially "closed." With it, the centuries of war, famine, disease, and genocidal policy brought the American Indian population to its lowest point in the history of North American settler colonialism. In 1928, in response to American Indian activists' demands, an extensive study, *The Problem of Indian Administration*, also known as the Meriam Report, found the Indian Bureau incompetent, corrupt, and murderous. Among its most egregious acts was mass starvation across reservations, as what little land remained for Natives to eke out a living was sold off to white settlers. Because of the disastrous

Dawes Act, between 1887 and 1932 allotment—and the "surplus" land sold to whites—devoured 91 million acres of Indigenous lands, leaving just 48 million acres for reservations. In order to limit the number of individual American Indians who could receive an allotment and become landowners, a racist federal "competency commission" issued patents based on racial mixture, disallowing "full-bloods" from becoming private owners, and instead keeping their lands in trust. This created conflict between landless "mixed-bloods" and "full-bloods" who kept allotments because they were deemed too "incompetent" to sell them to whites. Oklahoma tribes were hardest hit; for instance, the Osage lost 70 percent of their allotted lands during the oil boom of the 1920s. By contrast, the Oceti Sakowin lost 30 percent of their allotted lands overall; among them, Rosebud and Lower Brule experienced the greatest hit, losing 40 percent of their lands.[4]

The IRA provided a temporary reprieve to the onslaught by making three important reforms: First, it ended the catastrophic allotment policy. Second, it ended the draconian prohibition on dancing, improved Indigenous freedom of religion and speech, improved the reservation criminal justice system, and provided monies for land reacquisition and economic development. Lastly, it imposed Western-style governance through a BIA model constitution, which required reservations to adopt a constitution based on the US Constitution and pledge fealty to the United States. The last point was the most contentious. While Indigenous peoples desired increased political autonomy, they didn't want to replace existing governance, based on consensus and kinship, with colonial institutions. They also feared the competitive Western-style electoral system would further intensify political factionalism and create a class of reservation elites whose allegiance lay not with community councils but with an external authority—the US government—and whose political power would be kept in check by the BIA and the Department of the Interior.

In fact, the IRA's primary architect, Commissioner of Indian Affairs John Collier, saw the IRA as part of a global design of colonial administration. Collier drew inspiration from Lord Lugord's early-twentieth-century model for British colonial administration. Under this system national independence was prevented through its permanent suspension. In 1947 Collier even compared the US colonial administration of Indigenous peoples to its imperial annexation and colonial management of the Philippines, Puerto Rico, Hawaii, Alaska, the Pacific Islands, the Panama Canal, and the Virgin Islands.[5] The IRA was a New Deal program, but it was also part of global imperialism; the view that Indian policy is only "domestic policy" fails take this fact seriously, and normalizes colonialism by reproducing the notion that Indigenous peoples are domestic US subjects. Indian affairs were thus removed from the realm of international relations—from treaty making and diplomacy—and relegated to domestic, territorial rule, a process that should be challenged rather than reproduced.

National independence for colonized peoples was never the goal for US imperial endeavors. Nevertheless, the IRA lifted the Oceti Sakowin "from absolute deprivation to mere poverty, and this was the best time the reservation had," as Standing Rock Sioux scholar and activist Vine Deloria Jr. observed.[6] And for all its flaws, the IRA enshrined certain principles of self-government for Indigenous peoples and provided them with a federally recognized government. Not all reservations accepted the IRA, but those that did possessed a distinct advantage in years to come. For example, the Standing Rock, Cheyenne River, Lower Brule, and Crow Creek Reservations created IRA tribal councils. The Yankton Reservation adopted the IRA but never formally adopted a model constitution or tribal council. With no federally recognized government, the Yankton reservation and its trustee, the Secretary of the Interior, were completely bypassed by the Army Corps, which proceeded to seize Native property by right of eminent domain in order to construct the Fort Randall Dam. Yankton Reservation members had little to no recourse. In the end, while IRA governments were deeply flawed, without them the Oceti Sakowin would not have been able to negotiate Army Corps damages—nor to ultimately resist termination. But it was a false choice to begin with: adopt the colonizers' model fully; accept "self-determination" with permanent tutelage; or perish.

During this era, treaties were broken by statute rather than by brute force. In the Missouri River basin, the Pick-Sloan Plan destroyed more Indigenous lands than any other public works project in US history, affecting twenty-three different reservation communities. The project, writes Deloria, "was without a doubt, the single most destructive act ever perpetrated on any tribe by the United States."[7] The land taken and destroyed was the best land on the reservation: riverfront bottomlands that were heavily wooded on otherwise treeless plains, and full of wildlife and plants, including animals on which many Indigenous peoples still depended for sustenance. A third of the residents of Standing Rock, Cheyenne River, Lower Brule, Crow Creek, and Yankton reservations were removed to marginal lands on the open prairies or were forced to leave the reservation entirely; in either case, they could not reproduce the lives they lived in the lush river bottoms. In total, the United States took 550 square miles of Indigenous lands, an area half the size of Rhode Island.

During the nineteenth century, treaty making was deployed as a way to ensure Indian title over lands so they could later be ceded to the United States. D'Arcy McNickle, a Flathead scholar and Indian Affairs employee at the time of the Pick-Sloan Plan, argued that under eminent domain, Indian tribes became categorized as private landowners "against whom the state could proceed." In other words, the identity of entire Indigenous nations became nothing more than a dollar sign.

"The process, in time," McNickle argued, "can only lead to the extinction of the Indian people."[8] Unlike white farmers and landowners, who could easily reproduce their businesses and lifestyles elsewhere, Indigenous peoples and the favorable river environment upon which they depended could not be replaced.

This was a cruel reward for those returning from the Second World War. In every war from the First World War to present, Indigenous peoples have served and volunteered at rates higher than the US population. The US military has also purposely distorted Indigenous warrior culture for its own ends, often enlisting Indigenous names and motifs, such as the "Lakota" helicopter or the "Tomahawk" cruise missile, for imperialist endeavors. Natives have served not so much as "national minorities" but more often as separate, sovereign nations. During World War I, the Haudenosaunee Confederacy, for example, independently declared war on Germany in 1917, choosing to send their soldiers to fight for their own nation. They did the same during World War II, independently declaring war on the Axis powers. Initially, Native military service had much to do with the maintenance of Indigenous sovereignty, with Native soldiers fighting alongside an empire in which they were not citizens. Although widely resisted by Indigenous nations, American Indian citizenship would not be granted until 1924.

The Oceti Sakowin held similar views toward military service, maintaining an understanding with the United States that their military service was for the protection of their own homelands, and nothing more. They understood their service would not require deployment overseas against enemies named by the US empire that didn't directly threaten Indigenous livelihoods. "There was an agreement between the [US] Government and the Indian people," Lakota holy man Fools Crow explained in 1978, regarding Lakotas' volunteerism during World War I, "that they will only fight within their own country, in defense. They send him [Lakotas] overseas which is contrary to the agreement that was made. It is something unusual for an Indian to fight in a foreign country . . . When they come back they are not the same boys. They drink. They destroy themselves."

When thousands returned home after the Second World War, the enemy threatening their homelands was the very military they fought for. A country that demanded Natives sacrifice their lives in war now demanded the sacrifice of their best lands and their governments. What was coming up the river was a new round of dispossession, a new round of enclosure, that used the most precious resource—water—as its weapon to eliminate and destroy nations and the land on which they depended for life. However, the struggle for control over the river began not with the Army Corps, but with states like South Dakota, whose political elite became staunch advocates for termination. But like termination, river development met resistance.

By 1910 the state of South Dakota, barely two decades old, was at the forefront of the movement to develop the Upper Missouri. Other states such as Montana and North Dakota had their own plans, but none compared to the scale and organization of those in South Dakota. Early attempts had failed to garner federal support, especially from the US Army Corps of Engineers, who had final say over any river improvement projects. In 1924 the state designated Big Bend, the largest oxbow bend on the Missouri, as the site for a hydroelectric plant. A large multipurpose dam, according to this plan, promised cheap electricity and irrigation for the exclusive benefit of the nearby white-dominated border towns of Pierre, Winner, Chamberlain, White River, Mitchell, Huron, Redfield, and Murdo. Ignored were the very people most impacted: the Lower Brule and Crow Creek reservations. Although the dam targeted their lands and threatened their water rights, neither Indigenous nation was consulted, and both were disregarded entirely during the initial planning of the project. And when South Dakota's river development projects failed to gain the necessary federal support, the Upper Missouri Valley Development Association formed in the spring of 1933 to take up their campaign.

The Big Bend site was just miles south from where the Lakotas first discovered the Lewis and Clark expedition in 1804, attempting to trespass through their territory unnoticed. So too did boosters of river development attempt to bypass the scrutiny of the Oceti Sakowin. Like the expedition, their plan was soon discovered. On May 16, 1937, Lower Brule Tribal Chairman Ruben Estes wrote to South Dakota Republican Congressman Francis Case expressing support for a hydroelectric plant at Big Bend that could provide "labor and relief," and electricity to the Lower Brule town site. But Estes also expressed concern at the tribal council's exclusion from plans for the development of Lower Brule lands and water, invoking the new powers Lower Brule was willing to exercise under the IRA to challenge a state project initiated on tribal lands without their consent. Ultimately, he questioned if the state or the federal government had the right to develop water within reservation boundaries "without the consent of the people" of Lower Brule and Crow Creek, or perhaps any Indigenous nation living on the river.[9]

By 1935 the Lower Brule Sioux Tribe adopted the IRA, becoming the first tribe among the Oceti Sakowin to do so, and the second in the United States.[10] They did so for pragmatic reasons: to counter attempts by state and federal agencies to lay claim to and develop the Missouri River.[11] Without an IRA council, the Lower Brule had little power to halt river development, to apply for federal loans, or to employ legal counsel to defend its lands. In the first instance, the Lower Brule did not support the development of the river without their consent. But they did support plans in which they could determine what that development would look like, and to what extent it would provide much-needed relief in the form of employment, and electricity during the Great Depression.

On June 1, 1937, Case responded to Estes agreeing that the Big Bend site "is right there in your reservation and you are entitled to first consideration."[12] Lower Brule followed suit, passing a resolution seeking federal loans from the Bureau of Indian Affairs (BIA) to develop a small-scale hydroelectric plant. While the tribe had planned a smaller project for the immediate benefit of their community, Case had bigger ideas, in which the Indigenous communities were not considered or were minor players. Case claimed that the Big Bend site "could mean much to national defense, to Indian rehabilitation and to the general welfare of central South Dakota."[13] From 1937 to 1940, the Lower Brule requested approval for developing the site, and the secretary of the interior, Harold Ickes, favored the plan as a BIA-led project to increase the Department of Interior's influence and control over the river.[14] But the Army Corps rejected both the BIA and Lower Brule proposals, basing their decision on a "cost-to-benefit" analysis and the simple fact that they didn't want to relinquish any authority to tribes or the federal government.[15] On the surface, it may have seemed like bureaucratic conflict or a lack of political will. What South Dakota, the Army Corps, and BIA did agree on, however, was that river development would happen—with or without Indigenous consent.

Lower Brule's initial opposition was consistent with other Indigenous nations' earlier attempts to protect their water rights. In the 1908 *Winters* decision, the US Supreme Court ruled in favor of the Fort Belknap Reservation's claim to water rights over a white farmer's effort to control the flow of the Milk River, a tributary of the Missouri River in Montana. The court ruled that even if Fort Belknap had given up its fertile former lands in exchange for arid ones— which were, according to the court, adequate for "nomadic uncivilized people"—that their occupancy of those lands was inconsistent with the federal government's desire to have them "become a pastoral and civilized people."[16] Put simply, Indigenous peoples retained quantifiable water rights if, and only if, the water was used in accordance with the civilizing mission of the federal government. The decision became known as the Winters Doctrine. The doctrine holds that, however diminished current reservation boundaries may be, tribes retain senior, reserved rights to water flowing through the originally defined boundaries established by treaty, statute, or executive order.[17]

Neither the Lower Brule or any Indigenous nation challenging Missouri River development had ever invoked the Winters Doctrine. But they still possessed the power to do so. The doctrine's intended use illustrates limits to Indigenous water rights under settler law; nevertheless, state or federal alteration or disruption of the flow of the river for any reason without the consent of the tribes, such as through the construction of dams, violates the spirit of the Winters Doctrine.

The 1944 Flood Control Act, which authorized the Pick-Sloan Plan, permitted the Army Corps only to construct dams—not to expunge Indigenous jurisdiction, treaty rights, or water rights. In less-than-precise language, Section 4 of the act opened the river for "public use" and "recreational purposes." It didn't strip Crow Creek, Lower Brule, Standing Rock, Cheyenne River, Yankton, Fort Berthold, or any Indigenous nation, for that matter, of their political authority over their river. Regardless, from the 1950s to the 1960s the Army Corps condemned reservation lands under eminent domain and Congress awarded compensation to the affected reservations. Neither the Flood Control Act (which took the land) nor the congressional acts addressing damages (which rewarded compensation for taking the land) explicitly extinguished Indigenous jurisdiction; and neither authorized nor provided any compensation for the Army Corps' taking the Missouri River itself. Compensation was provided only for taking the land, but not for the water. Since then, the Oceti Sakowin have contended that the Missouri River and its shoreline were never legally ceded. And, according to statute, they are right: the Army Corps' alteration of the flow of the river by damming it directly violates both the Winters Doctrine and the 1868 Fort Laramie Treaty.[18] But, regardless of treaty rights and sheer legality, the Army Corps proceeded anyway.

For Dakotas and Lakotas, water rights are defined by treaty. For example, Article 2 of the 1868 Fort Laramie Treaty delineated the eastern boundary of "Sioux territory" as beginning at the "low-water mark" of the east bank of the Missouri River. In contrast, the tribal constitutions for the Cheyenne River, Standing Rock, and Lower Brule Reservations delineated reservation boundaries according to the 1889 Sioux Agreement. The agreement divided West River tribes into five distinct reservations (Pine Ridge, Rosebud, Cheyenne River, Lower Brule, and Standing Rock) and defined the eastern boundary of the three reservations bordering the river (Standing Rock, Cheyenne River, and Lower Brule) as beginning at "the center of the main channel of the Missouri River."[19] Regardless of the 1889 Agreement's diminishment of reservation lands, all these reservations and the Oceti Sakowin still possess powers under the Winters Doctrine to the Missouri River according to the original 1868 Treaty boundaries, as long as the water is used in a "civilized" manner.

Winters rights take effect on the date reservations are created by federal authority and are considered unquantifiable or, according to the court decision, "uncircumscribed," allowing for the perpetual benefit and use for a permanent Indigenous homeland. According to Diné scholar Melanie K. Yazzie in her analysis of the 2012 Navajo-Hopi Little Colorado River water settlement, subsequent Supreme Court decisions have interpreted this "uncircumscribed" quality to mean a "minimal need" required by the reservation. In other words, Indigenous nations are only entitled to water they can use for "civilized" purposes. Those purposes are quantified—or, put another way, Indigenous sovereignty is quantified according to water usage and degrees of "civilized" usage. Anything falling outside these qualifications is considered surplus, unused, or wasted. The rest can be measured and siphoned away to meet the need of non-Native interests. After each party quantifies their needs, water that flows through reservation or treaty lands is then, by no small feat of the imagination, not entirely "owned" by Indigenous nations. The result is that Indigenous nations can only use a restricted amount—in some instances, a fraction of a percentage—of the water flowing through their territory.

Settler agricultural interests in water, because they are so insatiable, have always outweighed the bare survival of Indigenous peoples. On the plains of the Missouri River basin, irrigation is necessary for agriculture, which as a mode of production personifies settler colonialism: it's sedentary and mostly permanent; it reproduces itself; and it always needs more land and water. As it expands, it eats away at Indigenous territory, destroying fauna and flora and annihilating Indigenous subsistence economies. This is not to say Indigenous peoples were not pastoralists, farmers, or ranchers before and during colonization. (Prior to colonization most Indigenous societies were agricultural, not "hunter-gatherer," with great affinities to domesticated plants such as corn.)[20] Indeed, by the time the Pick-Sloan Plan was proposed, Missouri River Indigenous nations had already developed successful Native-run cattle ranching enterprises and small-scale agricultural projects, often reflecting communal practices. These small-scale economies allowed Indigenous nations to resist and challenge the further diminishment of their reservation lands by preventing the need to sell it off to feed themselves.

Lanniko L. Lee, a Lakota writer and a citizen of Cheyenne River Reservation, remembers the river bottomlands before the floods. Drawing on memories of her childhood, she recalls what life was like before the Oahe Dam took her lands:

> I see a river shoreline of men and women, young and old, carry-ing water, picking berries, gathering firewood, fishing from the shore, wading in the sloughs for cattail root, gathering teas of so many kinds, making toys for children from the fallen leaves and branches, telling stories of how we came to be a people, making furniture, women telling river stories to their grand-children, children learning the gifts of the river. I hear men singing; I hear women, old and young, singing as they work and live among the trees. I hear children's laughter, too.[21]

Pick-Sloan's massive dam projects, for instance, quite liter-ally snatched the food from the mouths of Indigenous peoples. Indigenous sovereignty could be felt through the hunger in one's stomach, as was the case for the Oceti Sakowin who had their most productive lands taken. In this sense, Indigenous sovereignty can be calculated according to their water rights, which, according to Yazzie, face "unlimited limitations" in federal courts.[22] That is, settler law has never expanded the material basis of Indigenous sovereignty—land and water; it has only eroded it by placing upon it endless restrictions. When it comes to water rights, it is not just the legal character of "Indians" that is defined. "Settlers," too, become legal subjects with a vested interest in the taking of Indigenous water. Put differently, in cases where Indigenous peoples possess water rights according to federal statute, executive order, or treaty, settler communities, to fulfill their needs, are dependent on diminishing those rights—with or without Indigenous consent. Thus, Indigenous water rights are calcu-lated first and foremost according to settler needs.

The undercurrents of the Pick-Sloan Plan also originated from the centralization of the power of the federal government to imagine and enact theories of space through land policy.

The practice began as early as the 1785 Land Ordinance and continued into the nineteenth and early twentieth centuries as federal authorities worked to know, map, reorganize, and manage land as territory. Water management was vital to these policies, as westward expansion and the taking of Indigenous lands confronted the problem of creating irrigation systems to make settler life possible in arid environments. After removing Indigenous peoples, the first task was to induce colonization. Federal policies such as the 1862 Homestead Act encouraged agricultural settlement on dry western lands unsuitable for settler farming techniques developed in the east. Pushed by the railroad lobby to spur settlement and therefore the need for railroads to transport agricultural goods, the 1877 Desert Land Act amended the Homestead Act and provided federal money for western irrigation projects. The Northern Pacific Railway, for example, also opened colonization offices in Germany, Sweden, Denmark, Norway, and England to entice European immigrants to settle the Northern Plains and, therefore, to create a demand for railroad transportation.[23] Conservation policy, influenced by President Theodore Roosevelt at the turn of the century, led to the creation of the Bureau of Reclamation in 1902 to provide for the irrigation of arid lands in the West. Land policy was the legal justification for the sometimes-unwilling shock troops of colonization—white European settlers. Settlement and settlers literally made "legal" and operational contemporary water law that depends so heavily on the theft of Indigenous water.

"Public land" for "public good" was a highly subsidized federal endeavor for private enterprise, racial exclusion, and Indigenous elimination. One and a half million white families gained title to 246 million acres of Indigenous lands—an area nearly the size of California and Texas combined—under the Homestead Act, with the added value of federally subsidized irrigation. A quarter of adults alive today in the United States are direct descendants of those who profited from the

Homestead Act's legacy of exclusive, racialized property ownership and economic mobility, a legacy that categorically excluded Black, Indigenous, and other nonwhite peoples.[24] Access to Indigenous water was crucial for securing the ownership of Indigenous lands and generating wealth from these lands over generations. Thus, a single land policy has had a profound lasting political and economic legacy. It informs present disparities, which boil down to a single axiom: land is wealth and water is wealth. The Pick-Sloan Plan is part and parcel of this massive settler-colonial agricultural machine that greases its gears with water. Today, agriculture in the western United States accounts for three-quarters of all water usage.[25] Water is settler colonialism's lifeblood—blood that has to be continually excised from Indigenous peoples.

To meet incessant demands for irrigation, the Pick-Sloan Plan was made to appear inevitable. But it was not a dream manifested in a dusty federal office building in Washington, DC, to be handed down to unwitting agricultural communities. States, local governments, the Army Corps, and other federal agencies all pushed for Missouri River development in various ways, in spite of the consequences for Indigenous communities. Although most of the power was concentrated in federal authorities by 1944, "grassroots" organizations continued to play a significant role. By 1941, the Upper Missouri River Valley Development Authority had dissolved. In its place formed the Missouri River States Committee, an organization of governors from Missouri basin states. It is rather telling that the first states to enthusiastically join the committee (South Dakota, North Dakota, Montana, Wyoming, and Nebraska) encompassed thirteen Indian reservations whose lands either immediately included or bordered the Missouri River (the Omaha, Winnebago, Santee, Rosebud, Ponca, Yankton, Lower Brule, Crow Creek, Cheyenne River, Standing Rock, Fort Berthold, and Fort Peck Reservations). Later, Missouri, Kansas, and Iowa would join the committee.

Representation ranged from federal, state, and municipal agencies and officials to businesses and community organiza- tions. The channelization of the river benefited mostly down-river states, while upriver states would bear the heaviest burden by taking on the majority of the dams and reservoirs. Since most of the land to be flooded was Indigenous, this was a "burden" South Dakota and North Dakota politicians were willing to assume. In 1951 during an appraisal hearing, Standing Rock Chairwoman Josephine Kelly challenged this aspect of the Pick-Sloan Plan, and especially the Oahe Dam's appropriation of Standing Rock lands. Someone asked why the dams were not built in the lower basin states, who benefit-ted the most from flood control, to which Kelly responded bluntly, in front of Army Corps and federal authorities: "Because there are no Indians down in that country."[26]

At no time did the state committee solicit the attendance or input of a single Indigenous representative from the affected reservations. The committee would work closely with the Bureau of Reclamation and the Army Corps, in the words of its chair M. Q. Sharpe, "for the general develop-ment [of the Missouri River] for the multiple purposes of flood control, power development, irrigation, navigation, soil conservation, [and] wildlife and recreational development." As he went on to explain, "the Missouri River States Committee had really become the general over-all supervis-ing, coordinating, steering and representative committee for the development of the Missouri River basin on a valley-wide, over-all plan, representing all the sovereign states of the basin in their sovereign status and in a semi-official way."[27] Thus, states' interests didn't lay solely in river devel-opment; they also proposed the total liquidation of Indigenous political authority through termination.

The construction of the Fort Peck Dam on the Missouri River in Montana in 1933 set a precedent for the way the Army Corps would ignore Indigenous communities, treaties, and water rights. After destructive floods in 1927, the Army Corps conducted an exhaustive four-year hydrological study on the Missouri River. The findings were published in what was called the 308 Report, which became the go-to manual for all future developments in the basin, including the 1944 Pick-Sloan Plan. The report also designated Fort Peck (not to be confused with the Fort Peck Indian Reservation) as the best site for a massive reservoir. The project fell in line with New Deal labor relief and public work projects, and President Franklin D. Roosevelt quickly authorized the Fort Peck Dam under the 1933 National Industrial Recovery Act. The Army Corps built what was at the time of its construction the largest dam on earth, in the process providing much-needed employment for about 10,000 workers. Regional histories celebrate the dam as a historic engineering masterpiece, and it is considered instrumental in pulling Montana and the region out of the Great Depression. The successes of the Fort Peck Dam secured Army Corps control in planning and constructing future massive multipurpose dams on the main stem of the Missouri and, according to historian Michael Lawson, "greatly expanded its powers and functions beyond its constitutional limits."[28]

While the dam's history is well publicized and well remembered as an economic boon and engineering marvel, missing from these popular accounts is the largely untold and undocumented history of the removal of 350 Nakota, Dakota, and Assiniboine families on the Fort Peck Indian Reservation and the flooding of earlier Indian Affairs irrigation projects that had benefited Native farmers.[29] The Fort Peck project paved the way for the 1944 Pick-Sloan Plan and Flood Control Act, and a similar process would repeat itself: postwar employment and river development projects would come primarily at the sacrifice of Indigenous lives and lands.

In anticipation of the need for postwar employment, and on the heels of massive flooding, in 1944 the Bureau of Reclamation and the Army Corps, with the input and guidance of the Missouri River states, called for the construction of five earthen rolled dams that would create massive reservoirs on the river's main stem. In South Dakota and North Dakota, the dams flooded 611,642 acres of land. Just over a half of this land— 309,584 acres in all—belonged to the Yankton, Lower Brule, Crow Creek, Cheyenne River, Standing Rock, Rosebud, Santee, and Fort Berthold reservations. Oahe Dam flooded the Cheyenne River and Standing Rock; Fort Randall Dam flooded the Yankton and Rosebud Reservations; Fort Randall and Big Bend Dams flooded the Lower Brule and Crow Creek reservations, while Garrison Dam flooded Fort Berthold and Gavin's Point Dam flooded the Santee Reservation. As a result, from these five reservations alone more than 900 Native families, one-third of their overall populations, were forced to relocate. Entire communities were forever submerged. Indigenous communities were well aware of the Pick-Sloan dams but had little idea where they would be built and how much it would affect them. Some communities were even flooded twice and experienced two dislocations, such as Crow Creek and Lower Brule. Seventy-five percent of wildlife and plants, and 90 percent of all commercial timber on these reservations lands were destroyed.[30] By design, the Pick-Sloan Plan was a destroyer of nations.

The Garrison Dam inundated the Fort Berthold Reservation, composed of the Mandan, Hidatsa, and Arikara nations, taking 152,360 acres of their land. Thirty percent of the community populations from Lower Brule, Crow Creek, Cheyenne River, and Standing Rock would be removed. Although less land was taken by the Garrison Dam than by the Oahe Dam, Fort Berthold lost a quarter of its entire land base, including its agency at Elbowoods. Because of its smaller size and the greater concentration of its residents in the river valley, approximately 80 percent of its people (325 families) were removed and 94 percent of its agricultural lands were destroyed.[31] No care was exercised to minimize the damage to Indigenous lands. To protect the majority-white border town of Williston, North Dakota, from losing its land, however, the Army Corps modified the Garrison Dam. The dam was also built safely upriver so as not to flood Bismarck, a white-dominated border town and the state capital of North Dakota. (Such were the considerations the Army Corps made when planning the Dakota Access Pipeline: minimization of damage to white settlements was prioritized.) The reservoir that sits atop Fort Berthold lands was named "Lake Sakakawea," after the Shoshone woman, captured and sold by the Hidatsas, who gained notoriety for her services to the Lewis and Clark expedition and US empire.[32] According to historian Michael Lawson, the Pick-Sloan dams "destroyed more Indian land than any single public works project in the United States."[33]

Lanniko Lee remembers teary-eyed women and men, young and old, gathering near the shorelines to watch as Mni Sose, the Missouri River, slowly widened and the flood waters crept up the rolling gumbo hills. "Some of them were singing the ancient songs for mourning," she recalled. "They sang of the coming death to the river life that the people had known." To Lee, it was an existential question about Indigenous identity grounded in land and water: "Would we still be able to call ourselves Minnecoujou, planters by the water?"[34]

While Indigenous peoples mourned the loss of their river, US President John F. Kennedy celebrated the Oahe's construction. At a dedication ceremony for the dam on August 17, 1962, held in Pierre, South Dakota, Kennedy spoke to a crowd of thousands, including businessmen, politicians, and the very Indigenous peoples whose lands were sacrificed. His message was one of salvation—the triumph of lightness over darkness, civilization over savagery. "This dam and the rest of the dams on this river," he said, "which 30 years ago would have provided only floods and darkness, now provide irrigation and light."

Although the Army Corps proclaimed before Congress that they would negotiate with the affected reservations, they never did.[35] White landowners were dealt with on an individual, case-by-case basis, and Missouri River tribes were dealt with as separate reservations. In contrast to the treatment of white landowners, the entire tribe received compensation, rather than the individual tribal members whose allotments were directly flooded or condemned. The creation of separate reservations had already severely weakened national unity for the Oceti Sakowin. Allotment emphasized individualism, breaking up the tightly knit family units of direct kin and extended relations called the tiospaye, isolating them on different plots of land in distant parts of the reservation. Tiospayes were the fundamental political unit of Oceti Sakowin governance, and they were where each family collectively selected its own representatives for general councils; though individuals once identified by political affiliation (for instance, as Hunkpapapa or Sicangu), they now identified by reservation (as Standing Rock or Rosebud). Now, Pick-Sloan, by negotiating with separate reservations rather than individual allottees, further fomented disunity between reservations, individual tribal members, and their tribal governments.

Indigenous nations were, nevertheless, awarded more money per acre than their white neighbors; this was to better enable tribes to "throw off the shackles of Federal supervision," as South Dakota Congressman E. Y. Berry declared during a debate on the Cheyenne River settlement in 1954.[36] In other words, Berry wanted to terminate the reservations and extinguish treaty obligations, and the dams provided the perfect opportunity. The initial negotiations for taken lands and relocation resulted in a $34 million award to Lower Brule, Cheyenne River, Crow Creek, Yankton, and Standing Rock. But this came with strings attached—namely, that these tribes would eventually give up their political authority.

As early damages were still being calculated, on November 2, 1949, BIA Superintendent Frell M. Owl wrote to the Lower Brule and Crow Creek Tribal Councils advising them, perhaps for the first time, of the inevitable flooding of their lands. The two tribes no doubt knew about Pick-Sloan, but none fathomed the catastrophe it would bring. Owl told them Congress transferred to the Army Corps all the lands "required" for the Big Bend and Fort Randall Dams. Emphasizing Lower Brule and Crow Creek had no say in the matter, Owl wrote that the proposal to take their lands "is submitted to you not as a document that you should adopt but it, more or less, points out the events to come in the future." Owl later conveyed the convoluted negotiations process: the Army Corps would condemn the land and negotiate directly with Crow Creek and Lower Brule legal counsel. The BIA would then approve and submit estimates of damages, but Congress would hold final approval over all the negotiations and pass legislation awarding monetary compensation.[37] This lengthy back-and-forth process resulted in the tribes negotiating with three different entities—the Army Corps, the BIA, and Congress—often causing such a backlog in hearings and proceedings that tribes received their relocation money only after their lands were flooded.

In 1946 the BIA sponsored a two-year fact-finding mission, known as the Missouri River Basin Investigation (MRBI), to estimate damages to Missouri River tribes and estimate monetary awards for relocation, taken lands, and "intangible damages." In the process, they saw "opportunity" in Indigenous "removal," "relocation," and "rehabilitation," words that were synonymous with "termination." This would sever Native people from the one thing keeping them from "merging with the total population" and evolving beyond their "primitive status": the reservation and the land. Put plainly, the dams would speed up termination and relocation. Indigenous culture, a "self-contained and ingrowing" culture of poverty, the BIA investigation concluded, wanted for benevolent state intervention and the civilizing project. Indigenous nations had achieved a relative degree of autonomy under the IRA, but it was only through the liquidation of Indigenous political authority and federal trust responsibilities—undergoing destruction as nations—that they could receive the "gift of democracy."[38]

Most Indigenous river communities, as the MRBI put it, still depended on the "free goods of Nature"—such as hunting, trapping, and gathering—in the lush bottomlands where many Lakotas and Dakotas historically camped, and taking those lands would "force [Indians] into seeking cash income to make up for the substantial portion of income now represented in their use of natural resources of their present environment," the BIA concluded.[39] In other words, Indigenous peoples could only attain democracy once they were destroyed as nations.

The BIA made it sound like flooding agencies, the reservations' headquarters, constituted liberation from dictatorial rule. "Our Indian agencies are growths descended from the frontier," the report claimed. It called the towns "undemocratic" and stated that their end "might take the course of transferring most of the Federal Government's services to the States." The transfer of treaty obligations (federal services such as healthcare and education) to the states is termination in line with Public Law 280. The "wiping out" of the agencies, the MRBI concluded, was a "rare opportunity" that "may lead to significant discoveries which will have wide application to the conduct of Indian affairs in the United States." In other words, it was an experiment in democracy.[40]

"It takes the very heart out of these Indians," one congressman said, speaking candidly about the legislation. "When you take reservation land, you destroy not only the land that is taken, but you destroy the community life, [the] religious and civil life of the people. You destroy nations, as a matter of fact."

Agencies were the heart of these nations. Hospitals, health clinics, schools, and administrative offices—the very institutions necessary to continue on as a sovereign nation—were all located in agency towns. The damages are worth reviewing in full.

The Oahe Dam entirely inundated Cheyenne Agency, Cheyenne River's largest community. The agency had to reestablish sixty miles inland at the isolated prairie town of Eagle Butte. More than 180 families, about 30 percent of the population of the agency, were forced to leave their homes. Fort Yates, the Standing Rock Agency, remained above the Oahe Dam flood waters, but the land below it, where most of the community's population lived, was flooded. As a result, Fort Yates was made into an island that had to be connected by a bridge, and 170 families were forced to relocate—25 percent of the reservation population. At Crow Creek, the Fort Randall Dam flooded Fort Thompson, the agency headquarters for Lower Brule and Crow Creek and the largest community, dislocating eighty-four families from Crow Creek, thirty-five families from Lower Brule, and twenty families from Yankton. The combined agency headquarters from Crow Creek and Lower Brule were relocated to Pierre, the small capital city of South Dakota some sixty miles north of both reservations. Indian health services were relocated to Chamberlain, a notoriously racist, white-dominated border town twenty miles to the south.

Beyond the agencies, the damage to the rest of the reservations was no less diffuse. The Oahe Dam, the most destructive, destroyed 160,889 acres of Standing Rock and Cheyenne River, including 104,420 acres of Cheyenne River lands and 55,994 acres of Standing Rock lands. Nearly all the Cheyenne River lands taken were grazing lands; 75 percent and 60 percent of Native ranchers were displaced at Cheyenne River and Standing Rock, respectively. The most expensive and largest of the Pick-Sloan dams, the Oahe project cost $346 million, is 245 feet high, and generates 595,000 kilowatts of hydropower. The Oahe reservoir (Lake Oahe), stretching 250 miles from Pierre to Bismarck and storing 23.5 million acre-feet of water, is as deep as Lake Eerie and longer than Lake Ontario.

The second-largest, Fort Randall Dam, rises 160 feet high and destroyed 21,497 acres of Indigenous land. Crow Creek lost 9,418 acres of land in the flooding and had eighty-four families removed; Lower Brule lost 7,997 acres and had thirty-five families removed; Yankton lost 2,851 acres and had twenty families removed; and Rosebud lost 1,231 acres of land. The Fort Randall generates 320,000 kilowatts of hydropower and cost $200 million. The reservoir it created, Lake Francis Case (named after a South Dakota congressman and early river-development advocate) is 107 miles long and has a storage capacity of 5.7 million acre-feet.

In an incredibly stupid and cruel engineering calculation, the Big Bend Dam, the third-largest of those constructed under Pick-Sloan, flooded and dislocated Crow Creek and Lower Brule lands to which communities had been already relocated from the previous Fort Randall flooding. Both reservations would have to relocate twice. Ninety-four feet high and producing 468,000 kilowatts of power, the Big Bend Dam was built directly on the now-inundated Fort Thompson town site and directly on Crow Creek and Lower Brule lands, flooding 20,478 acres of each and destroying the Lower Brule Agency headquarters. Lower Brule lost 14,299 acres and had sixty-two families, more than half its population, removed. Half the remaining Lower Brule farms not destroyed by the Fort Randall project were destroyed by Big Bend. Crow Creek lost 6,179 acres and had twenty-seven families removed. The reservoir behind Big Bend, Lake Sharpe, was named after the appointed Lower Brule and Crow Creek attorney M. Q. Sharpe, who represented the two tribes during the Pick-Sloan negotiations. For his lifelong commitment, not to Indigenous peoples, but to the taking of their lands by flooding it, Sharpe is immortalized by the water that sits atop Lower Brule and Crow Creek lands.

The smallest and southernmost dam, Gavin's Point, took 593 acres of Santee lands. Gavin's Point created Lewis and Clark Lake, named for the two US explorers who famously branded the Oceti Sakowin as "the vilest miscreants of the savage race."

As much as the Army Corps already viewed the Missouri River as a technical problem to be managed and administered, the MRBI reduced Indigenous relocation and the trauma it inflicted to a set of technical questions and problems to be sorted out by the administration of federal and state services. Each of these problems had a solution, followed with a cash payment. By all accounts most of the Indigenous river communities, as the MRBI put it, still depended on the "free goods of Nature"—such as hunting, trapping, and gathering. This relationship was viewed as preventing full integration into the market economy. The BIA argued that taking the bottomlands would "force [Indians] into seeking cash income to make up for the substantial portion of income now represented in their use of natural resources of their present environment." "Income" calculated not only cash income from wage labor, but also what was harvested from the land for consumption, rather than for profit. The assessment of "intangible" and "tangible" resources would force Indigenous people to begin thinking in terms of the cash economy, rather than relying upon goods that were otherwise considered "free" and, if properly managed, naturally replenishing. "Substitutes for native products destroyed by the reservoirs will be commercial products acquired through cash payments," reasoned the MRBI.[41]

During a 1958 congressional hearing on the Oahe Dam, Standing Rock member Louis Thief compared the catastrophic impact of "intangible damages" to the delayed explosion of an atomic bomb—unfolding gradually over time and space rather than in a split second—forever destroying the land, and whose consequences could only be fully understood by future generations. The bomb killed the "little things" that had no market value, such as mice or mouse beans, which had prevented many Indigenous peoples from starvation on the reservations. Mouse beans, or makatomnica in Lakota, are ground beans that are highly revered in Indigenous culture. Lakota and Dakota women would sing special songs in which they asked the mice for permission to take their beans, promising to leave appropriate gifts. The beans were a major source of protein for many families and today remain nearly extinct.[42] Thief explained how the previous winter a man had dug up some of these mouse beans and had "enough to tide him over two weeks and [save] his family from starving."[43]

The loss of wildlife and plant life and the gardens also had a deleterious health impact. Prior to the dams, there was no diabetes. After the dams, diabetes rates soared. US Department of Agriculture commodity foods, such as canned meats and vegetables, white flour, and white sugar, replaced healthy foods. "Civilizing" the river landscape replaced a healthy diet of vegetables and lean meats with a high carb, sugar, and fat diet, causing generational health issues.[44]

Thief's testimony evoked the idea that Missouri Indigenous communities were also "energy sacrifice zones," a term that the Nixon-era National Academy of Sciences used to describe the Shoshone and Paiute lands that were taken for nuclear testing at the Nevada Test Site. With no small irony, the US Department of Energy created a 1,360-square-mile "reservation" where 928 nuclear bombs were detonated, making it the most heavily nuclear-bombed area in the world. The only difference was that while the Nevada Test Site sought to transform atoms into nuclear energy, Pick-Sloan sought to transform water into hydropower. Both made the landscapes uninhabitable. Despite MRBI attempts to calculate the costs of damage, the value of the land could never be replaced.

Also at stake was the future realization of life that sustained Indigenous lives, that kept families from starving to death. In this sense, the dams reached into the future to take human and nonhuman life, and literally drowned its potential reproduction. Calculations were not for immediate damages but future damages, demonstrating the MRBI's inability to realize relations with other-than-human life. For the Oceti Sakowin, the attempt at compensation for taking their future was not a new phenomenon. During the illegal annexation of the Black Hills, a federal official offered Red Cloud and his people $6 million for the Black Hills. When Red Cloud refused, the official asked him the value of the Black Hills. "The Black Hills [are] worth seven generations to me," Red Cloud responded.[45] In other words, it was not about money but about a viable future, something entirely unquantifiable. It was not merely about surrendering one's lands, but also surrendering one's future relations to that land. As Lower Brule Tribal Council member Richard LaRoche Jr. testified before Congress in 1955,

> We doubt if any group of strangers to this land, even though they may have some skill as appraisers[,] could come on to it and find all of the real values of it and appraise them accurately. We who have lived with it and owned some of it and worked it all of our lives, we think, are better able to tell you its true value.[46]

The BIA, seeking to account for the loss of "intangible" things like mice beans, wild plums, chokecherries, buffalo berries, wild game, plant medicines, and a bountiful timber supply, was estimating the "value of wild products" to be equivalent to "the grocery of food to replace the loss of wild products."[47] But many of the "wild products" lost also played central roles in seasonal ceremonial practices. One such practice involving women's coming of age required the use of buffalo berries, which would never again grow on Lower Brule land after inundation, thus ending the ceremonial practice. LaRoche was outraged at having to explain this and place a monetary value on the loss of ceremonial rites: "Well, the white man, he never cared about these things; he didn't even know what it was."[48]

In a 1958 congressional hearing on the Oahe relocation and rehabilitation program for Standing Rock, Josephine Kelly, no longer the chairwoman, expressed disgust at the way the United States government and the Army Corps ran roughshod over treaties. Frustrated congressmen told her in patronizing tones that the settlement would provide agricultural and community development loans. "We don't want loans," Kelly shot back. The congressman compared the loan to a gift from Santa Claus, as if Kelly was an entitled child. "We have been Santa Clauses, too, the Sioux Indians. We gave up our Black Hills and gave up our land," she replied, "and now we are down to bedrock, just like a bunch of beggars, and that is really sad."[49]

No matter. Human and animal life, BIA officials harshly explained, would "have to reestablish on the open upland plains where a less hospitable and more rigorous climate prevails."[50] And compensating land loss at "fair market value" was next to impossible because this sudden rise in demand for hospitable lands drove up real estate prices and market competition for prime ranchland.[51] As a result, many families had to subsist on a monetary compensation that arrived only after their homes had been flooded, "with the result that they run the real risk of ending up penniless and homeless."[52] And many did. Michael Lawson describes an all-too-familiar scene that unfolded at Standing Rock, which was also experienced by the Lower Brule and Crow Creek Reservations:

In January 1960, when the Corps of Engineers finally delivered the settlement funds to Standing Rock, it also served the tribe with an immediate eviction order. In the midst of a fierce Dakota winter, with temperatures falling as low as thirty degrees below zero, tribal families who lived within the Oahe reservoir taking area were forced to gather all their possessions and to leave their land. Because the federal government had not yet made funds available for either the construction of new homes or the relocation of old dwellings, these people were crowded into cold and cheerless trailer houses, which they had to maintain at their own expense until permanent housing could be prepared.[53]

Although the dams promised to hasten the death of Indigenous nations by destroying the land, they failed to accomplish this task, thanks to the Oceti Sakowin's ability to mobilize, unite, and defeat termination legislation—not once, but twice. However, it was an enormous task. During early Pick-Sloan negotiations, most of the politicians "advocating" for the Oceti Sakowin were also ardent terminationists and Pick-Sloan supporters, like South Dakota congressmen Karl Mundt, E. Y. Berry, and Francis Case; the Lower Brule and Crow Creek legal counsel M. Q. Sharpe; and the commissioner of Indian Affairs, Dillon Myer. From the time Myer took over as commissioner of Indian affairs, he was intent on overturning the progressive legacy of his predecessor, John Collier, who introduced the IRA. Myer was also the perfect man for overseeing the overthrow of Indigenous nations. Appointed by President Franklin Roosevelt as director of the War Relocation Authority, Myer earned his credentials, imprisoning more than 100,000 Japanese and Japanese Americans in concentration camps during World War II.

If facing imminent flooding were not a bleak enough situation for the Lower Brule and Crow Creek, they also had an enthusiastic Pick-Sloan advocate and terminationist representing them in the negotiations process. In June 1951, the consolidated agencies of Lower Brule and Crow Creek appointed M. Q. Sharpe as their legal counsel because his law practice was located near the reservations and he had political connections in Congress and within federal agencies—and, above all, because he was the most affordable lawyer. Indian Commissioner Dillon Myer had also refused to allow Crow Creek to hire separate legal counsel after they selected Lakota attorney Ramon Roubideaux.[54] When the failure to select a legal counsel for both reservations delayed negotiations, Myer intervened and made the decision for them.[55] In the course of the negotiations, Myer, as well as the South Dakota politicians, consistently tried to steer the conversation toward termination.

The issue arose of relocating the agency headquarters—the seat of the tribes' IRA government—off the reservation to nearby white-dominated towns, a move which would fulfill the dual purpose of providing a model for termination while also beginning the process of Indigenous relocation into surrounding white communities. Berry and Myer claimed that the leaders of the white-dominated border town Chamberlain offered up their town as a potential site for Lower Brule. This move, wrote Myer to Berry on August 31, might "result in some inconvenience to individual Indians," but in the longer-term, "many of the Indians who now take all their problems, great and small, to the agency superintendent might through necessity have to start taking care of some of them for themselves." The completion of Fort Randall Dam, Myer continued, might "become the starting point" for pushing them toward "more assimilation and integration"—and away from the "narrow and inbred way of life" that was "customary of reservation living."[56]

Local white leadership reacted virulently. Because Chamberlain was the seat of Brule County, the county commissioners adopted a resolution to thwart an effort by the BIA and Congress to force the members of Lower Brule and Crow Creek into integration at the public schools and into the community at large, claiming it "would place an intolerable financial burden on Brule County, South Dakota."[57] Chamberlain Mayor Herschel V. Melcher took an even more threatening tone, in a March 30, 1954, letter to Case and Berry, reminding them that carrying the "relief load for Indians" was the job of the federal government.[58] "We do not intend to let an Indian light around here at all. We do not want to live with them, we don't want them in our schools," he wrote. Impatient, he sent another letter just two weeks later, threatening racial violence. "Anybody who rents them any property will have to change his address and I would not want the insurance on his building. We do not feel that this town should be ruined by a mess like this and we do not intend to take this lying down."[59]

Crow Creek and Lower Brule also opposed the proposed relocation, adopting a resolution that barred Commissioner Myer from further obstructing the tribe's requests for legal counsel and to open negotiations with Congress and the Corps of Engineers.[60] But Myer refused to halt the proposed relocation, to allow the tribe to select its own legal counsel, or to open immediate negotiations for Fort Randall claims. This rebuff highlighted a larger failure of termination, and a persistent feature of settler colonialism's "Indian problem": white settlers want Indigenous lands, but they don't want Indigenous peoples. Federal agencies adopted a hands-off approach when dealing with tribes once their land bases were destroyed, with the BIA and Congress recommending a course of action, then standing back, leaving already hard-pressed Indigenous communities to fight for themselves against powerful federal bureaucracies and violently hostile white settlers. It was a tactic of neglect. The Pick-Sloan Plan created an opportunity to experiment with forced Native relocation and assimilation as a way of relinquishing federal wardship responsibilities. Ultimately, the experiment failed, but termination remained on the table.

In 1957 the South Dakota legislature introduced a bill to assume criminal jurisdiction over Dakota and Lakota lands, but the Oceti Sakowin fought back. The majority of the Lakotas and Dakotas whose lands were circumscribed by the state resoundingly rejected state jurisdiction in a 1958 reservation-wide referendum.[61] But the victory was short-lived. In 1963 South Dakota again introduced legislation to attempt to overthrow tribal governments under the auspices of Public Law 280, which did not immediately require Indigenous consent but mandated states to assume all the financial burdens of taking over Indigenous authority. Within weeks the Oceti Sakowin formed United Sioux Tribes (UST) and collected more than 20,000 signatures to put the legislation up for a statewide referendum. In 1964 UST mobilized both Native and non-Native communities with a savvy media and publicity campaign appealing to the "fairness" of state jurisdiction, which had been imposed without consent. Although they had never participated in large numbers in state politics, because of South Dakota's history of anti-Indian hostilities, nearly 90 percent of Natives in South Dakota turned out to vote. The referendum won in a landslide victory, with nearly 80 percent in favor (and therefore against termination) statewide.[62] South Dakota, which was deeply anti-Indian, wanted to take reservation land but could not fathom taking care of Indigenous peoples once they were "liberated" from federal rule, as the financial "burden" of termination and state jurisdiction was too much to bear. Nevertheless, the victory of the plebiscite killed the state's terminationist agenda, demonstrating the resiliency of the Oceti Sakowin.

Yet the Pick-Sloan dams endure, remaining disruptive structures on the riverscape whose longer-term impacts are hard to ascertain. Rob Nixon argues that environmental devastation, much like climate change, is difficult to understand because it unfolds over such a long duration. Violence is often viewed as immediate, explosive, and spectacular, like the Indian Wars of the nineteenth century. But Nixon sees environmental degradation as a kind of "slow violence": a violence that is neither "spectacular [n]or instantaneous."[63] Pick-Sloan might not have been an explicit attempt to overthrow tribal governments, but it nevertheless perpetuated "slow violence" on Indigenous people *as sovereign nations*—not simply as cultures. These are nations of people who need food, shelter, warmth, safety, and care, without which the nations cannot reproduce themselves or live as they choose. And this is far more than a question of cultural survival; cultural revitalization, while important, cannot bring back the stolen lands that once offered up food, clothes, materials for shelter, and medicines. Any cultural and spiritual connection to Mni Sose was also accompanied by a material connection: the river kept people from starving or freezing to death.

Indigenous peoples are more than cultures, they are sovereign nations. Thinking purely in terms of culture as a form of historical agency tends to neglect the concrete reality of Indigenous life. While Nixon's framework of "slow violence" as a steady accumulation—a gradual buildup—of violences through environmental contamination is useful for understanding the lasting impact of the Pick-Sloan Plan, there is also another kind of accumulation, one that is not always spectacular, nor instantaneous, but that nevertheless makes the endgame of elimination an impossibility: the tradition of Indigenous resistance. This accumulation is a radical consciousness and political practice, deeply embedded in history and place, and cannot be simply overturned by colonial fiat or by inundation with water. It cannot be killed. It endures the long game of colonial occupation. With the Pick-Sloan dams and the failed project of termination, a new generation of young people, thrown from their reservation homelands and shipped off to the city, took up the mantle of Red Power in the spirit of their ancestors and demanded freedom and justice in the face of this history of dispossession.

Water Protectors protest outside the White House
for the Native Nations Rise march and rally.
March 2017. Photo by author.

5

RED POWER

They can't stop the wind and they can't stop the rain. They can't stop the earthquake and the volcano and the tornado. They can't stop power.
—John Trudell, "We Are Power," Black Hills Survival Gathering, South Dakota, July 18, 1980[1]

Visions for Indigenous freedom coalesced into the Red Power movement in the 1960s. For the Oceti Sakowin, the American Indian Movement (AIM) became the militant vanguard for the 1868 Fort Laramie Treaty and Indigenous nationhood in the 1970s. Policies of termination, relocation, and the damming and flooding of the Missouri River had torn thousands of Indigenous peoples from rural reservations, scattering them in far-off urban centers. Many of them saw a direct link between the Pick-Sloan Plan, which took reservation lands in the 1950s and 1960s, and relocation policies. "I grew up along the Missouri River," Madonna Thunder Hawk told *Indian Country Today*, "and I saw that land go when it was flooded." The Oahe Dam flooded her home and community on the Cheyenne River Reservation. "I've never been able to take my children and grandchildren to where I grew up. That was probably one of the major events that put me on the road to activism."[2] She later joined AIM, following the 1969 Alcatraz takeover. The eighty-nine-day occupation of the federal prison island in the San Francisco Bay marked the beginning of a militant protest movement. "It was like a bomb that dropped, and we were scattered like shrapnel," Lakota and Ho-Chunk AIM activist Lakota Harden recalls.[3] The shrapnel that was Native life, which became radical activism, was scattered to places like Minneapolis, Chicago, San Francisco, Cleveland, Los Angeles, Denver, and other major cities.

In 1973, Thunder Hawk served as a leader and medic during AIM's armed takeover of Wounded Knee. But the hard work for her began once the occupation ended. She was central to organizing the Wounded Knee Legal Defense/Offense Committee, to combat the legal repression following the take-over; the We Will Remember Survival School, to provide an alternative education for Native youth; the International Indian Treaty Council, which advocates for the defense of Indigenous treaty rights at the United Nations; the Women of All Red Nations, organizing American Indian women around reproductive health, including against illegal sterilization and environmental contamination of Native lands; and the Black Hills Alliance, a Native and non-Native alliance formed to halt uranium mining in Black Hills. Lakota Harden, like her sister Marcella Gilbert (Thunder Hawk's daughter), came of age in the movement. As a student of the We Will Remember Survival School, she also became a leader. Each of these women had been impacted by genocidal Indian policy. Finding themselves flung far from their reservation homelands, instead of dissolving into the melting pot of settler society, they helped organize the twentieth century's most audacious Indigenous uprisings: Red Power.

Originally envisioned as a means to dismantle Native communities by removing them from the land and integrating them into mainstream urban society, relocation in fact had the opposite effect. Indians didn't simply stop being Indians once they left the reservation. Relocation, for all its malicious intent, helped birth a new movement that arose from both poverty-stricken urban ghettos and rural reservations. Natives on relocation found each other in the cities and at universities, forming pan-Indigenous organizations such as the National Indian Youth Council, United Native Americans, AIM, and many more. Their concerns, however, were fundamentally no different than those of their reservation-based relatives. They merged their respective rural and urban experiences into one, and what emerged was a radical, explicitly anti-colonial political consciousness that took the world by storm. It viewed the federal system as a colonial structure rather than as a solution. And, unlike youthful generational protests of its day, Red Power looked to older generations, the traditional reservation leadership, for guidance—the elders who had rejected federal administration and kept alive the "old ways."

In less than a decade from its founding in 1968, AIM would go from being a neighborhood patrol in the streets of Minneapolis, stopping police violence against Natives on relocation, to a far grander stage: the United Nations. To understand this trajectory, and how they wound up there, it is necessary to take a deeper look at the historical context of Red Power.

Powerful pan-Indigenous organizations, including the National Congress of American Indians (NCAI), preceded Red Power by nearly two decades. While it had led the fight against and successfully defeated termination legislation in the 1950s, which sought to end trust responsibilities to tribes, NCAI was ambivalent about the future of Native sovereignty, seeing it as heavily wedded to formal IRA governments and incremental reforms within the federal system. NCAI hoped to keep in place what a younger generation intended to end: colonial administration. Like its predecessors, many of NCAI's solutions pandered to the rampant anti-communism and flag-waving patriotism at the time. It was the height of the Cold War. To curb Soviet influence in the Third World, where colonial regimes were being violently overturned, the United States expanded its covert counterinsurgency campaigns in Latin America, the Middle East, and Southeast Asia. The justification was an intensifying ideological and economic struggle between Soviet Communism and Third World decolonization, on one side, and North Atlantic imperialism and capitalism, on the other. Humanitarian aid became empire's bargaining chip, a way to win hearts and minds, both at home and abroad. NCAI leaders understood this and appealed to domestic contests over the meaning of freedom and democracy. Black Americans had also pointed to the disparities in civil rights and racial injustice in the United States. In 1951 NCAI cofounder D'Arcy McNickle called for "a domestic Point Four Program for our Indian reservations." McNickle drew parallels with President Harry Truman's Point Four Program for international aid, which he undertook in the world's poorest countries in an effort to forestall the spread of communism.[4] Furthermore, McNickle understood that Natives shared "the world experience of other native peoples subjected to colonial domination."[5]

How could the United States defend its claims to moral superiority when Native people were not free and remained in an impoverished state, excluded from the wealth and bounty of the new global superpower? "The assertion of a global indigenous identity stands among the most potentially transformative aspects of the struggle for tribal sovereignty during the Cold War era (1945–1991)," writes Daniel Cobb.[6] The geopolitical realignment of the world created a sense of uncertainty and urgency. New nation-states emerged as old European empires were carved up, and more division was on the horizon as colonized people clamored for independence. Native people posed a parallel threat to the United States, and the fast-growing decolonization movement inspired Indigenous activists. During the Cold War, the Indigenous movement began to identify less with domestic policy solutions, instead starting to imagine itself as part of a larger political community of colonized peoples.

The more Native youth followed NCAI leadership, the more they became disenchanted with its limited vision for change. As part of President Lyndon Johnson's "war on poverty," NCAI's efforts had garnered funding from the new

Office of Economic Opportunity for rural and community development known as "Community Action Programs." Once Johnson's priorities switched from the war on poverty to the war in Vietnam, organizations like the National Indian Youth Council (NIYC) adopted more militant tactics, arguing for a more robust form of Indigenous autonomy that wasn't wedded to the Indian Bureau. NIYC was founded in Gallup, New Mexico, in 1961 after the fallout of an NCAI conference in Chicago, where young activists "grabbed the mic" to protest the conservatism of the older generation and demanded for more radical change. The young militants initially gained traction by supporting the "fish-ins," a drawn-out struggle for Pacific Northwest Native treaty rights where many were beaten, and some killed, by white vigilantes and state officials.[7] This generation of activists—including Hank Adams, Clyde Warrior, Shirley Hill Witt, Janet McCloud, and many others—pioneered a new era of Indigenous protest that called itself "Red Power." It deployed confrontational tactics that included sit-ins, occupations, and direct action, while also working within existing channels of power.

At its core, as Vine Deloria has suggested, Red Power was ideological, and it went beyond the facile settler politics of liberal versus conservative. In line with a flowering worldwide revolutionary spirit, Red Power was about Indigenous liberation. More so than others of his generation, Deloria read the pulse of Indian Country. His wit and relentless advocacy made him the most prolific and iconic Oceti Sakowin intellectual of the twentieth century. His 1969 classic *Custer Died for Your Sins* set aflame a generation of young Indigenous activists. Deloria's calls for a renewal of Native politics and culture spoke truth to everyday Native experiences. What's more, *Custer Died for Your Sins*'s main arguments still ring true today: Indigenous peoples are political by default. They continue to exist as nations when they are supposed to have disappeared, and they have to fight, not only for bare survival, but also for accurate representation. They incarnate the inconvenient truth that the United States was founded on genocide and the continuing theft of a continent. Deloria understood all this. He also came from a prominent family of scholars and activists—his aunt Ella Deloria was a prominent anthropologist who studied under Franz Boas; his father, Vine Deloria Sr., was a well-known reservation-based Episcopal priest; and his son Philip Deloria is a preeminent Native historian.[8] This pedigree, combined with the tumultuous years—in which, according to him, "the Indian revolution was well underway"—situated Deloria as the intellectual lightning rod for the burgeoning movement.[9]

Deloria's potent Red Power ideology—spelled out in his numerous writings—was fundamentally at odds with US and Western values and their corresponding economic and political systems. This new ideology sought to reclaim tribalism, not as a thing of the past, but as a modern political identity that existed both within and beyond the borders of the United States. From the reservation era onward, a collective Indigenous national identity had been targeted by assimilation and allotment policies and was seen as preventing individuals from achieving "civilization." The destruction of tribalism meant the eradication of nationhood, which worked in tandem with land theft. In a 1964 Senate hearing on termination legislation, Deloria, then the executive director of NCAI, charted a new path forward. "We suggest that tribes are not vestiges of a past, but laboratories of the future," he stated. For him, the difference between "civil rights" and Indigenous rights was that settlers "came over as individuals" and earned citizenship by converting Indigenous lands into private property. Indigenous peoples, on the other hand, had been brought into the US constitutional framework as separate nations through treaties—not by way of individual or civil rights. "We were here as independent nations," he proclaimed, "and treaties were made with us, and we each have traditions." Pan-Indigenous organizations such as NCAI and NIYC unified Indigenous nations, not in sameness, but in difference, with "independent relations to each other" as "a kind of miniature United Nations."[10] He envisioned Indigenous international relations as existing not only among themselves or within the United States, but also with nations from around the world.

Deloria was especially taken by the version of Black Power enunciated by Kwame Ture (Stokely Carmichael). Kwame Ture, the former leader of SNCC (the Student Nonviolent Coordinating Committee), had adopted a pan-African Black nationalism, which saw little use for civil rights or further incorporation into a white supremacist state. For Deloria, Black Power and Red Power weren't just repudiations of "the exploitation of land, people, and life itself" by capitalism, colonialism, and racism; they were also affirmations of *peoplehood*. "Peoplehood is impossible without cultural independence," Deloria argued, "which in turn is impossible without a land base."[11] The notion of peoplehood was a departure from civil rights discourse that called for equality under the law. Rather, Deloria's calls for peoplehood—an understanding of unique tribal or national status—were a step toward national self-determination: Black and Indigenous peoples taking charge of their own lives and destinies. To do so first required the restoration of Indigenous governance and territories, a project long in the making, as well as the abolition of the colonial system.

Deloria saw the 1960s and 1970s as "the third ideological American revolution." According to his thinking, major racial groups—Blacks, Mexicans, and Native nations—had been brought under the US constitutional framework not as individuals, but as entire groups of people and nations, making them more apt to wage struggle as whole peoples or nations (versus as alienated individuals). For example, the 1848 Treaty of Guadalupe Hidalgo ended the US–Mexican war and annexed Mexican territory and citizens; the end of the Civil War in 1865 made freed Black slaves citizens; and the 1871 abolition of Indigenous treaty making made Native nations an internal "problem" to be dealt with.[12] In each instance, each group had no say about citizenship or how they would be incorporated. It was thrust upon them, often without consent. The revolutionary potential of these colonized peoples had to do with the inability of the settler state to seamlessly "absorb" them into mainstream political and social life as individuals. At the same time, understanding Native grievances as simply linked to their economic status as poor people failed to account for how race and colonialism intersected with class; doing so also reproduced the "melting pot" theory that the United States is a "nation of immigrants." Native nations and Indigenous Mexicans had not migrated from elsewhere. Black slaves had come in chains. These people were not "immigrants." And even if economic inequality could be leveled, it would still be atop stolen Indigenous land. After all, Third World nations, at the time, had waged the most successful and widespread struggles, linking race, class, and colonialism. Why couldn't the same happen in the United States, where entire peoples had been incorporated into a colonial system against their will?

Indigenous concerns were, nevertheless, socioeconomic. The devastating poverty experienced both on and off the reservation was closely linked to centuries of land theft and forced removals. But the false promise of "equality" had also been guaranteed under termination. For Natives, "civil rights" frequently meant assimilation into settler society, and the language of civil rights had been the justification for termination. "Equality of the law" was the language of termination Utah Senator Arthur V. Watkins, a right-wing Mormon, used in 1954 when he invoked the Emancipation Proclamation: "I see the following words emblazoned in letters of fire above the heads of the Indians—THESE PEOPLE SHALL BE FREE!"[13]

"Restrictions" on Native property, so the argument went, held Native people back from "freely" selling their lands and lives to white people. Native concerns dealt specifically with the colonial relation that many saw enshrined in the 1871 abolition of treaty making. Prior to this, the United States had confirmed through its ratification of more than 370 Indigenous treaties that Indigenous peoples were in fact distinct, self-governing nations in control of their own territories. In total, the United States negotiated more than 500 treaties and agreements with Indigenous nations. As a result of treaty making, numerous other agreements, and the reservation system, more than 567 federally recognized tribes still exist as largely autonomous political entities. "The real issue for Indians—tribal existence within the homeland reservation—appeared to have been completely be ignored," Deloria observed, criticizing Martin Luther King Jr.'s 1968 Poor People's Campaign, which had not garnered significant Native support.[14] Poverty was only a symptom of the root problem: colonialism. And the Native struggle, for Deloria, "was one of historical significance, not of temporary domestic discontent."[15] If Native people truly were nations, then they should act like nations, make their own relations, and determine their own futures.

A fellow traveler, the fiery Ponca prophet and NIYC president Clyde Warrior, explained in a 1967 speech before a presidential committee on poverty that the very things holding back Native freedom were the systems in place to secure it:

> We are not free. We do not make choices. Our choices are made for us; we are the poor. For those of us who live on reservations these choices and decisions are made by federal administrators, bureaucrats, and their "yes men," euphemistically called tribal governments. Those of us who live in non-reservation areas have our lives controlled by white power elites. They are called social workers, "cops," school teachers, churches, etc., and now OEO [Office of Economic Opportunity] employees.[16]

The bureaucratic practices of the BIA, tribal governments, and state institutions were part of the same colonial structure, he argued, and therefore part of the same problem. Throwing money at the "Indian problem" wouldn't make it go away, especially when Congress determined the amount of money (which was never enough), and unelected bureaucrats determined how and where it was spent. According to Warrior, "the solution to Indian poverty is not 'government programs.'" Rather, the solution could only be self-determination: "Let poor people decide for once, what is best for themselves."[17] Centuries of paternalism dictated everyday Native life. It was engrained in the very institutions and ways of thinking that were meant to lift them out of poverty; it was an ideological force with real power that had to be reckoned with.

By contrast, Red Power was not just an abstract theory or an intellectual exercise. It was a practice of everyday Native people taking charge of their lives and their communities. It was a movement, a revolution. Education, paternalism, police violence and incarceration, and the false promise of citizenship all had to be challenged, if not entirely undone. Red Power, built upon centuries-old traditions of Indigenous resistance, sprang into action in rural reservations and urban centers alike.

In the coming years, Red Power galvanized around attention-grabbing occupations and protests, including takeovers of Alcatraz, the BIA headquarters in Washington, DC, Mount Rushmore, and Wounded Knee. While these actions often overshadow their origins, specifically in the 1960s and with NIYC, they also point toward a significant shift. The 1969 occupation of Alcatraz island, an abandoned federal prison, by Natives in the San Francisco Bay was the spark, and growing Native discontent was the kindling. Previously, in 1964, a group of Lakotas—Russell and Hank Means, Belva Cottier, Richard McKenzie, and others—attempted unsuccessfully to reclaim the island as federal surplus property when the prison shut down, under an alleged provision of the 1868 Fort Laramie Treaty. In fact, the island is Indigenous land belonging to the Ohlone people. Five years later, another group—organized by LaNada Means (War Jack), a Shoshone-Bannock student who helped organize the Third World Liberation Front strikes (calling for the creation of ethnic studies programs, among other things, at the University of California Berkeley), and Mohawk activist Richard Oakes (murdered in 1972 by a white man)—led a nineteen-month occupation of the island.[18] Calling themselves "Indians of All Tribes," the Alcatraz occupiers symbolized and practiced a pan-Indigenous unity that had been "long dreamed by our people." They saw themselves as a "new" but "old" movement, beholden not to government funding, but to the people. Its principles arose from desires and experiences of everyday Natives, both on relocation and in reservation communities. "New concepts based upon old ideas demand that new leaders emerge," their manifesto read. "Our children will know Freedom and Justice."[19] To be sure, the reclamation of the island and the plans to turn it into an "all-Indian university" constituted a major historical event and turning point. Although they never achieved their goals and were evicted by police under orders from the Nixon administration, the occupiers had galvanized the movement to go beyond merely seeking reform within the halls of power, turning power into the hands of poor, working-class Native people.

The formation of United Native Americans in the San Francisco Bay and the American Indian Movement in Minneapolis made the occupation possible. In 1968 AIM was founded by a group of Ojibwes—Dennis Banks, Clyde and Vernon Bellecourt, Patricia Bellanger, George Mitchell, and others—as a community patrol, partly inspired by the Black Panther Party for Self-Defense, founded two years earlier in Oakland. Like the Black Panthers, the original focus was on community empowerment and service programs, such as creating survival schools to educate urban Native youth about native history and culture. But AIM also confronted the institutions of the state, such as the police and education systems. At the time, police often swept Indian bars, making mass arrests and profiling poor, urban Natives, many of whom were on relocation. Through community organizing and AIM patrols, often involving violent confrontations with police that ended in the arrests of AIM members, they succeeded in bringing the practice to a near halt.

Even in its early days, AIM was more than a protest movement. It founded survival schools in Minneapolis, Rapid City, and Pine Ridge—an alternative for youth who had faced discrimination in public schools. By the 1970s there were about sixteen AIM survival schools in urban centers and reservation communities. The founders of these schools were all women, among them Miniconjou activist Madonna Thunder Hawk and Ojibwe activist Patricia Bellanger. According to the We Will Remember Survival School, founded in Rapid City, South Dakota, in 1974 and then moved to the Pine Ridge Reservation, the school didn't accept government funds. "If we are to learn the truth about the history of the Lakota since the start of colonization and its results called genocide," the teachers and students wrote in a collective document, "we must maintain our independence. To learn the true meaning of Native American Sovereignty, we must have full control of what our young people are taught."[20] AIM also provided legal advocacy for parents and children against state welfare programs that incarcerated Native youth, or otherwise removed them from their homes and placed them in the custody of white families—a practice that continues, to a large degree, to this day.[21]

As in every revolutionary movement, women's roles in AIM are nearly forgotten, with men taking center stage as leaders. The feminist slogan "women hold up *more* than half the sky" was equally true for AIM and has been for Indigenous movements, in general. When the FBI began targeting AIM men, AIM women filled the vacuum and kept the movement going. As in the past, Indigenous women were not seen as leaders by the media or by state institutions; this relative invisibility, however, also provided freedom and security in ways not granted to male leadership. "The women of AIM then realized that we could just about do anything under the eyes of the feds and press because we were invisible," Madonna Thunder Hawk recalled.[22] "The stability of our people has always been with the women, regardless of what disease has come along, whether it has been religion, or federal Indian policy."[23]

Nevertheless, Indigenous women participated and filled leadership roles in all major AIM actions, takeovers, and campaigns. In 1977, after attending an international conference on ending apartheid and colonialism, and seeing other women's committees with other revolutionary movements, the AIM women decided to create their own. The next year in Rapid City, with the motto "Indian women have always been in the front lines in the defense of our nations," Thunder Hawk, Young, Bellanger, Lorelei DeCora Means, Agnes Williams, Lakota Harden, and Janet McCloud formed Women of All Red Nations (WARN).[24] "We are *American Indian* women, in that order," their manifesto read, which was read by Oglala activist Lorelei DeCora Means. "We are oppressed, first and foremost, as American Indians, as peoples colonized by the United States of America, *not* as women." Moreover, what defined American Indian women's struggles was decolonization—the end of the continual destruction of Native life and land—which Means declared as "the *only* agenda that counts."[25] Within the movement, WARN argued that colonialism had different consequences for American Indian women than it did for men. Both on and off the reservation, women faced forced sterilization, malnutrition among young children, and high levels of domestic violence and abuse.

But ultimately, AIM came to be known more for its high-publicity protests. After Alcatraz, AIM grew rapidly: by 1973, there were seventy-nine chapters, eight of them in Canada.[26] When the movement swept through Oceti Sakowin country, it adopted a specifically nationalist character, focusing on the 1868 Fort Laramie Treaty and the Oceti Sakowin. In 1970, AIM, United Native Americans, and Lakota activists from South Dakota occupied Mount Rushmore in the Black Hills to bring attention to the 1868 Treaty and the fact that the land upon which the monument had been built was stolen. Activists pointed out that the monument itself was a form of vandalism—not "a shrine of democracy" but "a shrine of hypocrisy." Each president—Washington, Jefferson, Lincoln, and Roosevelt—had participated in Indigenous genocide and land theft. The Haudenosaunee Confederacy called Washington "Town Destroyer" for his role in the extirpation of their villages. Jefferson had advanced Indigenous removal policies and begun the expansion of the US empire west of the Mississippi. Lincoln had ordered the hanging of thirty-eight Dakota patriots after the 1862 US-Dakota War and oversaw the 1864 Long Walk for Navajos in the Southwest. Roosevelt had "nationalized" millions of acres of Indigenous lands for national parks. While symbolic, there was a growing militancy to the tactics of takeover and occupation. Across the United States, BIA headquarters became the targets for protest. Among the protestors' many concerns was the failure to uphold treaties. Critics in the federal government viewed treaty claims as mere rhetoric.

As the war in Vietnam intensified, by 1972 a full-throated treaty movement had crystallized. Eight Native organizations—including AIM, NIYC, and the Canadian National Indian Brotherhood, among others—led a coast-to-coast caravan of thousands of Natives to Washington, DC, gathering participants in each city and reservation along the way, and occupied the BIA headquarters from November 3 to 9. The occupation and the negative media it attracted overshadowed the real issues of the caravan. The Trail of Broken Treaties, as it was known, intended to disrupt the presidential election by drawing attention to unfulfilled treaty rights. Organizers drafted a document, primarily authored by Hank Adams, called the "Twenty Points." The first point demanded, "Restoration of Constitutional Treaty-making Authority: This would force federal recognition of each Indian nation's sovereignty."[27] The most salient points proposed the restoration and enforcement of treaty making. Although the federal officials promised to look into the demands, their response led to no action. A genius document, the Twenty Points was presented in 1977 at the United Nations, forming the basis of the 2007 UN Declaration on the Rights of Indigenous Peoples.[28]

After the Trail of Broken Treaties, AIM regrouped and continued working on urban Native rights, or what Paul Chaat Smith and Robert Warrior call its "border town campaign."[29] In February 1972, in brutally harsh winter conditions, four white men—Melvin and Leslie Hare, Bernard Ludder, and Robert Bayless—kidnapped fifty-one-year-old Oglala man Raymond Yellow Thunder, stripped him naked, beat him, forced him to dance as a "drunk Indian" for the entertainment of whites in a dance hall, and left him to die in Gordon, Nebraska. The town is on the southern border of the Pine Ridge Reservation. In common vernacular, the white-dominated settlements—cities and towns—that ring Indian reservations are called "border towns." In border towns, persistent patterns of anti-Indian exploitation, discrimination, violence, and criminalization define everyday Native life. Gordon was such a place. AIM was called to investigate the death by Yellow Thunder's family, who were worried that the authorities would chalk it up as "just another dead Indian," an all-too-frequent sentiment for dead Natives found off the reservation. Because of AIM's advocacy, Leslie and

Melvin Hare were charged with manslaughter and sentenced to prison. Yellow Thunder was immortalized in the "Raymond Yellow Thunder Song" that became the AIM anthem.[30] The successful campaign earned AIM the respect of the Oglala elders and traditionalists in Pine Ridge, who called upon AIM again in 1973 to take a stand at Wounded Knee.

Despite the horrific nature of the crime, it is important to turn to career anti-AIM critic and journalist Stew Magnuson who has cast doubt on Yellow Thunder's murder. He criminalizes Red Power activists much in the same way Yellow Thunder's killers targeted him for violence: they were all Indians off the reservation and deserved what they got. For example, Magnuson's award-winning 2008 book, *The Death of Raymond Yellow Thunder*, purposefully questions calling a "murder" what even an all-white jury had unequivocally decided was one. Like generations of journalists before him, Magnuson peddles a myth of white settlers and friendly Indians as victims of "criminal, "militant," and "hostile" "Sioux warriors." In this view, there are "good Indians" and "bad Indians." AIM members were the "bad Indians." Magnuson's narrative has less to do with the historical and brutal reality of colonialism than it does with an obsession with the bravado of AIM men. In the book's opening pages, he describes a 1999 protest against alcohol sales in White Clay, a notorious border town less than a mile south of the reservation, with a population of about a dozen. White Clay liquor stores sold millions of cans of beer a year, entirely to residents of Pine Ridge, where alcohol is banned. A frequent site of protest until relatively recently after liquor stores closed, countless Native lives have been consumed and destroyed by such profiteering of death and suffering on the part of White Clay and border towns like it. "Everyone feared the young men," Magnuson writes of the protestors as they descended on White Clay—a description evocative of the common trope of settlers being surrounded by lawless Natives.[31] By casting the settlers as victims—in this case, a handful of white liquor store owners—he makes colonialism look like self-defense. The description also invokes the fearsome image of AIM warriors descending on racist border towns, like they did in Gordon and elsewhere in the 1970s.

Despite its racial undertones, Magnuson's "angry Indians" stereotype is useful for understanding what AIM was trying to accomplish and how they became criminalized for it. AIM consisted primarily of Natives "off the reservation." "Off the reservation" is an American English idiom that took on murderous meaning with the creation of Indian reservations. The Oxford English Dictionary defines the phrase as meaning "to deviate from what is expected or customary."[32] The expression is also current in military and political spheres to describe someone who defies orders, who is unpredictable and therefore ungovernable. Those who "go off the reservation" are rogues or mavericks in military jargon—the ones who "cross the wire" of military bases (called "reservations") or enter hostile territory (called "Indian Country").[33] For Natives, to "go off the reservation" refers to those who historically refused reservation life or refused to respect its borders, where they could be contained and managed. Those willfully crossing borders were considered renegades, outlaws, or hostiles and were usually hunted down and summarily shot, hanged, or imprisoned. It is no coincidence the phrase arose from the language of the nineteenth-century Indian Wars and the murderous consequences inflicted upon those who refused reservation life. In this way, to go "off the reservation" is to question territory and sovereignty, and a political practice. To evoke Kahnawà:ke Mohawk scholar Audra Simpson, Native trespass into the domain of what is considered "settled" territory calls into question the legitimacy of settlement—asserting that indeed it is anything but settled.[34] In other words, Natives off the reservation are the unfinished business of settler colonialism—the ones who refused to disappear, refused to sell their lands, and refused to quit being Indians.

In Rapid City, South Dakota, such sentiments thrived and became a target for AIM's border town campaign. The city occupies the moral and political universe of the Oceti Sakowin, He Sapa, the Black Hills, and, like the towns of Gordon and White Clay, is within the territory of the 1868 Fort Laramie Treaty. As they had for generations, most Natives in Rapid City lived in squalor in shantytowns near Rapid Creek, the downtown area next to the railroad district, or in Sioux Addition, the "Indian ghetto" (or "Red ghetto") outside city limits and built upon remaining trust lands of the Rapid City Indian School, an off-reservation boarding school that closed its doors in the 1930s.[35] The "Indian problem" had returned in the form of "urban Indians" who left the reservation.

To curb and control off-reservation migration into white towns, in 1939 South Dakota passed a series of "warning out" laws that required "transient" populations to fill out and sign "certificates of non-residence" that excluded them from poor relief, public welfare, voting, and establishing permanent residency. In Rapid City, Pennington County, and South Dakota more broadly, warning-out laws specifically targeted off-reservation Natives, barring them from legally residing within certain communities or receiving basic housing, social, welfare, educational, and medical services. Ramon Roubideaux, a Sicangu attorney from the Rosebud Reservation, described the practice at a 1962 civil rights hearing: "In Rapid City they follow that program religiously. They serve transient Indians . . . a nonresident notice. This is what they call it. In other words, by service of this notice on the individual, you prevent him [sic] from acquiring, as the statute says, a *legal settlement*."[36] Often county social service and health officials issued nonresident certificates when Natives applied for services, or they were simply denied services altogether. The labeling of Natives off reservation as "transient" did important work. It normalized the practice of settling—home ownership, citizenship, paying taxes, employment, and so forth—as a prerequisite for person-hood, as opposed to the lifestyle of a "nomadic" or "transient" Indian. Questions of personhood and citizenship came to a head in 1972. It began with a flood.

On June 9, fifteen inches of torrential rain clogged the Canyon Lake Dam, which burst early the next morning, sending a wall of water down Rapid Creek. In a matter of hours, the flood swept away more than 1,300 homes, 5,000 automobiles, and 238 lives. Hardest hit were the poor—both Natives and whites—who lived near the creek in mobile homes and dilapidated structures. Although Natives made up 5 percent of Rapid City's population, they accounted for 14 percent of those who perished in the flood, and a significant number of those displaced. The city received $160 million for disaster relief and urban renewal programs.[37] The relief money, however, was allocated along racial and class lines. While all flood victims were equally entitled to relief, Mayor Don Bartlett, a liberal Democrat, observed, "That doesn't mean that we just divvied up the money equally all around. The Indian who lost a shack and few sticks of furniture didn't get as much as somebody who lost a $40,000 house with 25 years of accumulated possessions."[38] More relief was dispensed to white, middle-class homeowners and business owners. Discrimination didn't end there. Many Natives fled to live with relatives elsewhere, including on the reservation, making them ineligible for relief. For those who stayed, temporary shelter was offered but was segregated.[39]

While white residents re-sheltered within city gymnasiums and churches, hundreds of Natives were concentrated at "Camp Rapid" at the National Guard base, on land originally belonging to the Rapid City Indian School. The camp housed Natives in militarized conditions that were intensely policed and they were kept under constant surveillance, in what amounted to little more than an open-air concentration camp. "The segregating of HUD [Housing and Urban Development] trailers, we believe, was partly done out of prejudice against the stereotype (drunken, troublemaking) Indian," described Lakota housing activist Edgar Lonehill. "It was done, we think, so that it would be easier for the white police and HUD to 'keep an eye on us.' Further proof of this is offered by the fact that the Indian trailer courts are floodlighted at night."[40]

Relief was slow, uneven, and often used to collectively punish the Native community. Camp Rapid was supposed to be temporary, but months passed before all the Native families were given homes, although many white families had already been rehoused. HUD homes were made available at Sioux Addition for Native families—which became the federal housing project Lakota Homes—outside city limits. Yet, community harassment and policing intensified because Natives were now cordoned off into a designated neighborhood—a permanent fix to the city's perpetual "Indian problem." It wasn't leaving the reservation but rather leaving the "Red ghetto" that made the Indian suspect.[41]

The flood accomplished what could not be done previously: it gave the city a clean slate, as the built environment that had kept everyone in their place was destroyed. City officials viewed the flood as a social equalizer that leveled not only homes but also race and class divisions. Yet, the flood also cleared the way to reinforce structural racism in new ways. It removed (and killed) the undesirable, poor, and Native people concentrated in the city center, literally forcing them out of town to make way for the business community's "urban renewal" program to rebuild the destroyed downtown area. The practice aligned with federal housing policies and community development programs in targeting low-income families and disenfranchised communities. Housing activists call this "gentrification"—the process, often backed by wealthy business interests, of removing poor, racialized urban communities to make way for middle-class and wealthier neighborhoods and businesses that raise real estate values. High rent and housing prices make it nearly impossible for poor communities to return to or inhabit these "renewed" neighborhoods. Typically, activists and scholars see such practices as taking place in larger cities, most famously in New York City's Lower East Side during the 1970s. But gentrification doesn't only happen in cities, and it doesn't only mimic colonial processes—it *is* colonialism. Settler colonialism, whether in border towns, rural areas, or urban geographies, is fundamental to the history of US expansion that has required the removal, dispossession, and elimination of Indigenous peoples. Rapid City is thrice-stolen land—first, in the illegal seizure of the Black Hills; second, in the theft of remaining Indian trust lands from the Rapid City Indian School; and third, in the taking of Native and poor communities by the flood and the subsequent imposition of exploitative housing policies. But the colonial parallels don't end there.

A 1974 article in HUD's serial publication, the *Challenge*, promoted "urban homesteading" inspired by the 1862 Homestead Act that gave rural acreage to farmers for free under the condition they migrate to it and improve it. "Just as nineteenth century homesteaders required government aid to hack out an existence as they helped to develop the West," the article reasoned, "people who are willing to undertake a difficult and rugged experience in the urban wilderness require aid designed to make the communities around them viable." In other words, urban homesteading sought to revitalize and repurpose land and housing "not worth maintaining because disease, crime, and lack of public services have made it too depressing and dangerous for anyone to live in."[42] Former slums and abandoned neighborhoods would be made anew. It was a civilizing effort. Rapid City utilized this program to deal with its own "urban wilderness," the savage Indians who refused to go away and who brought down property values because they embodied the disease and crime of what Lonehill identified as the criminal, "drunken, troublemaking Indian." Nevertheless, the city rebuilt itself and became an HUD success story. Meanwhile, Native resentment simmered against enforced gentrification and further segregation. In fact, the fundamental "challenge"—that the city sat atop stolen land—was never addressed, and was only exacerbated by the influx of federal programs meant to "improve" Native lives by granting community self-determination and autonomy through subsidized housing.

While federal housing policies re-entrenched Native-settler boundaries within border towns such as Rapid City, vigilantes, police, and everyday settlers defended (often with violence) against the hyperbolic threat of Native invasion. The figure of the "drunk Indian" became a specific target. The murderous practice of "Indian busting"—the targeting of intoxicated Native men for beating, torture, and homicide—was a weekend pastime and sport for white settlers in border towns. In January 1973, after Wesley Bad Heart Bull was stabbed to death by a white man in Buffalo Gap near Custer, South Dakota, 200 AIM members descended on Custer to demand murder charges be brought against the accused. After being denied access to the courthouse where Bad Heart Bull's murderer was being arraigned for manslaughter, a violent confrontation with police ensued. Several police cars were set ablaze. Dozens were arrested.

The Custer fight spilled over into Rapid City's bar district, where Natives faced violent discrimination from both white vigilantes and the police. The figure of the "drunk Indian" is seared into the popular settler imaginary. Although being "drunk" or "Indian," or both, as not definitively illegal, constructing Natives off the reservation as drunk, militant, and violent is a classic example of the political art of policing. Native presence in border towns, therefore, is always conflated with criminality and lawlessness. "I don't think any of us go out on purpose to arrest Innuns [*sic*] for being drunk, but chances are an Innun's on the street by himself, he'll be arrested, because chances are he's got no place to go. A drunken white man'll have a home," explained a Rapid City police officer in 1973. "Of course that makes our record for arresting Innuns look pretty high."[43]

To counter this, AIM called for actions in Rapid City bars and saloons—where Natives had been victimized by vigilantes and the police—to "keep the people stirred up."[44] Mayor Bartlett described AIM's campaign as creating "a sense of uncertainty and fear."[45] On February 6, 1973, just weeks before the armed takeover of Wounded Knee, AIM stormed a hearing of the Racial Conciliation Committee, a commission created partly to resolve ongoing discrimination in housing and employment (exacerbated by the flood) and to improve "race relations." About 200 Natives packed the meeting. "They weren't committed civil rights people," Bartlett described the crowd. The officials sank in their seats as AIM leadership gave fiery speeches calling for revolt if their demands for equal housing, more Native police officers, and the hiring of a Native city attorney were not met. AIM leader Dennis Banks stated that they were prepared "to declare war on every town in the Black Hills" if demands were not met. The committee agreed to host a series of meetings to discuss the demands—some of which were carried out, although most were not.[46]

In response, Bartlett reminded the Native community that if they participated in "uncivil" disobedience and didn't follow the liberal doctrine of level-headed, rational dialogue, he would respond with violence. "If [AIM] wanted Rapid City to be as famous as Selma, Alabama I could take care of that in about 15 minutes," he said. AIM didn't relent. Neither did Rapid City. For several nights AIM members took to the streets after their demand to close the bars for thirty days, while they negotiated with city officials, was not met. Street fights broke out. Riot cops were deployed and hundreds were beaten, arrested, and driven out of town. Bartlett even directly participated in strong-arming AIM members from local motels and out of downtown.[47] White elites were on high alert as the tenuousness of their claims to the land were made clear.

The same month that AIM took Rapid City by storm, they also occupied Wounded Knee. In February 1973, the Oglala Sioux Civil Rights Commission (OSCRC), a grassroots organization, along with a group of traditional leaders, called upon AIM to take a stand. Richard "Dick" Wilson, the elected tribal councilman of Pine Ridge, had become increasingly authoritarian, terrorizing political opponents with his paramilitary "GOON" squad (which stood for "Guardians of the Oglala Nation"). In particular, the grassroots people opposed the Indian Reorganization Act government and called for the restoration of the treaty councils and customary leadership. At this time, ceremonies such as the sun dance were still criminalized and were practiced underground. People wanted a return of the "old ways," the return to treaty relations with the United States, and the end to the rampant violence on the reservation. They saw the successful publicity received by AIM as potentially useful for inspiring a political and cultural revitalization of the Oceti Sakowin. More importantly, they wanted the means for their own self-defense against the GOONs and the rest of Dick Wilson's regime, which was backed by federal marshals.

On February 27, in a late-night meeting in Calico, a small village in Pine Ridge, the OSCRC and a council of customary chiefs—Red Cloud, Iron Cloud, Fools Crow, Bad Cob, and Kills Enemy—met with AIM and deliberated on what was to be done. But it was the elder women who proved decisive. While the men discussed in the public forum, Oglala elders Gladys Bissonette and Ellen Moves Camp spoke directly to the AIM warriors, pleading with them to take a stand. The two recalled how those who protested Wilson were mostly elders and women who strongly believed in traditional governance. Moves Camp asked, "Where are our men? Where are our defenders?"[48] Their impassioned plea worked, and Fools Crow asked Russell Means, an Oglala leader of AIM, to take his warriors to the hamlet of Wounded Knee, the site of the 1890 massacre at the hands of the vengeful Seventh Cavalry. AIM would make a stand for the life and liberation of all Indigenous peoples. The message was heard around the world.

While the media trailed AIM and the Red Power movement from one action to another, the FBI also followed. Informants infiltrated the organization, and a smear campaign began. In 1956 the FBI began its Counterintelligence Program (COINTELPRO) to infiltrate, disrupt, and destroy the Communist Party. By the 1960s and 1970s, COINTELPRO also targeted civil rights leaders, student antiwar movements, the Black Panther Party, and the Black freedom movement in general. According to an internal 1967 memo titled "Counter Intelligence Program Black Nationalist-Hate Groups," the program's stated goal was to "expose, disrupt, misdirect, discredit, or otherwise neutralize" targeted groups and "their leadership, spokesmen, membership, and supporters, and to count the propensity for violence and civil disorder."[49] After reports were leaked to the press about COINTELPRO, it was officially terminated in 1971. It was later revealed, however, that the FBI had infiltrated AIM and begun its own COINTELPRO operation to discredit and neutralize the organization and its leadership.

The seventy-one-day takeover of Wounded Knee revealed to AIM and the world the lengths to which the United States was willing to go to crush the Indigenous movement. Armed mainly with shotguns and hunting rifles, AIM faced off with the paramilitary GOON squad and federal marshals armed with fully automatic weapons and armored personnel carriers. Fire fights broke out daily. On AIM's side, Frank Clearwater and Lawrence "Buddy" Lamont were killed by law enforcement. Despite the heavy-handed police tactics, AIM, OSCRC, and the Oglala traditional leadership declared the Independent Oglala Nation under the authority of the 1868 Fort Laramie Treaty, and with it the need to end the colonial relationship between the United States and the Oceti Sakowin and Indigenous peoples.

Coincidentally, the five-year anniversary of the My Lai Massacre occurred during the 1973 Wounded Knee takeover. It was hard to miss the similarities between Wounded Knee in 1890 and the US Army's wanton slaughter of hundreds of Vietnamese villagers. Military historian John Grenier defines what he calls "the first way of war" as frontier violence: "From both military necessity and hands-on experience, successive generations of Americans, both soldiers and civilians, made the killing of Indian men, women, and children a defining element of their first military tradition and thereby part of a shared identity."[50] What D'Arcy McNickle in 1949 termed "the Indian war that never ends"—the perpetual conflict between Natives and imperial dispossessors—clearly had global implications.[51] It's been said that the war was "brought home" to America in the 1960s and 1970s, but it had always been "home" in occupied Indigenous lands. The US empire's counterrevolutionary wars to crush the decolonization campaign, the Viet Cong in Vietnam, and Black Power and Red Power activists in the United States employed tactics first used in its "irregular wars" against Indigenous people— the original enemies of empire. Vigilante murders and rampant police violence against Indigenous peoples in border towns were simply the modern face of the military tradition of frontier homicide. AIM had painstakingly linked the everyday policing, surveillance, and criminalization of Indigenous peoples in border towns to the global anti-colonial struggle and treaty rights. The takeover of Wounded Knee was the continuation of this struggle.

For seventy-one days, Wounded Knee was an independent Indigenous territory, attracting worldwide attention and the support of revolutionary movements. For the first time, American Indians had a captive and sympathetic international audience, the awareness of which attracted a harsh military and police response. In the aftermath of Wounded Knee in 1973, the FBI and Dick Wilson waged a dirty war against their opponents in Pine Ridge in what became known as the "reign of terror." Dozens were murdered. Hundreds were imprisoned. On June 26, 1975, ninety-nine years after Custer Jumping Bull ranch. The two FBI agents entered the property over a reported theft of a pair of cowboy boots. AIM had set up camp on the property to protect the Jumping Bulls, an elderly couple, from GOON and FBI harassment. They had also constructed a culture camp there for youth. A firefight broke out, in which agents Ronald A. Williams and Jack R. Coler were killed. In the ensuing battle with FBI and BIA officers, Joeseph Stuntz Killsright, a young Native man, was killed by sniper fire. A massive manhunt ensued. AIM leader Leonard Peltier was later charged and condemned to two life sentences for the murder of the FBI agents. Federal prosecutors and agents manufactured evidence, hid proof of innocence, presented false testimony, ignored court orders, and lied to the jury about Peltier's involvement in the murders. Since his incarceration, former FBI agents and federal prosecutors (including the head of the prosecution team that convicted him), along with numerous civil rights and human rights organizations, have found faults on the FBI's handling of Peltier's case and called for his clemency. Twice Peltier's case has come close to presidential pardon or clemency. In both instances, the FBI led a smear campaign against AIM and Peltier, showing that the Indian War continues unabated. Most recently, President Obama denied Peltier's clemency application during the efforts to halt Dakota Access Pipeline at Standing Rock, after issuing more executive clemencies than the past thirteen administrations. He could not let go of neither his commitments to the oil and gas industry, nor to the continued imprisonment of an innocent Indigenous freedom fighter.

As a result of the loss of life at Wounded Knee in 1973, AIM has been blamed for the murderous crackdown and the increased deprivations of Indigenous communities that followed. The dirty war that came after in Pine Ridge left forty-five unsolved homicides of AIM leaders and organizers. Among the more well known was the execution of Anna Mae Aquash, a Mi'kmaq activist, whose murder resulted in the conviction, years later, of two Native men associated with AIM. While the rumors swirl about Aquash, the other forty-five killed, mostly Lakotas who were less well known, left behind families, relatives, and children who are to this day without answers.[52] While Red Power attracted a heavy response from the state, historian Jordan Camp notes that "those focusing on the criminalization of street protests rarely connect it to the everyday and routine policing, surveillance, and criminalization of the racialized poor."[53] In other words, those struggles—whether on the part of AIM or the Black Panthers—seek to undo the state violence inflicted on them each day. AIM's border town campaign, which confronted rampant police and vigilante violence head-on, is a case in point.

Pervasive anti-AIM sentiment persists, especially in places like South Dakota, where state politicians, including William Janklow, have made careers out of arresting and demonizing Indigenous activists. In 1974, after being elected attorney general on a wave of anti-Indianism, Janklow remarked: "The only way to deal with the Indian problem in South Dakota is to put a gun to the AIM leaders' heads and pull the trigger."[54] But instead of killing AIM members, in 2003 the two-time state governor and South Dakota senator killed a white man, Randy Scott, with his Cadillac. Janklow subsequently resigned from politics, serving one hundred days in jail for manslaughter, and died in disrepute in 2012.

Anti-Indianism has also been reinforced under neoliberalism—the restructuring of politics and economy towards privatization, including the widespread defunding of public education, transportation, healthcare, and public sector employment—

services that in other parts of the world are considered fundamental human rights. But the role of the US state in reproducing anti-Indianism has also increased since the mid twentieth
century, including through the expansion of the military and
prisons. For example, the prison population increased from
about 200,000 in the late 1960s to 2.4 million in the 2000s;
as of 2018, there are 6.9 million adults in jail, in prison, or on
probation or parole. Most are nonwhite and poor. In South
Dakota, incarceration rates are among the highest in the
nation. In spite of an overall decrease in crime nationally and
statewide over the last two decades, South Dakota's imprisonment rate is ten times higher than the national average, growing over 500 percent from 1977 to 2012. Native inmates make
up over 30 percent of the total population while only consti-
tuting about 9 percent of the state's population.[55] The rise in
incarceration rates directly correlates with increased Native
political activity in the 1970s. The historical process of elimination as a tool for political repression—removing Natives
from the land and imprisoning them—has taken the new
form of mass incarceration. The "Indian problem" was thus
solved not through granting treaty rights—such as access to
healthcare, employment, education, and social welfare—but
through the use of police and prisons.

Today, in Rapid City, South Dakota—a city located in the
cosmological and political center of the Lakota universe, He
Sapa (the Black Hills)—Natives (mostly Lakotas) make up 12
percent of the urban population. Yet, more than half of the
Native population lives below the poverty line—a rate higher
than in most reservations.[56] Three-fourths of the city's homeless are Native. Natives also make up half the city's jail population and are five times more likely to get arrested or receive
traffic citations.[57] These statistics reveal a general pattern of
police violence against Natives in the United States. According
to The Guardian's "The Counted," an online database of
police killings, 2016 was a particularly deadly year for Natives.

Police killed twenty-four Natives, more than they had the previous year and at a rate higher than any other group. Almost all the killings were at the hands of non-reservation law enforcement.[58] Police are the instrument employed to manage the political, social, and economic crisis that is Indigenous life, especially off reservation. The intense police violence directed against the #NoDAPL movement at Standing Rock was no aberration: most, if not all, arrests of Water Protectors protesting the pipeline were at the hands of non-Native, off-reservation law enforcement agencies.

From the perspective of the United States, it has been more realistic to increase incarceration and law enforcement budgets than it has to uphold the basic tenets of treaties—international agreements—made with Indigenous nations. Despite the violent backlash, AIM and Red Power turned their sights elsewhere (as noted earlier in this chapter), to the United Nations, to let the world judge the United States for its criminal behavior. But the legacy of AIM remains incomplete and underappreciated to this day. In 1981 Nisqually activist Janet McCloud (Yet-Si-Blue) noted that "AIM's brave and daring effort to uplift the lives of their people, to challenge a powerfully hostile enemy, and to promote a better social order for all Indian people" inspired not only Native people but the oppressed of North Vietnam, Northern Ireland, the peasants of Southern France, and the aboriginal peoples of Australia and Africa. But "the greatest beneficiaries of the American Indian Movement are the tribal council leaders who are always quick to seize opportunities created by the Movement, and to claim unwarranted credit for the positive social changes won for Indian people." Yet many others benefited too: Native youth who enjoy "new cars, live longer, have better health, are bettered educated, have well-paid jobs," she said.[59]

The formation of the International Indian Treaty Council in 1974—another outcome of Wounded Knee and the rise of AIM—also paved the way for Indigenous internationalism at the UN and laid the groundwork for the 2007 Declaration on the Rights of Indigenous Peoples. In 1980, AIM returned to the Black Hills and Rapid City. This time, however, Women of All Red Nations, an AIM contingent of women leadership, formed the Black Hills Alliance (BHA), a coalition of white ranchers and Native activists to halt uranium and coal mining in the Black Hills. Eleven thousand people from around the world gathered, succeeding in halted mining operations altogether. After the Alliance dissipated, AIM formed a short-lived encampment on the outskirts of Rapid City, named "Yellow Thunder Camp" (YTC), after Raymond Yellow Thunder. Their goal was to begin to reclaim the Black Hills region under the 1868 Fort Laramie Treaty. Unlike the previous border town campaign, BHA and YTC garnered local white support under the umbrella of environmentalism and treaty rights. For example, a union of Black Hills gold miners supported both campaigns, citing the inviolability of Lakota treaty rights and concerns regarding corporate energy development that jeopardized "the health and welfare of working people."[60]

The alliance with white working people and farmers—historic enemies of Lakotas—proved vital because it demonstrated that working-class settlers and Natives shared a common struggle against corporate exploitation. Fighting for Native land rights and sovereignty was also necessary to protect the lands upon which both groups depended for their continued existence. If dispossession was the primary mode for exploitation in Rapid City and the Black Hills, then liberation for both Native and settler required upholding, at bare minimum, the 1868 Fort Laramie Treaty. For a while, white sentiments toward Natives in border towns actually improved. Even one of AIM's main detractors, Mayor Bartlett, conceded that in the wake of the uprisings, "quietly behind the scenes there is an effort being made without headlines" to improve the lives of Natives in Rapid City.[61]

A signpost at Oceti Sakowin Camp shows the diversity
of movements and Indigenous nations represented at the
camps, an outcome of decades of international work.
November 2016. Photo by author.

6

INTERNATIONALISM

As we came with this Pipe, also we come with the Treaty, the 1868 Treaty. That Treaty is bloody. It was made over a hundred years ago. It was our elders who told us that this was a good Treaty. But somebody spilled blood on this Treaty. And they said, "You are going before the world with your Pipe, and you will offer it to the world, the world community, and if they accept, then together we can help to clean this Treaty."
—Larry Red Shirt, Palais des Nations, Geneva, 1977[1]

In the late summer of 1977, a small group of Indigenous elders from Canada's Six Nations, the Oceti Sakowin, Hopi, Panama, Guatemala, the Amazon, Mexico, and Chile led a delegation of 120 through Geneva, Switzerland. The march bore the marks of history. Having survived centuries of genocide and punitive colonial policies of assimilation and land theft, they also carried with them the aspirations of hundreds of millions of Indigenous peoples from around the globe to gain a seat at the United Nations. Geneva and the UN had never seen anything like it before, and probably have not since. Dressed in their traditional regalia, the delegation sang the "Raymond Yellow Thunder Song," (widely known as the "AIM Song") to honor the Oglala elder brutally murdered by white vigilantes in 1972. The procession wound through the quaint mountain town, arriving at the Palais des Nations. UN security guards opened the tall double doors as they approached. The singing grew louder as they ascended the stairwell to the second-floor council chambers, where world leaders had met to decide the fates of colonized peoples, and where generations of American Indians had been categorically denied entry as nations. Fifty-four years earlier at this exact location, the Cayuga leader Deskaheh (Levi General) from the Haudenosaunee Confederacy made an unsuccessful appeal to the League of Nations in defense of Indigenous rights and nationhood, in protest of the overthrow of the Six Nations government by the Canadian state. This time, however, with the support of Soviet bloc countries, Third World nations of the Non-Aligned Movement, and national liberation movements such as the South African anti-apartheid struggle and the Palestine Liberation Organization, Indigenous peoples had, to a large degree, provincialized the influence of North Atlantic powers to dictate their diplomatic relations "outside" the settler colony. Consequently, US media and diplomats largely boycotted the conference that laid the groundwork for what became the touchstone document of international Indigenous rights: the 2007 Declaration on the Rights of Indigenous Peoples, a document four Anglo settler states—the United States, Canada, New Zealand, and Australia—initially refused to endorse.

While Indigenous representation has become a permanent feature at the UN, its radical origins are less well known. The historic 1977 Geneva gathering was preceded by a simpler, but no less monumental, gathering in Standing Rock, along the banks of the Missouri River. In the heat of the Northern Plains summer, 5,000 people from more than ninety-seven different Indigenous nations met from June 8 to 16, 1974. By the end of the week, the International Indian Treaty Council was founded as an international arm of the American Indian Movement (AIM), tasked with gaining international recognition at the UN for Indigenous peoples of the Western Hemisphere. The Treaty Council's founding document, the "Declaration of Continuing Independence," foregrounded nationhood and treaty rights as central features of an American Indian political identity. "We condemn the United States of America for its gross violation of the 1868 Fort Laramie Treaty in militarily surrounding, killing, and starving the citizens of the Independent Oglala Nation into exile," it read, in reference to the brutal crackdown on AIM following their occupation of Wounded Knee in 1973. The Treaty Council appealed to "conscionable nations" to join "in charging and prosecuting the United States of America for its genocidal practices against the sovereign Native Nations; most recently illustrated by Wounded Knee 1973 and the continued refusal to sign the United Nations 1948 Treaty on Genocide."[2] Following the seventy-one-day siege, AIM leadership had been arrested and tied up in court proceedings. Then came the brutal repression under the infamous FBI Counterintelligence Program (COINTELPRO) that nearly destroyed Indigenous, Black, and revolutionary movements in the United States. The strategic turn to international human rights law largely saved the Indigenous movement from utter collapse in a moment of intense state repression.[3]

The Treaty Council, however, was not the first or only version of what historian Daniel Cobb calls a "global Indigenous identity."[4] Rather, it belonged to and drew from a long tradition of Indigenous internationalism.[5] Prior to European contact, Indigenous nations had often entered into relations with each other for alliance, kinship, war, peace, or trade. As shown in previous chapters, agreements were made not solely between human nations, but also among nonhuman nations as well, such as the buffalo and the land. Such treaties were, and continue to be, the basis of diplomacy and the evidence of a prior and continuing status of Indigenous nationhood. Sovereign nations do not enter into international relations or treaties with domestic or "internal" populations. On the contrary, the very basis of sovereignty is the power to negotiate relationships between those who are seen as different—between other sovereigns and nations. But concepts of "sovereignty" and "nation" possess different meanings for Indigenous peoples than for their European-derived counterparts. And they are not entirely consistent, either, with the aspirations for a nation-state that came to define decolonization movements in the Third World. While doing important defensive work, on face value these Western and Third World concepts only partially reflect traditions of Indigenous resistance.

Far beyond the project of seeking equality within the colonial state, the tradition of radical Indigenous internationalism imagined a world altogether free of colonial hierarchies of race, class, and nation. This vision allowed revolutionary Indigenous organizations such as the Treaty Council to make relatives, so to speak, with those they saw as different, imagining themselves as part of Third World struggles and ideologies, and entirely renouncing the imperialism and exceptionalism of the First World (while still living in it). They were *in* the First World but not *of* it—much like American Indians are in, but not entirely of, the United States. Indigenous peoples across North America and the world have fought, died, and struggled to reclaim, restore, and redefine these powerful ideas. Their goal has been to take their proper place in the family of nations.

Radical Indigenous internationalism, however, predates AIM and the Treaty Council. Contemporary pan-Indigenous movements were a result of more than a decade of Red Power organizing that began in the early 1960s, nearly a decade before the creation of AIM. Earlier, in the 1950s, Flathead scholar and writer D'Arcy McNickle and the National Congress of American Indians had explored a similar intellectual and political terrain of internationalism. And before that, the Society of American Indians advocated for a seat at the table during the 1919 Paris peace talks and representation at the League of Nations. Each distinct instance posed a similar question: If Indigenous peoples are nations, why are they not afforded the right to self-determination?

Two strands of thinking about self-determination for the colonial world prevailed following the First World War. In the first, US President Woodrow Wilson argued for self-determination with a limited set of rights that would not radically upset the colonial order. Such liberal internationalism, however, glaringly omitted Indigenous peoples, as they understood themselves as nations that existed prior to the formation of settler states. Rarely were Wilson's principles applied to North America or the United States; nor were they ever intended to extend to Indigenous peoples.

A second, more radical vision put forward by Communist revolutionary V. I. Lenin argued for the right of colonized nations to secede and declare independence from their colonial masters. This view was echoed by the Third World decolonization movement, as part of a global Socialist and Communist revolution, and it has frequently been applied in the Asian, African, and South American contexts. But this view remained almost entirely absent in North America, except among radical Indigenous, Black, Asian, Caribbean, and Chicanx national liberation movements.

The Treaty Council advocated Indigenous nationhood as part of this global anti-colonial movement and in line with Third World liberation movements. After decades of experiencing land loss, enduring bare survival, attempting to work with federal programs, filing court cases, defeating termination legislation, and facing mass relocation, an assertion of Oceti Sakowin sovereignty went from ambition to prescription. Few avenues remained other than the pursuit of international treaty rights. Treaties made with the United States were proof of nationhood. But what legal institution would uphold this position if the United States refused to? If the goal was to reverse the unjust occupation of an entire continent, the advancement of Indigenous rights through the very legal and political systems that justified that occupation in the first place had proven limited in some instances, and hopeless in others.

To survive, AIM and the Treaty Council therefore had to look elsewhere to make their case—beyond the confines of the most powerful political construct in world history, the nation-state.

Prior to and during colonization, Indigenous nations had self-organized into deliberate confederacies, alliances, and governments. The Nation of the Seven Council Fires (the Oceti Sakowin), for instance, is a confederacy of seven different nations of Lakota-, Dakota-, and Nakota-speaking peoples in the Northern Plains and Western Great Lakes. They are hardly unique; in North America alone there are the Creek Confederacy in the Southeast, the Haudenosaunee Confederacy of Six Nations in the Northeast, the Council of Three Fires (made up of Ojibwes, Odawas, and Potawatomis) in the Great Lakes region, the United Indian Nations in the Ohio River valley (under the Shawnee leadership of Tecumseh), the All Indian Pueblo Council of the Southwest, and the Iron Confederacy of the Northern Plains. Many other political confederacies also flourished prior to, alongside, and in spite of settler states in North America.[6] And their legacies are hardly relegated to the primordial past.

Modern Oceti Sakowin internationalism, for instance, traces its origins to the early twentieth century, an era generally viewed as a low point for Indigenous activism and resistance. In North America alone, an estimated precolonial population of tens of millions of Indigenous peoples had been reduced to about 300,000, and for Flathead historian D'Arcy McNickle, writing in 1949, two processes contributed greatly to this decimation: the institution of private property and the destruction of Indigenous governance that once held land in common. Indigenous nations at the time also possessed little in the way of either collective property or political power, as Indigenous territory had been drastically diminished, and the reservation system had overthrown or almost entirely dissolved customary governments. If Indigenous peoples once constituted the tree of the Americas, whose roots deeply entwined in the land, the cultivation of "growth from the severed stump," McNickle argued, was the pivotal challenge of the twentieth century.[7]

Physical extermination and the repression of Indigenous political power verified the United States' genocidal intent, but these had not accomplished their purpose. And despite otherwise stating pluralistic claims to inclusion, McNickle concluded that the United States simply "can not tolerate a nation within a nation." If Natives were to be assimilated, they would be assimilated as individuals and not as nations. In the popular imaginary, Natives disappeared into the wilderness of history, were never truly nations, and had been overpowered by a superior civilization. If they were nations, they were eclipsed and replaced by the *real* nation—the United States. Such erasure notwithstanding, vibrant Indigenous political traditions persisted. But to the untrained eye, nothing was awry. From the severed stump began to regrow the tree of life—the tree of resistance that would blossom into revolt decades later.

Two Dakota activists of the early twentieth century stand out as forbearers to current Indigenous internationalism, but they are by no means the only ones. The first was Ohiyesa, or Charles Eastman, a Mdewakantonwan medical doctor born and raised in buffalo hide tipis in his Dakota homelands. At age four, after the Dakotas were violently expelled from Minnesota Territory during the 1862 US-Dakota War, Eastman and his family fled to Canada. He later attended a Christian mission school, graduating from Dartmouth College in 1887, then from Boston University with a medical degree. Dr. Eastman was among the first American Indians to practice European medicine as a licensed physician, becoming a BIA physician who treated casualties of the 1890 Wounded Knee Massacre in Pine Ridge.[8]

The other was Zitkala-Ša, née Gertrude Simmons, an Ihanktonwan writer, musician, and activist born the same year as the Battle of Greasy Grass, along the Missouri River in the Yankton Reservation. Quaker missionaries plucked Zitkala-Ša from her homeland when she was a child and sent her to a Christian mission school in Indiana. A product of government- and church-run boarding schools, Zitkala-Ša became an instructor at the Carlisle Indian School and also one of its staunchest critics. Her biting wit and strident Indigenous nationalism launched her literary career and lifelong commitment to restore her nation to its proper place in history. More so than her peers, including Eastman, Zitkala-Ša advocated Indigenous cultural renewal and a radical form of political self-determination, which made her, according to one biographer, "a forerunner of Red Power."[9] Both were, however, unique products of their time: boarding school–educated, but firmly rooted in Indigenous history, culture, and politics. Eastman and Zitkala-Ša both joined the ranks by attending the first meetings of the formally educated American Indians known as "Red Progressives."

In 1911, Oglala treaty council member Henry Standing Bear joined with Charles Eastman to form a national organization to bridge grassroots treaty council organizing with the younger generation of boarding school–educated American Indians. On Columbus Day, the Society of American Indians (SAI) emerged with the aim of combatting the continued dissolution of Oceti Sakowin lands, which had dwindled from 13 million acres to 8 million in less than a decade. Foremost among their grievances was He Sapa (the Black Hills), which was "taken by the gun," in the words of James Crow Feather, a Cheyenne River leader, after the so-called 1876 Black Hills Act.[10] Predating the workers' councils—or soviets—that formed in revolutionary Russia in 1905 and took power in 1917, Oceti Sakowin grassroots leadership formed treaty councils in North America as early as 1887 (the same year as the Dawes Allotment Act) to oppose a reservation system dominated by federal Indian agents. (Zitkala-Ša later joined to serve as SAI's secretary and editor of its quarterly publication, *American Indian Magazine*.)

In many ways, the treaty councils—which were primarily formed around historical leadership structures based on kinship—were the political collectives that passed on traditions of Indigenous resistance from the generations who made and signed treaties to those who Indian agents designated "assimilated" by the boarding school system. As the name suggests, central to the councils' political identity were treaties made between the United States and Indigenous nations. Treaties, in this case the 1868 Fort Laramie Treaty, were therefore proof of international relations and separate nationhood status.

Although short lived (officially disbanding in 1923), SAI became the first entirely American Indian–led, national professional organization, and an ideological predecessor to the National Congress of American Indians, which would be founded in 1944. SAI is typically compared to its Progressive Era contemporaries, such as the Black-led NAACP, formed two years earlier. But the organizations differed in their understandings of how to get free. Foremost among SAI's goals were the abolition of the Indian Bureau, the end of allotment, the upholding of treaty rights, and the granting of US citizenship to Indigenous peoples. But the fulfilment of treaty obligations, on the one hand, and US citizenship, on the other, didn't—and still don't—neatly fit within Black and white racial binaries. Whereas the former is about racial inclusion and democratizing the settler colony, the latter stands in for opposition to the US occupation, invasion, and colonization of Turtle Island.

Calls for citizenship and formal equality under the law could be viewed as assimilationist—and in many cases they were. Some Indigenous nations, such as the Haudenosaunee Confederacy, asserted their sovereignty by flatly rejecting settler citizenship in the United States and in Canada. For others citizenship was not about complete surrender to the nation-state. At its first annual meeting in 1912, for instance, SAI framed the "Indian problem" as one of being "doubly wronged" and "held in the grip of false conditions." On one hand, the return to a "former condition" of absolute independence was impossible under colonial rule. On the other, US citizenship had been denied. American Indians were "neither citizen nor foreigner." "Contracts made with his 'nation' are dignified with the title of 'treaty,'" SAI argued, "yet he is unable to exercise the rights of a nation or to enforce the provisions of the treaty."[11] Eastman scoffed at the absurdity of devolving from "an independent foreign nation" to a "domestic dependent nation." He preferred, as a more accurate description, a "perpetual inhabitant with diminutive rights," citing Chief Justice John Marshall's ruling in the 1823 *Johnson v. M'Intosh* decision.[12]

Thanks to the 1887 Dawes Act, US citizenship could be achieved only by *individual* Natives, by privatizing their land—thereby, diminishing *collective* treaty lands. Once individual Natives proved "competence" through land stewardship and agriculture, they were eligible for citizenship, which was granted to American Indians in 1924. Land allotment formally ended in 1934 with the Indian Reorganization Act. This made citizenship a form of elimination because it required individuals to relinquish collective rights, collective property, and a distinct political identity in order to become private landowners and citizens. They were not considered permanent members of nations in control of their own territory and destinies. On the contrary, "after negotiating treaties as an equal," Eastman commented, the Indian was "strangely born again a child—incompetent, irresponsible, and unable to think for himself."[13] Despite this unequal position of ward to guardian, he affirmed, "we must try the highest obligation of all civilized nations; treaties; the highest obligation; the international law."[14]

The paradox of settler citizenship and the perpetual colonial condition didn't stop SAI from working within the framework of US racial politics, or what were dubiously called "race relations." Eastman had befriended Black intellectual and activist W. E. B. Du Bois, who no doubt influenced Eastman and the early direction of SAI, of which Du Bois was the only non-Native voting member.[15] In 1911 Eastman published *The Soul of the Indian*, whose title was inspired by Du Bois's 1903 book *The Souls of Black Folk*. While different in scope, each book shared a similar commitment to crafting a racial imaginary in which the souls of a white nation and those who it excluded were both at stake. "Between me and the other world there is ever an unasked question," Du Bois famously wrote. "How does it feel to be a problem?" The question cut to the bone of Black experience in the United States under Jim Crow: that of being considered a problem to be dealt with. This definition of the "Negro problem" was an issue for Du Bois because it was dissociated from what actually constituted racism—the legacies of slavery, institutions of segregation, lynching, and racial terror. His diagnosis of the "Negro problem" was that Blacks had developed a "double consciousness," "two souls, two thoughts, two unreconciled strivings"—one "American" and the other "Negro." This racial imaginary extended beyond the United States; as Du Bois famously declared, "The problem of the twentieth century is the problem of the color-line—the relation of the darker to the lighter races of men in Asia and Africa, in America and the islands of the sea."[16]

Du Bois looked to the South for a history of the color line. In his narrative he navigates the "Black Belt" by train, inviting fellow travelers to witness US history from the vantage of a segregated "Jim Crow Car." The train cuts through the "ancient land of the Cherokees—that brave Indian nation which strove so long for its fatherland, until Fate and the United States Government drove them beyond the Mississippi." He summarizes the history of the Black Belt with mentions of Hernando de Soto, the Georgia slave trade, the Creek

Confederacy, the Haitian Revolution, and Cherokee presence and removal. According to Du Bois's account of Southeastern Indigenous resistance, "the war-cry was hushed and the Indians glided back into the west."[17] While perceptive of race in the binary, Du Bois could not make sense of the vexed history of settler colonialism, nor of the continued existence of Indigenous nations in the South and elsewhere.

Relegating Native presence to a past or "ancient" culture is a popular convention in history and contemporary politics. To counter this, in *The Soul of the Indian*, Eastman embraced "the human, not the ethnological standpoint." He dismissed ethnographies written by "strangers" that reduced complex Indigenous social systems to a "matter of curiosity," and he didn't see Indigenous peoples as the last vestiges of a dying race, far removed from their homelands and from the modern world. During this time, anthropologists flooded Indian reservations, intent on preserving this "ancient" people they believed to be always on the brink of extinction. Knowledge of this vanishing race had to be extracted through their stories and by digging up their remains, in what amounted to little more than grave robbery under the guise of "archeology." In contrast, Eastman aimed "not to pile up more bones, but to clothe them with flesh and blood." Put simply, Indigenous peoples were humans with rights, and Eastman desired to engage the world on terms of cultural integrity and self-determination. He compared Native religion against Christianity, emphasizing the fallacy of Europe's impulse to civilize, which was merely the "lust for money, power and conquest so characteristic of the Anglo-Saxon race." Under the moral authority "of their God," the United States made treaties with Indigenous nations that "were promptly and shamelessly broken." Indigenous history could not be simply grafted onto Black–white racial dynamics. It missed what Eastman characterized as "not only the anger, but contempt" for earlier crimes and ongoing colonialism.[18]

Such erasure is not Du Bois's alone, and it still persists today. Despite his conceptual shortcomings, Du Bois himself was more ally than antagonist to American Indian rights. As race progressives, Eastman and Du Bois didn't confine their activism to just US audiences. In 1911, the same year SAI formed, Eastman was chosen to represent American Indians at the Universal Races Congress in London, held from July 26 to 29. He was the only Indigenous person invited from the Western Hemisphere. According to conference proceedings, the gathering proposed to address "the problem of the contact of European with other developed types of civilization." Most discussion, however, focused on East–West binaries, as though colonization and imperialism were happening everywhere other than North America. The debates were framed as ethical and barred any presentations of "a political character" or any "particular scheme for reforms."[19]

In London, Eastman presented during the same session as Du Bois. In his talk, Eastman attempted to establish racial identity for Natives as a way to be counted among the minorities of the world. But he was quick to note the "pauperising effect" of the reservation system as a "miserable prison existence." Under this system, the world could ignore the imprisonment of Indigenous peoples while praising their culture, making them "like that of a wild animal confined in a zoological garden."[20] His solution to the "Indian problem" was not a return to the past. US citizenship and the abolition of the Indian Bureau were all that prevented the fulfilment of treaty rights. But citizenship and equality didn't imply becoming the same as the settlers. Rather, Indigenous identity could be simultaneously "American" and distinctly "Indian." But identity was as far as Eastman ever went. His vision was one of spiritual awakening, and a reconciliation of the Native identity with the modern world. Eastman admitted that he was an advocate "in this new line of defense of the native American, not so much of his rights in the land as of his character and religion."[21]

Zitkala-Ša and the later phase of the SAI took a more robust and confrontational approach. When the United States entered the First World War in 1917, SAI began adopting the language of nationalism, internationalism, and anti-colonialism. Natives volunteered for military service at rates far surpassing any other group, even though most were not considered US citizens—circumstances much like those of other colonized peoples serving in white Europe's bloody civil war. An astounding 25 percent of all adult Native men served in some capacity, compared to 15 percent of men in the US overall. Most were drawn from the ranks of off-reservation boarding schools—such as Carlisle Indian School where Zitkala-Ša was once a teacher—where pupils had been indoctrinated with military discipline and US patriotism.[22]

Yet the war and Wilsonian internationalism provided the possibility of a new terrain of Native struggle. For many Red Progressives, Wilson's Fourteen Points, in which he outlined his vision for long-term peace in Europe, gave meaning to US and American Indian involvement in the bloody war. Wilson argued the sacrifice of lives and resources and the creation of an international body would prevent another great war. The principal vision was the right to self-determination and the abolition of colonial regimes. Because of military service, SAI thought the United States would live up to its democratic commitments to Indigenous peoples and help them attain representation in a world forum alongside other colonized peoples. "The sunbursts of democratic ideals cannot bring new hope and courage to the small peoples of the earth without reaching the remotest corners within America's own bounds," wrote Zitkala-Ša in SAI's quarterly *American Indian Magazine*. "As America has declared democracy abroad, so must we consistently practice it at home."[23] Wilson's stance, however, ran contrary to the strong isolationism of the United States, and, in the end, Congress rejected membership in the League of Nations.

Celebrations of Wilson's internationalism overshadow other histories or futures that could have been. This is not to mention that Wilson, a so-called "progressive," also resegregated the federal civil service and valorized the Ku Klux Klan—positions entirely consistent with his foreign policy, which included the military invasions of Mexico, Cuba, Haiti, and Nicaragua. The Russian Revolution, however, offered an alternative vision for another world: proletarian and anti-colonial revolution. What came immediately was imperial counterrevolution; and what came later was a decolonization movement that toppled colonial regimes. For American Indians, following the Second World War, an anti-colonial nationalism came in the form of Red Power. Yet none of this could have become possible without Zitkala-Ša's unrelenting advocacy for American Indian political renewal and self-determination during the early twentieth century.

The war—and with it the draft—was also a turning point in the political direction of SAI. How could a country conscript those it did not consider citizens? Apache medical doctor Carlos Montezuma, a former SAI member who left the organization as his politics became more radical, argued that a Native draft was morally wrong. Intensely suspicious of the Indian Office and the federal government, Montezuma became a strident opponent of forced conscription. "The Indian Office keeps us Indians from our rights," Montezuma wrote in 1917, the year the Selective Service Act was passed. "It tells the country that we are competent soldiers, but are not competent citizens . . . We are nothing but wards; we are not citizens and we are without a country in this world . . . The wards are called upon to protect their Protectors!"[24] His fiery rhetoric and activism attracted the attention of the US Bureau of Investigation (which would later become the FBI). That same year the Espionage Act made anti-war activity a criminal offense punishable by imprisonment, while the 1918 Sedition Act did the same for those using "disloyal, profane, scurrilous, or abusive language" toward US institutions such as the Indian Bureau or national symbols such as the flag. Thousands of draft resisters were either deported or imprisoned. Most famously, six-time Socialist presidential candidate Eugene V. Debs was charged in the summer of 1918 and swiftly sentenced to prison. Perhaps fearing reprisals against its own members, SAI adopted a nationalist stance on the war. One member went as far as to denounce the 1917 Green Corn Rebellion in Oklahoma, which was a Native-led armed uprising of poor whites, Blacks, Seminoles, and Muscogee Creeks against the Selective Service Act.[25]

In spite of its best efforts, however, the *American Indian Magazine*, under the leadership of Zitkala-Ša, came under fire for subversive content. After US entry into the war and during the same month of the October 1917 Bolshevik Revolution, Zitkala-Ša's opening editorial read, "BREAK THE SHACKLES NOW, MAKE US FREE." The controversial special issue, called "The Sioux Number," detailed the horror the Oceti Sakowin endured during the brutal military campaigns after the 1862 US-Dakota War, at the 1890 Wounded Knee Massacre, and the legacy of the United States' broken promises contained in the 1868 Fort Laramie Treaty. The editors also called for the abolition of the Indian Bureau, the creation of a comprehensive program that allowed individual Indigenous nations to opt for or against US citizenship, and the upholding of treaty rights, especially the 1868 Treaty. Only once these bold demands were met could the United States retain moral authority in the world— or so they believed.[26]

The special issue also targeted US military aggression. A sarcastic play on the patriotic anthem "My Country, 'Tis of Thee," Zitkala-Ša penned a rebuke of US nationalism in her poem "The Red Man's America." She changed the verse "Land where my fathers died / Land of the pilgrims' pride / From ev'ry mountainside / Let freedom ring!" to "Land where

OUR fathers died / Whose offspring are denied / The Franchise given wide / Hark, while I sing."[27] In another poem, "A Sioux Woman's Love for Her Grandchild," she depicted the courage of a grandmother who refuses to leave her grandchild behind as they are overrun by US soldiers, noting the courage of the Oceti Sakowin and the tyranny of the military.[28] Other contributors joined her in condemning militarism. "Why proclaim the sacredness of a treaty, or cry 'Shame!' to the German invasion of Belgium?" Eastman asked, attacking the hypocrisy of US military intervention in Europe, when the US continually violated the 1868 Treaty (among others).[29]

This brutal honesty unnerved policy makers and allies with "unmixed horror." Critics accused Zitkala-Ša of becoming the "rankest Bolshevekist" who had descended into "Apacheism," a derogatory term for criminal gangs. "If we were severe," Zitkala-Ša reminded critics, "the faults we saw were still more severe."[30] She clarified her position in a 1919 editorial titled "The Black Hills Council." In it, she argued that if "[the Sioux] were good enough to fight and die for world democracy," then they were "worthy of full American citizenship and the protection of the law under our constitution."[31] The eagerness of Congress to send noncitizens to war but to ignore their legitimate grievances over treaty rights infuriated Zitkala-Ša. While they sent their sons overseas to fight and die, Oceti Sakowin treaty council leaders—all respected elders—pleaded their case before Congress and drafted bills that would allow them to take the Black Hills claim to court. "One after another these bills failed passage by Congress," she recalled, "while access to the Court of Claims to all other Americans was comparatively easy, types of men like the IWW [the Industrial Workers of the World] and the Bolsheveki [were] not excepted." Clearly referencing the attacks on SAI and its magazine, Zitkala-Ša spoke a simple truth: even the anarchists, socialists, communists, and draft resisters—all considered enemies of the state—had their day in court, a national headline, and some protections under

the law. But any talk of Indigenous treaties, stolen land, genocide, the Black Hills, or citizenship was rejected as treasonous,
or simply ignored. Those issues could not even be entertained
in a court room, because the United States refused to recognize
its own criminal behavior—and it refused to recognize the
Oceti Sakowin as either citizens or their own nation. "Small
wonder that Immortal Justice must be blindfolded upon her
marble pedestal lest her tranquility be marred by the Red
Man's dilemma!" Zitkala-Ša remarked.[32] But SAI offered other
possibilities beyond the United States, as the promise of a new
political order arose at the conclusion of the Great War.

As peace approached, SAI members, including Eastman,
Zitkala-Ša, and Montezuma, were undeterred by Congress's
stubbornness and seized upon Wilson's principles to defend
Native rights. "Under the new sun an epoch is being staged.
Little peoples are to be granted the right of self-determination!" exclaimed Zitkala-Ša in 1919.[33] Montezuma was more
critical. "There is no picture as black as the history of our
race. You may speak about abuses and mistreatment received
by the Belgians, Bohemians, Poles, Serbians and other nations
of the old country, their griefs and wild kings are no comparison to the treatment of the Indians at the hands of the
American Government," he wrote in a 1918 piece, provoca-
tively titled "Another Kaiser in America."[34]

Eastman, however, echoed Zitkala-Ša, arguing that the
scourge of wardship was thoroughly undemocratic, stunted
the renewal of Indigenous autonomy, and ran counter to
Wilson's principles of self-determination. "The whole
system reminds of the story of Two-Face in the Sioux
legend. He stole a child to feed on his tender substance,
sucking his blood while still living, and if anyone protested
or aroused by the baby's screams, attempted a rescue, he
would pat it tenderly and pretend to caress it," he wrote. A
vampiric Indian Bureau, if not stopped, would continue to
wither away Indigenous life and land. But Eastman

cautioned, "We do not ask for territorial grant or separate government. We ask only to enjoy with Europe's sons the full privileges of American citizenship."[35]

Despite their best efforts, Eastman, Zitkala-Ša, and SAI could not break the mold that cast them. Conservative factions within prevented SAI from petitioning President Wilson to attend the peace conference. Non-Native supporters viewed SAI as novelty, rather than a serious political organization. Slowly, the organization descended into obscurity, officially disbanding in 1923, a year before the passage of the Indian Citizenship Act, which unilaterally imposed citizenship upon all individual Indigenous peoples without consent. The criticism leveled at the Indian Bureau did, however, result in a sweeping investigation and report of its practices. The publication in 1928 of *The Problem of Indian Administration*, also known as the Meriam Report, was a massive indictment of federal Indian policies of assimilation and allotment. Whether as an intentional or unintentional outcome, the report found, Natives lived in destitution, poverty, and misery, and they had access only to highly deficient education and health services. The Indian Bureau became the focus of a massive reform under the Indian New Deal, which ended allotment, along with some bans on Native cultural and religious ceremonies. SAI's ideas, especially those of Zitkala-Ša around cultural and political renewal, were taken up by John Collier, who is often credited with envisioning the 1934 Indian Reorganization Act. It is clear that many elements of the IRA drew inspiration from SAI, but none of its members received credit.

Having failed to gain entry to the Paris peace talks and the League of Nations, and likewise failed to garner support for the treaty claims (despite overwhelming numbers of American Indian servicemen), Zitkala-Ša penned a final rebuke of the United States in 1923, the year SAI collapsed. "It were better to slay this greedy octopus for a museum exhibit, before it sucked all the life blood of helpless Indian victims," she

scathingly wrote of the Indian Bureau in an unpublished tract
called "Our Sioux People." "In spite of all the efforts to segre-
gate and differentiate the human family by color, and a sea of
names," she continued, "at heart they are all the same." It
was the white man who with "his Bible under one arm and
gun powder under the other" had excluded himself from any
true claim to humanity. The Sioux had not been militarily
defeated but "subdued by starvation," forced to surrender
lands "filled with the stench of putrefying carcass of buffalo
herds wantonly killed by paid sharp shooters, [the] outcome
of the white man's broken promises to the Sioux weeping over
little cold lifeless bodies in their weak arms, their little
darlings dead from hunger and fever." After relentless imperial expansion, "the Sioux were driven into smaller reservations, out of which they were never to go again without a
pass—never again as free men." Segregated by reservations,
"the course of their evolution, determined by their own initiative, and according to their own philosophy, has been inter-
rupted." Yet, those who held most tightly to their political
traditions—those of the treaty councils—were rendered
"criminal" and "the most backward." The treaty councils,
nevertheless, were "the most helpful because of their reluc-
tance to cast aside our native culture." This fact didn't necessarily prevent American Indians from taking part in society.
What prevented that success was the Indian Bureau, whose
legacy was one "of absolute tyranny over America's aboriginal people, and a despoliation of his land and native culture."
The more serious crime of "treaty mutilation" had been the
cause of great wars in this country when Sioux people, who
successfully resisted, were tricked by "good faith" but were
"trampled underfoot when the wild lust for gold stampeded
white men across the place to the Black Hills, into the country
of the Sioux." Subsequent laws disallowed them the right to
interpret the very documents that were meant to guarantee
their freedom. "Who owned America before the white man

came?" Zitkala-Ša asked. "And by what process has the ownership vested in the United States?" These were supposed to be "pertinent questions" of any "highly civilized nations" wishing to represent "the universal laws of justice." The United States, thus, is the antithesis of civilization and justice. To Zitkala-Ša, America is the root of war.[36]

Angered by Collier's dismissal of her work and activism, and concerned that the IRA didn't go far enough, Zitkala-Ša organized her nation, the Yankton Reservation, to oppose the IRA. Although Yankton ultimately accepted the IRA, they never adopted an IRA constitution. Instead, a council of Ihanktonwan traditionals, organized by Zitkala-Ša, drafted a different constitution, with a broader vision of sovereignty that granted voting rights to off-reservation members and self-appointed tribal officials, and allowed the tribal council full veto power over any federal decisions over tribal lands, jurisdiction, and members. Effectively, the constitution virtually eliminated any influence of BIA and federal government interference over internal tribal affairs. Of course, Collier and the secretary of interior opposed the new constitution, which left the Yankton Reservation without a formally recognized council—a decision that had dire consequences when the Army Corps flooded their lands in the 1950s.[37] Even by today's standards, Zitkala-Ša's visions for Indigenous nationhood and sovereignty are radical and beyond the imagination and will of most tribal governments. In spite of her monumental contributions to traditions of Indigenous resistance, she died exhausted, poor, and unrecognized. Her death certificate ingloriously read. "Gertrude Bonnin from South Dakota—Housewife."[38]

In the end, SAI never accomplished its major goals. But the organization nevertheless succeeded in carrying forward previous notions of Indigenous nationhood and sovereignty. Against the background of anti-colonial movements, their internationalism was at best aspirational, as it failed to imagine itself outside the nation-state. On one hand, SAI's nationalistic rhetoric was strategic, given the intense climate of repression; but on the other, it descended into blind patriotism. The political visions of Zitkala-Ša and Eastman were nevertheless far reaching. Treaty rights, human rights, and governance continue to be central challenges facing Indigenous nations; and central to each of these issues was the failure of the United States to live up to its agreements in the 1868 Fort Laramie Treaty for peaceful coexistence. Both envisioned an Indigenous sovereignty that existed alongside US state sovereignty, but that could, at the same time, refuse US colonial rule because it represented a prior (and therefore superior) form of governance and authority. Those bold visions, however, would not come to fruition for the Oceti Sakowin in the international arena until the 1970s, with the creation of the International Indian Treaty Council.

After the SAI failed to accomplish its goals of attending the 1919 Paris peace talks and gaining the recognition of the League of Nations, in 1923, Haudenosaunee hereditary chief Deskaheh (Levi General) took his nation's grievances against the United States and Canadian governments to the League of Nations. Although unsuccessful, the Treaty Council picked up where Deskaheh and SAI left off. They, too, attempted to transcend the colonial bureaucracy and assert treaty rights to a wider world, transposing the frontlines of struggle from armed barracks to the US courts and, finally, to the international arena.

In the aftermath of Wounded Knee 1973, many tribal governments wanted nothing to do with the American Indian Movement. They could hardly go anywhere without attracting negative attention. Nevertheless, the Standing Rock Tribal Council unanimously passed a resolution inviting AIM to the reservation to form a council to take the treaty issue to the World Court and the United Nations Committee on Colonialism.

Standing Rock spelled out its intentions unambiguously: "The Great Sioux Nation does not want money damages and is determined to enforce the Treaty of 1868 for all Sioux people."[39] The treaty meeting also had the blessing of the Oglala Treaty Council, the same group of traditional elders who invited AIM to Wounded Knee. The Oglala Treaty Council demanded "total recognition of the treaty—nothing less" and the remuneration of all lands and resources that had been taken either by the Pick-Sloan flooding or goldmining in the Black Hills. Acts on behalf of the United States subsequent to the 1868 Treaty, the council determined, "did not diminish our inherent right to govern ourselves as a sovereign nation"; also, "all actions taken by the US government on the 1868 treaty has been illegal and contrary to the practices of international law and the usual relationship between sovereign nations."[40] Further, they pushed the United States to sign and ratify the 1948 Genocide Convention. In spite of its prior hostility toward IRA governments, AIM now had the backing of the traditionalists, the grassroots people, and Standing Rock's IRA tribal council.

The coalescence of forces was truly historic, yet the June 1974 treaty meeting attracted hardly any media attention. This was in part due to Indian Health Service misdiagnosing a case of hepatitis at the gathering. Immune booster shots ran out on the reservation, forcing many UN observers and media to cancel their participation.[41] However, this made the gathering no less important for its 5,000 attendees, representing ninety-seven different Indigenous nations. To mark the landmark occasion, Hunkpapa elder Evelyn Gabe—a direct descendent of John Grass, the Hunkpapa chief and treaty council leader who led the successful resistance against allotment in 1887—welcomed AIM and thanked them for coming to Standing Rock. "We have agreed to make a stand in unity with the most valid treaties, one of which is the 1868 treaty," she told the crowd in attendance.[42] As a result of Standing Rock's support, the 1868 Treaty became the tip of the spear for the UN work. With this reminder of why they had come, they posed these questions first: How was Indigenous law to be judged by a court of non-Indigenous peers? Who were peers to Indigenous knowledge keepers, the lawmakers and elders?

It was decided that only other Indigenous peoples could determine their peers, and that other colonized peoples could be their peers, along with any nation willing to recognize them—since the United States wouldn't. To get the UN to work for them, Jimmie Durham, who was later appointed executive director of the Treaty Council, suggested following the lead of African revolutionary Amílcar Cabral, whom he had befriended in Geneva. To get his message across to the UN and to the European world, Cabral had "to make speeches and use 'white' ideals and pretentions."[43] Those "white" ideals and pretentions included speaking in the language of sovereignty, culture, and nationhood. Pressed by their legal counsel that they would need "concrete evidence of sovereignty" at the UN, Santee AIM member John Trudell responded, "The treaties are our evidence."[44]

For Russell Means, Indigenous treaties and culture were only stepping-stones to a larger goal. Recognition, whether cultural or political, was pointless if it didn't entail the destruction of the colonial system and, above all, the restoration of treaty lands and Indigenous modes of governance. Although Means never knew Amílcar Cabral, the two shared a similar vision of decolonization. Throughout the Treaty Council documents, meeting notes, and newsletters, Cabral's thoughts and visions of anti-colonial struggle were occasionally cited. Cabral, who founded the African Party for the Independence of Guinea and Cape Verde (or PAIGC), a Marxist revolutionary party, proposed that colonized Africans "return to the source." That source was a distinct African culture that was preserved primarily by those most oppressed by Portuguese colonialism—not urban elites, but the villagers and the tribal people who lived in the forest. The power of the latter lay in their culture of resistance, which had held at bay complete domination by a foreign culture. Revolution, for Cabral, didn't mean becoming a European society or a European-style state, but becoming a society that reflected its own culture and values. Yet more than cultural resistance was at stake. These Indigenous cultures also exemplified horizontalism, as they were free of arbitrary hierarchy and abundant with self-rule.[45]

On the last day of the Standing Rock Treaty Council meeting, Russell Means took the microphone. Throughout the day, he had been reading various communiqués from the Irish Republican Army, the Organization of African Unity, and several Arab nations in support of the Standing Rock gathering. There was some tension about the direction the Treaty Council would take. Most of AIM's leadership was still tied up in the courts from the Wounded Knee arrests, so how could the organization fight for recognition at the UN? More importantly, people who had no experience with international law or human rights were in charge of their destinies but had no clue about the maze of UN decision-making processes. The path ahead was daunting and uncertain, and the tenor of the meetings sober. This was clearly a departure from the past one-off actions. Means stated that the Treaty Council must look to all potential allies, "the United Nations, the Organization of American States, the Organization of African Unity, the Arab countries, the communist bloc and whatever is necessary for us to get our treaties in court and would give the world forums a chance to hear us." Moreover, Means emphasized the historic character of American Indian struggle as it related to the rest of the world. "What we are into is revolution, turning that cycle of life always back," he said. It wasn't just about Turtle Island, because "in the history of the world the successful struggles for independence and the struggles which are still going on for independence all involve land, *all* involve land—whether it's in Africa or Asia or Southeast Asia or the [Mediterranean], or in the Middle East, or in

Ireland and the United States or Canada or South America or Central America, or Micronesia or Puerto Rico." In the nineteenth century, the Oceti Sakowin had no way to enlist the aid of other countries, or even the people of the United States. Now the Treaty Council had a global forum and allies worldwide. "If we are going to struggle for our land, it can't be just with words, just with paper," Means solemnly declared. "It has to be with our lives."[46]

The outcome of the conference was the "Declaration of Continuing Independence," which was in large part written and framed by Phyllis Young—the Standing Rock leader who, decades later, stood defiant against the Dakota Access Pipeline (see chapter 1). The declaration called for (1) the recognition of the United States' violation of Indigenous treaties; (2) acknowledgment of the "inviolate international relationship" between Native nations and the United States; (3) restoration of treaty land; (4) eschewal of violence, except in self-defense; (5) rejection of all legislative and executive acts since 1871; and (6) entry into international diplomatic relations with the United States and colonial states through UN recognition and membership. Above all, the 1974 Declaration cited violations arising from the failure of the United States and other colonial states to adhere to international human rights standards, which it charged had not yet been adequately extended to Indigenous peoples, or to abide by Convention on the Prevention and Punishment of the Crime of Genocide.

While these were bold statements, AIM leadership was still hamstrung by the courts. Hundreds of cases still had to be resolved. The traditional leadership suggested near the conclusion of the treaty meeting at Standing Rock that these cases be resolved before moving on with the international work. And there was one more request. AIM should try one last time to get the federal courts to recognize Oceti Sakowin sovereignty.

With its high-risk, attention-grabbing protests, including the siege at Wounded Knee in 1973, AIM had won in the court of public opinion, or at least held its attention. But the movement soon found itself and its aspirations for freedom on trial in the courts of the conquerors—a situation that was immobilizing for an organization sustained by constant action. By the end of 1973, arrests from Wounded Knee had tied up most of the AIM leadership in federal and state courts for months, and sometimes years. The case against Dennis Banks and Russell Means was one of the longest criminal trials in US history at the time; following a nine-month trial, Federal Judge Fred Nichols threw out all charges against Means and Banks on the grounds of government misconduct. After the tanks rolled away from Wounded Knee, a team of volunteer lawyers rolled in, forming the Wounded Knee Defense/Offense Committee, led by attorney Ken Tilsen, to represent to the hundred-plus AIM members. Five defendants initially cooperated with federal prosecutors, pleading guilty in exchange for the dismissal of the other hundred-plus cases. However, the Justice Department would have none of it, and the trials continued on for nearly two years. The US lawyers came down heavy. Nevertheless, for all their efforts, only two of the five AIM members who took the plea deal served any jail time. Because of a committed legal defense and the weak nature of the charges, most of the other cases were thrown out.[47]

In another well-known case, some sixty-five AIM defendants argued that the United States lacked criminal jurisdiction in Oceti Sakowin territory protected under the 1868 Fort Laramie Treaty. Because the defendants were charged with alleged criminal acts in the Pine Ridge Reservation and were within the 1868 Treaty boundaries, the legal defense team moved for dismissal. The Lakota patriots and their allies who made their stand at Wounded Knee had also asserted sovereignty based on the 1868 Treaty. "I went to Wounded Knee only because of that Treaty," declared Russell Means. "The first night we were in there, we [sent] out a copy of the 1868 Sioux Treaty to the FBI and said that was why we were at Wounded Knee."[48]

The hearing became known as the "Sioux Treaty Hearing." Vine Deloria Jr., along with lead defense attorney John Thorne, engineered the treaty defense. Deloria cited the accuracy of oral tradition as the basis for the Oceti Sakowin's understanding of treaties. These oral histories were just as accurate as US records of treaty proceedings and provided a point of view often overlooked. "You can't imply that the Sioux[,] in signing any treaty, ever thought that they were submitting to a process whereby they would someday be in a federal court with endless appeals leading up the United States Supreme Court," argued Deloria. "We cannot say that the United States has ever legally taken jurisdiction over the Sioux Nation of Indians."[49]

For the defense, the 1868 Treaty was undeniable evidence of Oceti Sakowin sovereignty and nationhood, not only because Natives said so, but also because the United States itself said so. Nothing could be clearer than Article 6 of the US Constitution, which unequivocally states that "all Treaties made, or which shall be made, under the Authority of the United States, shall be *the supreme Law of the Land*."[50] If the United States had abrogated its responsibility or changed the terms of the treaty, Deloria reasoned, it had done so without the consent of the Oceti Sakowin, which was beyond the original intent of the agreement. Treaty signing was also not an acquiescence to a superior sovereign; rather the United States has interpreted it that way, despite the mountain of evidence to the contrary. In spite of its strengths, the treaty defense was a bold and controversial claim with little chance of success.

Questions of Indigenous survival were of pressing concern during the thirteen-day hearing. In December 1974 in a Lincoln, Nebraska, courthouse, Federal Judge Warren Urbom listened attentively to the testimony from Lakota and Dakota elders, scholars, and activists. The hearing was unique and groundbreaking. Among the forty-nine "expert witnesses" on the defense's witness list were historians, anthropologists, activists, and Indigenous elders and traditionalists. The list was the who's who, not just of AIM, but of the entire Indigenous movement and its organic and new intellectuals, including Leonard Crow Dog, Vine Deloria Jr., Roxanne Dunbar-Ortiz, Russell Means, Dennis Banks, Edith Bull Bear, Beatrice Medicine, Irma Bear Stops, Severt Young Bear, Alex Chasing Hawk, Evelyn Gabe, Francis He Crow, Gladys Bissonette, Robert Yellow Bird, Frank Kills Enemy, Ted Means, Nellie Red Owl, Faith Traversie, Matthew King, and many more. Breaking with tradition, witnesses could swear to the truth over the Canupa (a Lakota ceremonial pipe), rather than the Bible. Because the hearing didn't require a jury, Lakota and Dakota elders and traditionalists filled the empty jury box. For the first time in a US court of law, as Roxanne Dunbar-Ortiz contends, "it was the Great Sioux Nation sitting in judgment on America, not the reverse."[51] The issues presented—treaty rights, sovereignty, colonialism, and genocide—were matters of survival for all Indigenous peoples, not just the Oceti Sakowin.

While a sympathetic US public expressed concern for the abuse of Native peoples and the heroic patriots of Wounded Knee 1973, they tended to—and, to a large extent, still do—view Indigenous issues as just another civil rights movement. But the testimony threw into question the very legitimacy of the United States' control of the continent, positioning the Oceti Sakowin and, by default, all Indigenous peoples, in the camp of other colonized people unjustly subjected to US and European colonialism.

It was a long shot. Everyone knew it. In the end Judge Urbom ruled against the defendants' dismissal. The Oceti Sakowin, Urbom decided, "were once fully sovereign people. They are not now and have not been for a long time. Whether they ever will be again is dependent upon actions of the Congress and the President of the United States and not of the courts."[52] While not the desired outcome, the hearing forced Urbom to confront the inherent conservative nature of his profession, especially when it came to Indigenous peoples. US law, and the entire Western legal tradition for that matter, is conservative—and not in the binary political sense of liberal versus conservative. Western court law is conservative because in the absence of "good" legislation, it frequently draws from crude and archaic expressions of its own past to determine "justice" in the present, therefore setting precedent for future cases. Only congressional or executive action can redirect the course of law away from its inherent conservativism, avenues that have provided little relief for Indigenous peoples. Otherwise, as is often the case for major Indian court decisions, a "bad" decision becomes doctrine. By following its own legal traditions, the arc of the Western moral universe never bends toward Indigenous justice. At best, it ignores it. At worst, it annihilates it.

To justify conquest, enslavement, and genocide under European law, Indigenous peoples, and the darker nations, have been categorically excluded from the realm of humanity—a principle that has been little challenged.[53] For example, in his ruling Urbom questioned, but reaffirmed, the basis of federal Indian law as defined by Chief Justice John Marshall in the early nineteenth century, when the United States was a fledgling nation. "Every lower federal court is bound" by Marshall's assertion in the 1823 *Johnson v. McIntosh* decision, he argued. In that decision Marshall held that under US law, Indigenous nations cannot be considered fully sovereign, because prior to European contact, Indigenous peoples were "fierce savages, whose occupation was war, and whose subsistence was drawn chiefly from the forest. To leave them in possession of their country, was to leave the country a wilderness."[54] And only "civilized" people can be fully sovereign. Such logic virtually mandates settler colonialism to "civilize" "fierce savages" and their "wilderness" landscape. Nevertheless, every court is expected to uphold this view— even if it has never been factually true, and even if the world no longer views it as legitimate. Urbom was merely keeping with tradition.

All was not lost, however. The defense viewed the decision as a partial, if not significant, victory. While he dismissed the main jurisdiction claim, Urbom agreed that the 1868 Treaty was proof of an international relationship between the Oceti Sakowin and the United States, a relationship no US court had the authority to resolve. To the casual observer, this may not seem important. But it was why AIM members risked their lives at Wounded Knee against the US government, and why North America's poorest people faced off with the greatest military power the world had ever known. In his fiery closing statement, defense attorney John Thorne compared the Oceti Sakowin's aspiration for international recognition to that of other oppressed nations like the Palestine Liberation Organization, Northern Ireland, Black South Africa under apartheid, and within the United States, the Black Panther Party, La Raza, and the United Farm Workers.

"They talk about oppression, and they talk about a better life. They move and they act. In response, we build bigger and better prisons, appoint more and more judges, more police officers, and make more arrests," said Thorne to Judge Urbom. "I want you to be bound by moral law."

"Whence comes my authority?" asked Urbom.

"To do what?"

"To do anything. I am a judge. Where did I get my authority?" Urbom shot back.

"Exactly the same place that the [1868] Treaty between the United States and the Sioux Nation gained its status as a solemn agreement," Thorne reminded the court.[55]

"Feeling what was wrong does not describe what is right," Urbom reasoned, as if the colonial reality were in the past. "Anguish about yesterday does not alone make wise answers for tomorrow."[56]

Urbom spoke as if the Indigenous elders who had for two weeks stood before the judge sharing their stories had walked out of a history book. Nevertheless, the defendants had gotten what they came for: admission that Indigenous treaties were rooted in international law. The next step was to take the struggle to the world.

Indigenous nationhood is often misunderstood as an exclusive project—the sole aspiration of just Indigenous peoples—or as confined within narrow definitions of the nation-state. This is similar to the way the "Indian problem" is treated as solely an *Indian* problem. According to the International Indian Treaty Council that first met at the Standing Rock Indian Reservation in 1974 and drafted the "Declaration of Continuing Independence," the problem was not Indigenous peoples; the problem was, and always has been, imperialism. The aspiration for nationhood set the Treaty Council apart from other Red Power movements that sought the freedom associated with nation-states. It looked instead to the global South, to the darker nations. The Treaty Council made common cause with Third World movements (including within the US) to gain recognition for Indigenous peoples at the United Nations. In response to more than a decade of Red Power protests beginning in the 1960s, in the 1970s President Nixon authorized Indian self-determination as domestic policy, thus ending termination and granting more powers to tribal councils to manage their own affairs and increasing "nation-to-nation" relations. But the Treaty Council had bigger dreams.

In its early days the Treaty Council faced several obstacles. The first was the lack of media publicity in the United States. While they maintained strong connections with grassroots communities (their base) and some tribal councils, the broader public was largely unaware of their important work. Second, according to its "Declaration," the Treaty Council was a national liberation organization that desired full representation at the UN. The Indigenous nations the Treaty Council represented, however, were not recognized as independent sovereign states by the world community—a prerequisite for entry into the UN. Still, the Treaty Council filed for non-governmental organization (NGO) status with the UN Economic and Social Council, gaining consultative status in 1977. To some, the channeling of energy into an NGO—arguably a non-revolutionary and non-sovereign entity—seemed in contradiction to their larger project.[57] A 1977 Treaty Council communiqué titled "Decolonization, Liberation and the International Community" offered their explaination of the NGO strategy: "Decolonization, or a better term, liberation, is a slow, painstaking process. What the colonialists accomplished over the past four centuries cannot be overcome easily."[58]

The Treaty Council also faced two obstacles in seeking international recognition. First, the United States simply could not tolerate Indigenous rights, let alone sovereign Indigenous nations, and it did everything in its power to thwart their efforts. Second, the very internal mechanisms of the UN prevented the delivery of full Indigenous sovereignty that was on par with that of states. The formal process of decolonization, outlined in UN decolonization charters, didn't account for, nor did it recognize, Indigenous peoples as potential nations. Typically, colonized nations gained their independence through a combination of armed struggle and international recognition. After Wounded Knee, AIM had eschewed the former in favor of the latter, but international legal frameworks ultimately proved inadequate. Allies elsewhere in the world had to be sought and maintained. Only by winning world opinion could international recognition be achieved.

Immediately following the 1974 Treaty Council meeting, two offices were set up—one in San Francisco and the other across the street from the UN in New York City. The slow process of gaining international recognition began. A Treaty Council delegation attended the International Conference of Solidarity with the Independence of Puerto Rico in Havana at the invitation of the Cuban government, where the Treaty Council was recognized alongside seventy-six other nations and fourteen liberation movements from around the world. Thus began a close collaboration with Third World independence movements and Socialist countries. Soon Treaty Council delegations visited the Eastern bloc and nations of the global South in North Africa, South America, and the Middle East in an effort to garner support. At their second gathering in the Yankton Reservation in June 1976, the Treaty Council drafted a "Red Paper," condemning the United States for ongoing practices of genocide and imperialist intervention across the globe. The Treaty Council directed international delegations to make friendly relations with other countries and to ask them to recognize the 1868 Fort Laramie.[59]

The delegations were well received by their hosts, especially in the Soviet Union and Eastern bloc countries, who were eager not only to support Indigenous causes but also to point out the hypocrisy of US "humanitarian" intervention abroad while it denied freedom to its own people. During a 1977 visit to the Soviet Union, Kazakhstan, Mongolia, and West Germany, Treaty Council representatives—Allene Goddard, Bill Means, Greg Zephier, and Bill Wahpepah—met with Iraqi, Algerian, and Namibian delegations. "I think because we got to know our brothers from the south better on these tours, we understand more than before that we are one people," observed Wahpepah.[60] Sherry Means, the fifteen-year-old daughter of Russell Means, found the tour of the Eastern bloc eye-opening. In contrast to the United States' treatment of Indigenous peoples, "these countries believe strongly in human rights," she reported.[61] The warm reception by Eastern bloc countries in Europe was in part due to a prolific Indian hobbyist culture. Under Socialist regimes such as the German Democratic Republic (or East Germany), Indian hobbyist clubs received state funding and played a significant role in providing transnational solidarity to American Indian causes. Much like the European Socialist regimes supported Black revolutionaries like Angela Davis, who was imprisoned by the state of California and later released, Eastern bloc countries provided genuine transnational solidarity to American Indian struggles.[62] More importantly, where Indigenous peoples found a hostile audience in North America, they found a welcoming one abroad, especially among Socialist nations and other colonized peoples. The "red nations" of Europe and Asia now provided a platform of support for the Red nations of North America.

Treaty Council delegations were frequent, and the relationships they fostered were lasting and deep. For example, in 1979 when the Iranian Revolution erupted, revolutionary students took hostage fifty-two US diplomats and citizens, holding them at the US embassy for more than a year. By taking US hostages, revolutionary students hoped to prevent the US-backed dictator, Shah Mohammad Reza Pahlavi, from returning to power. Nearly forgotten, however, is the Treaty Council's role in helping to peacefully end the situation, as well as the mail exchange program they ran for the US hostages. According to Russell Means, after the 1977 Geneva conference AIM's ties to the Palestine Liberation Organization (PLO) gave the Treaty Council "some credibility in that part of the world." Since Means was barred from leaving the United States as part of the terms of his parole, John Thomas, a Dakota AIM member and Means's second in command—"a witty, lovable guy who gets along with everybody"—served as a "roving ambassador" in Lebanon, Iran, and Egypt. The Treaty Council sent Thomas to Tehran after the Revolutionary

Guards took over the US embassy "to see what he could do." Ultimately, the students only allowed packages and mail to be delivered in person by an AIM member.[63]

In one instance, Thomas arrived at the embassy with a bag of 150 letters. Iranian students welcomed him, and he was allowed to see one hostage, Army Sergeant Joseph Subic Jr. "You have our deepest sympathy. Our people [American Indians] have been held in bondage for 150 years by the US government," Thomas told the sergeant.

"I know. Thank you for coming," Subic answered.[64] For their efforts Bill Means, John Thomas, and the Treaty Council received a formal "thank you" from the UN secretary general, commending the mail exchange for helping in "the negotiation of a peaceful settlement."[65] Although the mail exchange didn't receive widespread publicity, the humanitarian diplomatic mission showed that American Indians were at odds with the US government and its colonial policies, but not with US citizens in general. That it was authorized to carry out such a unique humanitarian mission also revealed the level of trust the Treaty Council had developed with the UN, Third World regimes, and national liberation organizations.

While the Treaty Council brought the struggle of Turtle Island to the world, the world also came to Turtle Island. International delegations were often guests of Indigenous nations in the United States, and Palestinian and Indigenous solidarity was particularly strong and visible. Both Palestinians and American Indians were unrecognized nations, stateless peoples, who were fighting settler-colonial regimes occupying their lands. At nearly every major Treaty Council event, Palestinians were in attendance. And it wasn't just political meetings. Elizabeth Cook-Lynn recalls their presence at powwows in the 1970s and 1980s. "Groups of thirty, forty, fifty Palestinians with their guns, with their uniforms, came after the prayers in the morning, after and before the grand entry, and when people could go to breakfast and [were] having coffee and getting organized, the Palestinians were out on that tarmac doing military maneuvers," she recalls. "They were invited there by our tribes."[66]

While American Indians sometimes referred to themselves as the Palestinians of North America, in the sense that they had been invaded and were being replaced by a foreign occupying power, not all Palestinians saw themselves as American Indians. To some, American Indians were a fait accompli—a lesson to Palestinians that they could end up stateless, unrecognized, in exile, or permanently placed on reservations if they did not overturn occupation. In the 1980s, when asked how he felt about the comparison, PLO Chairman Yasser Arafat responded, "This is one part of our struggle—to ensure that we do not suffer the same fate of the American Indians at the hands of the Yankees."[67] His implication was not that American Indians were beneath Palestinians. But Palestine and Turtle Island have different histories and are experiencing different stages of settler colonialism. From 1516 to 1918, Palestine was part of the Ottoman Empire. In 1920 it was placed under British authority as part of the League of Nations mandate system that allowed states (primarily European ones) to administer overseas territory. In 1948 Israel became a "Jewish homeland," and their expulsion of more than 700,000 Palestinians (around 85 percent of the Arab population) from their homes became known as the Nakba—the "catastrophe." Israel soon attacked surrounding Arab states, leading to three major wars in 1956, 1967, and 1973, resulting in the Israeli occupation of Eastern Jerusalem, the West Bank, the Gaza Strip, and the Golan Heights. In other words, Palestinians were still engaged in direct combat with Israeli settlers at this time, much in the same way the Oceti Sakowin had fought to repel settler invasion a century earlier. Like the tens of thousands of Oceti Sakowin who were displaced by military occupation, flooding, and industrial development, today there are around 6 million Palestinian refugees who do not have the right of return to their homelands.

Palestine, with a landmass the size of New Jersey—smaller than some Indian reservations—was like a microcosm of nineteenth-century settler colonialism in North America. So, in some ways Arafat was correct: Indigenous peoples of North America were the evidence of the advanced stages of settler colonialism, today making up less than 1 percent of the total population and possessing less than 3 percent of their original land. Yet Palestinians had something American Indians didn't have in the nineteenth century: access to the UN, an international body founded in 1945—partly to end colonialism— where they could attempt to change world opinion. At the height of their physical elimination and removal, American Indians didn't have an international institution to which they could bring their grievances. They couldn't even enlist the aid of US citizens, who were benefiting from and actively participating in their elimination.

Not all American Indian activists supported this close relationship with Palestine. A common trope used to explain the existence of Indigenous peoples in the Americas, since the Bible made no mention of them, was that they were a lost tribe of Israel. Many American Indians, having been indoctrinated into Christianity, accepted as a matter of biblical doctrine the legitimacy of the state of Israel as a "Jewish homeland," much in the same manner the United States has commonly called itself a "Christian nation." Vine Deloria Jr. stands out during this time as a promoter of this view of Zionism—an ideology, on par with Manifest Destiny, that calls for the reestablishment and the protection of a Jewish nation, Israel. In his 1974 book *Behind the Trail of Broken Treaties*, Deloria predicted the rise of the international Indigenous movement, but he argued that full Indigenous sovereignty and autonomy wouldn't radically threaten the political and territorial sovereignty of the United States. Israel and Zionism, he asserted, were prime examples of how traditional, historical claims to specific territory as the sovereign heritage of a particular people could become legitimate. "If the US is capable of recognizing Jewish rights to sovereign land in Israel, it must be capable of acknowledging a similar right for American Indians in the US."[68] The opposite was true, however, and Deloria's views were entirely out of step with radical Indigenous internationalism at the time. Palestinian American scholar Steven Salaita argues that the Israeli Zionist project was not so much a departure from US Manifest Destiny as it was an extension of it. The dog (the US) wags its tail (Israel)—not the other way around. Both were different versions of what he calls a "holy land in transit"—the usage of biblical references and imperial ideologies to map a European "old world" onto a Native "new world" of Turtle Island and Palestine, and to erase the histories and presence of both native peoples.[69]

Tellingly, Israel (like the US at this time) sided with the white supremacist South African apartheid regime when the rest of the world condemned it. Israel also adopted settler-colonial tactics similar to those of the United States in order to expel, remove, contain, and ultimately eliminate Palestinians; at the same time, the United States has politically, economically, and culturally backed the Israeli occupation of Palestine, effectively making the colonization project an extension of US domestic and foreign policy and intervention in the Middle East. In this way, each struggle was bound to the other. And this view wasn't unique to American Indians. Scholar Alex Lubin, for instance, describes the interconnection of global struggles as "geographies of liberation." The Black Panther Party's concept of "intercommunalism," which resembled radical Indigenous internationalism at the time, also moved away from efforts to win equality within the nation-state. In this way, Lubin argues, these disparate struggles all sought to imagine a world that was fundamentally different—one absent of class, race, national, and colonial hierarchies.[70]

In its publication *Oyate Wicaho* (voice of the people), Dakota AIM frequently published interviews, short stories, poetry, and reports from Palestinians resisting Israeli occupation, even referring to Palestinians as "relatives." Indigenous internationalism, as Means spelled out in his 1974 speech at the first Treaty Council meeting, was bound to the struggles of those fighting for the emancipation of their lands. And in the end, these alliances with the global South and national liberation organizations proved the most productive for the Treaty Council. When the world turned its back on AIM after Wounded Knee, the world's colonized reached out and helped launch Indigenous peoples' rights to the international level. The very notion that the Treaty Council met with Third World and Socialist regimes offended even some of their Indigenous and non-Indigenous allies, especially those engaged in the UN campaigns. Other organizations, such as the World Council of Indigenous Peoples and the Indian Law Resource Center, chose to ally themselves with the North Atlantic states (the traditional imperial powers) and take money from their own colonial governments—both moves that AIM and the Treaty Council vehemently eschewed. But the alliances made sense, pragmatically and ideologically. And there was also the issue of funding: to avoid being beholden to private or government donors, the Treaty Council depended mostly on donations from church groups to exert autonomy from settler states.

The Treaty Council also faced a greater challenge: there were no appropriate working definitions of Indigenous peoples under international law. Until then, the UN categorized Indigenous peoples as internal "populations." At the urging of Indigenous activists, "indigenous peoples" was included as a category in the first UN Decade for Action to Combat Racism and Racial Discrimination, which began in 1974. The corresponding UN resolution also called out South African apartheid and Israeli Zionism as forms of racism.[71] For this reason, US presidents from Jimmy Carter to George

W. Bush boycotted both the first and second iterations of the UN "Decade" program, spanning from 1974 to 1993.

The crucial event, however, was the 1977 International NGO Conference on Discrimination against Indigenous Populations in the Americas at the UN headquarters in Geneva, Switzerland, from September 20 to 23. The Treaty Council initiated the conference and the NGO Sub-Committee on Racism, Racial Discrimination, Apartheid, and Colonialism organized it. At the invitation of the Treaty Council, more than one hundred Indigenous representatives from across the hemisphere attended, including Indigenous delegates from Argentina, Bolivia, Canada, Chile, Costa Rica, Guatemala, Ecuador, Mexico, Panama, Paraguay, Peru, Suriname, Venezuela, and the United States. Representatives also joined from Australia, Cuba, France, Iraq, Mongolia, Syria, and Yemen, among others. Notable NGOs and international organizations in attendance included Amnesty International, the World Alliance of YMCAs, and the Muslim World League.[72]

The conference was a monumental achievement and was covered widely by the international press—unsurprisingly, the US press boycotted the entire affair. In all-night sessions, the Indigenous leaders hammered out a collective document, called the "Draft Declaration of Principles for the Defense of the Indigenous Nations and Peoples of the Western Hemisphere." It contained thirteen principles, defining the parameters of Indigenous nationhood under international law, the right to Indigenous independence and autonomy, the upholding of treaties and other agreements with colonizing nations, Indigenous legal and territorial jurisdiction over their lands and members, a process to settle disputes with colonizing states, rights to environmental protection, and the rights to define Indigenous membership. The first principle urged that "Indigenous people shall be accorded recognition as nations" if they possess the requirements of nationhood under international law—namely, a permanent population, a defined territory, a government, and the ability to enter into relations with other states. The Oceti Sakowin, by this point, had long since checked all the boxes for nationhood status.[73] These points built upon the Twenty Points of the 1972 Trail of Broken Treaties that demanded the return to Indigenous treaty relations—that is, international relations—with the United States. The Indigenous movement came full circle. Roxanne Dunbar-Ortiz argues that the draft declaration may be "the fundamental political document of the international Indigenous movement."[74] But it would not be until four decades later, in 2007, that the UN adopted the Declaration on the Rights of Indigenous Peoples.[75]

In 1987, under mandate from the UN, Cuban special rapporteur Miguel Alfonso Martínez led a ten-year investigation into the status of the treaties and agreements. He concluded that colonial powers like the United States, by virtue of treaties such as the 1868 Treaty, have unjustly claimed authority over Indigenous nations and lands. Martínez calls this the "domestication" process, whereby Indigenous nations were "removed from the sphere of international law and placed squarely under the exclusive competence and internal jurisdiction" of settler states.[76] In spite of continued US aggression toward Indigenous nations, Martínez argues that treaty rights have ongoing effective status under both domestic and international law. Verifying his claim, some legal decisions have, in fact, come down on the side of the Oceti Sakowin.

In 1980, the US Supreme Court confirmed the Oceti Sakowin's claim that the Black Hills had indeed been stolen. "A more ripe and rank case of dishonorable dealing will never, in all probability, be found in our history," the ruling stated.[77] As a result, the court awarded a $106 million settlement. The Oceti Sakowin responded nearly unanimously under a popular slogan: "The Black Hills are not for sale!" In the spirit of Standing Rock and the Treaty Council's original

1974 contention, they considered a full restoration of the illegally taken lands to be the only just solution. And this gets at the heart of the matter. The Oceti Sakowin's struggle for its land is not about getting reparations, apologies, or reconciliation. It is about justice and ending the settler-colonial system. Still, many settlers cannot imagine the return of lands—or, for that matter, future peaceful coexistence of the more than 500 distinct Indigenous nations. While many will agree that colonialism is wrong, they cannot imagine a future without it.

During a 1999 civil rights commission hearing in Rapid City, South Dakota, renowned Lakota environmentalist Charmaine White Face reflected upon the fact that when the US Supreme Court issued its ruling on the 1868 Treaty, many of South Dakota's "non-Indian" people feared losing their land. "Are they remembering the fashion in which many of their ancestors forced the loss of the homes and livelihoods of Lakota people and think the same will happen to them, or are they afraid that the federal government will turn on them also as it has turned on Lakota people?" she asked.[78]

White Face was identifying the implicit admission from non-Natives that indeed this land was stolen by force and coercion. This also implies a limit to the project of settler justice, which can extract an admission of wrongdoing, but cannot reorder the world or redistribute wealth, especially land, back to its rightful owners. Non-Natives believe that somehow Indigenous peoples will do to settlers what they did to them. But the opposite is true. The example of the Black Hills Alliance in the previous chapter demonstrates that when Indigenous and poor settlers organize around treaty rights, they can beat multinational energy corporations and take control of their lives. The same happened during the 2013 protests to stop the Keystone XL Pipeline and the 2016 efforts at Standing Rock to defeat the Dakota Access Pipeline. Although both projects remain active, a diversity of forces, from environmentalist groups, to farmers and ranchers, to labor unions—what Zoltán Grossman calls "unlikely alliances"—have put up significant obstacles.[79]

Renowned Pawnee jurist Walter Echo-Hawk sees contemporary Native nations as "simply coasting under the Indian Self-Determination Policy initiated by President Nixon in 1970," suggesting that they have failed to adequately address "indigenous conditions, problems, or rights in over thirty-five years."[80] But the much-lauded accomplishment of the 2007 United Nations Declaration on the Rights of Indigenous Peoples (UNDRIP) is testament to Indigenous internationalism's commitment to seeking self-determination beyond nation-state solutions. The Non-Aligned Movement, the Eastern bloc, and the Soviet Union provided a check to Western aggression. The decline of each hindered the work of the radical Indigenous internationalist movement, as they lost allies at the UN. Where visions of Indigenous freedom had eclipsed the confines of the imperial nation-state, they were now forced once again to seek recognition and rights from the colonizer. Even though the United States, Canada, New Zealand, and Australia voted against UNDRIP's passage, all three states have reversed their decisions—a possibility because of the "non-binding" aspect of UN declarations. More troubling, however, was what accompanied the United States' 2010 decision to reverse its vote against UNDRIP—an official apology resolution as part of the 2010 Defense Appropriations Act.

In 2009, Congress approved the largest and most expansive defense appropriations bill in world history. Defense expenditures totaled $683.7 billion for fiscal year 2010. This exorbitant sum has served as a benchmark that continues to justify the US-led "war on terror," which has extended covert military actions abroad and increased national security and surveillance programs domestically. Buried in the 2010 Department of Defense Appropriations Act, which Obama signed into law in 2010, is an official "Apology to Native

Peoples of the United States"[81]—what has been called "the world's quietest apology."[82] More importantly, the "Apology" stipulated, "Nothing in this section (1) authorizes or supports any claim against the United States; or (2) serves as a settlement of any claim against the United States."[83] Within a single bill, billions of dollars were devoted to policing the world, but not a cent went toward upholding the original treaties, the original promises, made with North America's first nations.

In a 2012 report, *The Situation of Indigenous Peoples in the United States of America*, the UN special rapporteur on Indigenous people, James Anaya, discusses the general lack of awareness of the 2010 "Apology" resolution. Moreover, Anaya links the lack of concrete action on outstanding Indigenous land claims to devastating social realities such as poverty, domestic and family violence, youth suicide, and lack of education or adequate healthcare. Chief among the Oceti Sakowin's outstanding claims is the Black Hills, of which the 1868 Fort Laramie Treaty is the "emblematic" and "visible reminder of their loss."[84]

The theft of Indigenous lands and the subdual of Indigenous nations is an essential part of global imperialism. Recognizing this, the international Indigenous movement continues its work today (though often quietly). This is necessary because the Indian Wars have never truly ended. The Treaty Council saw its sacred duty as ending imperialism abroad by ending it at home, and at Standing Rock in 2016, this spirit of internationalism was visible once again as a parade of Indigenous nations from around the world showed up in solidarity.

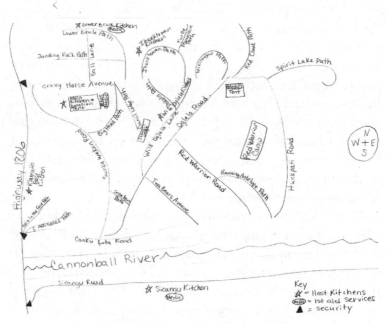

A hand-drawn map of Oceti Sakowin Camp given
to new camp arrivals. Map by author.

7

LIBERATION

At Greasy Grass on June 25, 1876, Lakotas, Cheyennes, and Arapahos blew out the birthday candles a week before the United States celebrated its one hundred years of "liberty." The Plains Indigenous alliance annihilated Custer and 268 of his men. Custer had launched the surprise attack on the large encampment to kill Indians and force them back onto reservations, in a perfect expression of the settler state's death culture. The Indigenous encampment was, in contrast, a life culture, celebrating the annual renewal of life with a sun dance—a humble ceremony in which dancers sacrifice their bodies by fasting without food or water for four days in order for their nation and the world to live. Indigenous peoples from reservations had slipped away to join their relatives at the camp and enjoy a brief taste of freedom. US history books and popular culture typically depict the battle as "Custer's Last Stand." "The very earth seemed to grow Indians," Colonel Marcus Reno later reported, "running toward me in swarms, and from all directions." Put simply, they were surrounded.

In their book *The Undercommons: Fugitive Planning and Black Study*, Fred Moten and Stefano Harney draw from Michael Parenti's anti-imperialist study of Hollywood films, which always portray colonization "upside down": invasion looks like self-defense, and the settlers, hiding in their militarized forts, are the "real" victims of an encircling native aggression. Such a reversal of roles, in which aggressor becomes victim, is a make-believe national narrative that began when settlers first invaded Indigenous lands in North America and repeats itself every time the United States invades or bombs another country in its overseas imperial project. Yet, Moten and Harney argue, it is simultaneously very much true that the settler is, in a way, surrounded and outnumbered.[1] While Indigenous peoples have been rendered a statistical minority within their own homelands, the power of Indigenous lifeways and resistance has always surrounded settlers in North America, along with their tenuous claims to land ownership. The perpetual threat of Indigenous nations is that they are a reminder of the settler's own precarious claims to land and belonging.

Ancestors of Indigenous resistance didn't merely fight *against* settler colonialism; they fought *for* Indigenous life and just relations with human and nonhuman relatives, and with the earth. When Custer and his men descended on the sun dance at Greasy Grass, the ancestors were dancing, as they have since time immemorial, to make the tree of life in Black Elk's vision bloom, and to ensure the rebirth of their people and the earth. In 2016, as construction of the Black Snake—the Dakota Access pipeline—began, they danced again, this time on the shores at Oceti Sakowin Camp and at Sacred Stone to protect Mni Sose (the Missouri River) and Unci Maka (Grandmother Earth). Indigenous resistance is not a one-time event. It continually asks: What proliferates in the absence of empire? Thus, it defines freedom not as the absence of settler colonialism, but as the amplified presence of Indigenous life and just relations with human and nonhuman relatives, and with the earth. To invoke the Kahnawà:ke Mohawk scholar Audra Simpson, the refusal to accept the impossible condition of banishment and disappearance from one's homelands, and outright dispossession, structures the Indigenous political practice of return, restoration, and reclamation of belonging and place.[2]

Ancestors also danced during the initial planning stage of the Pick-Sloan dams on the Missouri River, before their sun dance grounds were flooded. Indian reservations and

Indigenous life were entirely absent from the original Army Corps maps and plans. When the Army Corps flooded our homelands and agency headquarters twice, our nation, the Lower Brule Sioux Tribe, was forced to imagine how to reconstruct itself after flooding and relocation, and how to do so in a way that would reflect our values. We drew, and redrew, the layout of our community. New roads and water pipelines had to be planned and constructed. Entire cemeteries—our dead ancestors—had to be disinterred and relocated along with our living ancestors to higher ground. Planners ultimately chose a half-moon-shaped community structure, a symbolic gesture to traditional camp arrangements with an open community center surrounded by tipi lodges whose entrances opened east to the rising sun. In the center of the newly planned Lower Brule community was a school, emphasizing the importance placed on education. Fanning out from there were municipal and administration buildings, churches, a juvenile detention facility, and several outer rows of housing. While imprisonment and Christianity were foreign institutions to traditional Oceti Sakowin societies, the modern relocated community made and imagined space for youth incarceration and churches.

Like the Army Corps (and often working alongside them), the planners of the Dakota Access Pipeline (DAPL) imagined building a pipeline in a world where Native people did not exist. And they had to imagine us out of existence to justify trespassing on Indigenous territory and protected treaty lands. When the pipeline risked interfering with white residential areas in Bismarck, North Dakota, it was rerouted such that the danger of water contamination was outsourced to the downriver Native nation of Standing Rock. When DAPL sought protection of its private property and investments—the rights of way across the land—police and private security stepped in on their behalf, imagining Indigenous peoples as the threat. These were modern-day settlers surrounded by an Indigenous-led uprising. DAPL's trespass through unceded treaty territory and the militarized crackdown on Water Protectors was made to look like self-defense—settlers in the fort, surrounded by hostile natives.

Police, military, and private security set up their own bases and planned their own theater of operations to wage low-level warfare against the prayer camps. In emails published by the *MuckRock* watchdog website, Toby Schweitzer, a helicopter contractor from Bakken Western, a quick-response oil spill and environmental cleanup company operating out of Mandan, North Dakota, sent an email on September 14, 2016, with the subject line "Israeli Crowd Control Method" to North Dakota probation officers working the #NoDAPL protests. "U tube [sic] crowd control. Have a great day!" Schweitzer wrote to the police officers. In the email, sent prior to the major police attacks and raids that would later make national headline news, he suggested the cops policing pipeline protest invest in "skunk spray"—an Israeli chemical weapon invented to degrade and humiliate Palestinians by dousing them in a nauseating, putrid biomedical odor that takes days to remove. "Forget the wall," he wrote. "Just put sprayers all along the southern border with sensors. Might have saved lots of store fronts in Baltimore and Ferguson. The US needs to get some of this for the looters in any out of control demonstrations. Israelis crowd control method. NOW WE ARE TALKING. BRILLIANT. Skunk spray!"[3] Such comments add insult to injury for Palestinians defending their homes against demolition or protesting the killing of loved ones.

In other emails, officers shared a Federal Emergency Management Agency "Field Force Operations" manual, which guided police officers in correct "crowd control" methods, "pain compliance" techniques, and application of "riot control agents," including chemical weapons and projectiles such as rubber bullets and beanbag rounds. These "non-lethal" weapons were deployed against unarmed protestors with ritualistic brutality, taking two individuals' eyesight and one woman's arm, while wounding and traumatizing countless others. The connections were clear: local law enforcement and private security imagined themselves participating in a global counterinsurgency against civilian populations that extended from Palestine to Baltimore, Ferguson, the US–Mexico border, and now Standing Rock. The war was against Black life, Palestinian life, migrant life, and Native life.

The tactics employed by TigerSwan, the murky mercenary security contractor hired by DAPL, were also confirmation that this was a global war. The security company had cut its teeth in the United States' never-ending "war on terror," in which it was deployed to run counterinsurgency operations against civilians in Iraq and Afghanistan. TigerSwan now applied the same techniques to Water Protectors. The *Intercept* reports that security personnel frequently referred to Water Protectors as "terrorists," planned prayer actions as "attacks," and the camps as a "battlefield." They also tracked the presence of Water Protectors of Middle Eastern descent, noting specifically the presence of Palestinians in the camps. TigerSwan went so far as to describe the Indigenous uprising as a "jihadist insurgency." When TigerSwan briefed local law enforcement on the camp activities, they frequently referenced aerial photography, which they used to monitor the growth and movement of the camps. In one situation report, an image of a gorilla is superimposed atop the camp. This was Harambe, the gorilla killed at the Cincinnati Zoo when a Black child fell into his cage. On one hand, white supremacists have used the killing of Harambe to mock Black people online, charging that the gorilla had to be killed because the Black parents are careless. On the other, the comparison of Black people to monkeys and gorillas is a well-established racist trope. Now, TigerSwan was evoking this anti-Black history to racialize, mock, and degrade Water Protectors with tropes of primitivism. To DAPL and law enforcement, the camps were a place of death, a place to be destroyed, a place that threatened to expose the illegitimacy of settlement.

In the orientation pamphlet for new camp arrivals at the #NoDAPL camp was a hand-drawn map of the site. Roads had been named for Indigenous revolutionary heroes, such as Red Cloud and the Red Warrior Society. Indigenous nations had set up their own camps on site, and their locations were also shown. The map indicated where to find camp security, who were tasked, in part, with keeping out drugs and alcohol; it also showed where to get food, medical care, and camp supplies. This reflected the values of the new community: that Indigenous peoples not merely survive, but thrive. #NoDAPL offered a brief vision of what a future premised on Indigenous justice would look like. For all its faults, there is something to be learned from the treaty camps at the confluence of the Missouri and Cannonball Rivers. Free food, free education, free health care, free legal aid, a strong sense of community, safety, and security were guaranteed to all. Most reservations in the United States don't have access to these services, nor do most poor people. Yet, in the absence of empire, people came together to help each other, to care for one another. The #NoDAPL camps were designed according to need, not profit. (There were no prisons or armed bodies of the state.) That's what separated them from the world of cops, settlers, and oil companies that surrounded them. Capitalism is not merely an economic system, but also a social system. And it was here abundantly evident that Indigenous social systems offered a radically different way of relating to other people and the world.

Drawing from the Black radical tradition, Ruth Wilson Gilmore calls the creation of this kind of world a form of "abolition geography" that "starts from the homely premise that freedom is a place."[4] Indeed, Indigenous freedom was, and is, a place; and for a moment, it took shape in the form of the #NoDAPL camps. The #NoDAPL camps didn't just imagine a future without settler colonialism and the oppressive institution of the state, but created that future in the here and now. They were a resurgent geography that reconnected Indigenous peoples with the land. Unlike the cynical and exclusive world of the settler, who had removed, confined, erased, and dispossessed Indigenous peoples from place, this place capaciously welcomed the excluded, while also centering the core of an Indigenous lifeworld—relationality. At its center was the resurgence and reunification of the Oceti Sakowin. Much like the First Palestinian Intifada, anti-colonial resistance began by de-linking the community from the settler state. From 1987 to 1993, Palestinians built alternative economies, popular education models, healthcare services, and women's committees. Palestinian women also used the revolution underway to challenge heteropatriarchy, which was as anathema to Palestinian liberation from Israeli occupation.[5] During the #NoDAPL camps, women, LGBTQ, and Two-Spirit activists challenged settler colonialism, and did so according to their own customs, calling on cis Indigenous men to recognize that heteropatriarchy was just as untenable as the US occupation, or as the destruction of land and water.

Beyond the Dakota Access Pipeline, a growing international movement is fighting the expanding network of pipelines across North America. The Kinder Morgan, Keystone XL, Enbridge Line 9, Bayou Bridge, and TransCanada Energy East, among a whole host of others, connect Indigenous nations and frontline communities. The appearance of each new flashpoint of struggle indicates a growing anti-colonial resistance, led by Indigenous peoples against settler colonialism and extractive capitalism. New pipelines are creeping across the continent like a spiderweb, with frightening speed, but in the process, they are also connecting and inciting to action disparate communities of the exploited and dispossessed. Each pipeline exists in relation to other pipelines, and while DAPL technically only extends from North Dakota to Illinois, it is fundamentally a transnational project, interlinking with other pipelines and infrastructure to ship oil to a global market, crossing the boundaries of settler states and trespassing through Indigenous territory.[6]

A vast array of solidarity networks supported the #NoDAPL struggle. Black Lives Matter, Palestinian justice organizations, religious groups, military veterans, and many more from other social locations and movements galvanized support for the Indigenous-led resistance from far beyond the physical geography of the Standing Rock Indian Reservation. #NoDAPL was reminiscent of other allied struggles that have enriched the Indigenous struggles in the past, including the International Indian Treaty Council and Indigenous internationalist movements of the twentieth century. Countering settler colonialism's own physical infrastructure—trade routes, railroads, dams, and oil pipelines—is the infrastructure of Indigenous resistance, its ideas and practices of solidarity. The resistance camps may have been temporary, but the struggle for Native liberation continues, and the fort is falling.

Given that the western frontier of US expansion closed in 1890 (the nineteenth-century Indian Wars fought and won), Indian citizenship was imposed in 1924, a formal apology was issued in 2010, the tribal "Self-Determination Era" was inaugurated by Nixon in 1970, past wrongs were "settled" under the recent *Cobell* lawsuit, and "nation-to-nation" rhetoric and policies increased under Obama (along with the placement of Indigenous leaders in key roles within his administration), why was there the need to create a new movement?

One way of answering this question is to look to the movement marching under the banner of "Black Lives Matter." Why did it arise under the Obama administration? Anti-Black police violence didn't profoundly increase under Obama's presidency, but it did not dramatically decrease either. Nevertheless, Obama's presidency brought into sharp focus the limits of racial inclusion under the rule of liberalism and capitalism. Consider the 2015 police murder of Freddie Gray in Baltimore. Freddie Gray was killed by Black police officers, and neither a Black district attorney, a Black mayor, nor a Black president could save his life. No matter who's in charge, as Keenga-Yamahtta Taylor points out, the current political system cannot save Black lives.[7] The same could be said for Indigenous peoples and the warming planet. Obama's 2010 "new energy security plan"—greatly enhanced under Trump in 2017—incentivized and dramatically increased domestic oil and gas production, opening up previously protected federal lands managed by the Department of the Interior. Under capitalism, neither Democrat nor Republican can save Indigenous lands or Black and Indigenous lives. The continuation of state-sanctioned racial terror against Black and Native people, from police violence to energy development, from one administration to the next demonstrates only radical change in the form of decolonization, the repatriation of stolen lands and stolen lives, can undo centuries of settler colonialism.

The continuing legacy of the Pick-Sloan dams also thwarts the possibility of a liveable future for the Oceti Sakowin and the millions of people who depend the Missouri River for life. The dams personify settler colonialism—their concrete and rolled earth endowed with the will to disrupt, flood, dispossess, remove, and ultimately eliminate Native society. The Dakota Access Pipeline echoed this process. The full force of the settler state—politicians, police, private security, banks, and private companies—carried out the will of Energy Transfer Partners, the corporation building the $3.7 billion pipeline that would tunnel under the Missouri River twice, the Mississippi River once, and cross four states (South Dakota, North Dakota, Iowa, and Illinois). Today, their tools are more sophisticated: assault rifles, arrest warrants, rural county jails, felonies, misdemeanors, body armor, armed drones, tear gas, mace, armored Humvees, the National Guard and state patrol, Black Hawk helicopters, Caterpillar earthmovers, and media censorship. But the Water Protectors draw from the history of past Water Protectors who fought to protect the same relative, Mni Sose. While corporations take on legal personhood under current US law, Water Protectors personify water and enact kinship to the water, the river, enforcing a legal order of their own. If the water, a relative, is not protected, then the river is not free, and neither are its people.

Mni Wiconi, as much as it reaches into the past, is a future-oriented project. It forces some to confront their own unbelonging to the land and the river. How can settler society, which possesses no fundamental ethical relationship to the land or its original people, imagine a future premised on justice? There is no simple answer. But whatever the answer may be, Indigenous peoples must lead the way. Our history and long traditions of Indigenous resistance provide possibilities for futures premised on justice. After all, Indigenous resistance is animated by our ancestors' refusal to be forgotten, and it is our resolute refusal to forget our ancestors and our history that animates our visions for liberation. Indigenous revolutionaries are the ancestors from the before and before and the already forthcoming.

Perhaps the answers lie within the kinship relations between Indigenous and non-Indigenous and the lands we both inhabit. There is a capaciousness to Indigenous kinship that goes beyond the human and that fundamentally differs from the heteronuclear family or biological family. "Making kin is to make people into familiars in order to relate," writes Dakota scholar Kim TallBear. "This seems fundamentally different from negotiating relations between those who are seen as different—between 'sovereigns' or 'nations'—especially when one of those nations is a militarized and white supremacist empire."[8]

The Water protectors also ask us: What does water want from us? What does the earth want from us? Mni Wiconi—water is life—exists outside the logic of capitalism. Whereas past revolutionary struggles have strived for the emancipation of labor from capital, we are challenged not just to imagine, but to demand the emancipation of earth from capital. For the earth to live, capitalism must die.

Hecetu welo!

Afterword

ANCESTORS OF THE FUTURE

I will not die
not truly
you will see me
when the cottonwoods bloom and blow
in the soft falling plumes and under the dappled shade
there I will live
forever.
> —Mark K. Tilsen (Oglala Lakota), "If I Fall in Battle,"
> *It Ain't Over Until We're Smoking Cigars on the Drill Pad*:
> *Poems from Standing Rock and the Frontlines* [1]

The Indian trader Andrew Myrick might have thought himself
a poet for once telling a group of starving Dakota people, "If
they are hungry, let them eat grass." This was in the summer of
1862, after he had refused to extend them store credit to buy
food. In 1851, starving Dakotas had signed two treaties ceding
millions of acres. Dakotas were hungry for food; whites were
hungry for land. European settlers had flooded Mni Sota
Makoce (the "Land Where the Waters Reflect the Sky"), killing
most of the game and preventing Dakota people from feeding
themselves. The exchange that mediated Native-white relations was straightforward: land for food. What little remained
of that territory wasn't enough to eke out a sustainable harvest
or hunt. Like many white men of their time, Myrick and his
brother Nathan built a lucrative enterprise dealing in Dakota
misery by selling goods on credit, then claiming the monthly
cash payments guaranteed to individual Dakotas. Treaty
money first lined the merchant brothers' pockets before it ever

made it into the hands of Dakotas. And once the federal dollars stopped, so too did the extension of credit. No credit, no food. Let them eat grass. Like Marie Antoinette, Myrick would pay with his life for such bad poetry.

Dakotas possessed poetry, too, which, for their enemies, they adorned with irony. It was midsummer 1862 when their uprising began. After returning empty-handed from a hunt, four young Dakota men entered the property of a white store owner to steal some chicken eggs. Deprived of their dignity, they shot and killed five settlers to prove they feared no white man. The backlash would be swift and brutal. Taoyateduta, the Dakota leader known as Little Crow, led his people into a bloody war he believed was unavoidable. Before this incident, he had warned government officials and traders: "We have waited a long time. The money is ours, but we cannot get it. We have no food, but here are these stores, filled with food. We ask that you, the agent, make some arrangements by which we can get food from the stores, or else we may take our own way to keep ourselves from starving. When men are hungry they help themselves." Dakotas faced two choices: starve to death or expel those who brought ruin upon their nation. Once fighting was underway, Dakotas looked no further than Andrew Myrick's well-stocked storehouse in Lower Agency, among the Dakotas who lived by the Bible and the plow. Warriors shot the white trader dead as he made a hasty getaway, jumping from a second-story window; the shop was looted and burned. According to some accounts, Myrick's decapitated body was found later, his mouth stuffed with grass. "I am inclined to call this act by the Dakota warriors a poem," writes Oglala Lakota poet Layli Long Soldier.[2]

Poetry—be it an act of violence or otherwise—can preserve a memory that belongs to the future. Not all poems are literature. Some are composed in the lyric of resistance. Others, the prose poetry of colonial legal documents. The change and adaption of a language, whether by verses or verb, reflects a larger archive of historical experience: it encodes oppression and liberation alike. Writing was the technology that helped facilitate land dispossession through transactions or treaties that supposedly sanctified agreements between Native and settler. The written word—through popular literature, such as novels and newspaper accounts—also helped a colonizing society imagine that the peoples and territories in far-off locations needed civilization. It facilitated a culture of property and possession.

During this time, the Dakotas weren't entirely illiterate, though many couldn't read or write—let alone speak or understand—English. Before ever signing a treaty, however, many had learned how to draw an "X" in a clerk's ledger next to their names when buying goods on credit. While soldiers, traders, and government agents often bear the brunt of criticism for facilitating dispossession, Christian missionaries transformed the Dakota language into a written script, thus attempting to colonize Dakota thought by changing the meaning and intent of words, thus attempting to alter the relationship of people to the land. Sicangu Lakota scholar Sarah Hernandez writes that, from 1843 to 1877, missionaries such as Stephen Riggs, Gideon Pond, and Samuel Pond "deconstructed the Dakota oral storytelling tradition story by story, sentence by sentence, word by word, and letter by letter so that they could reconstruct and revise these tribal land narratives to reflect the new settler colonial land narrative" that privileged the expansion of the United States at the expense of the Oceti Sakowin.[3] First, they improvised a Dakota orthography based on English alphabetic script, allowing them to compile the first Dakota dictionary and grammar. With this writing technology, the Pond brothers with Riggs created two Dakota-language newspapers that took Dakota oral stories and reimagined them through Christian themes. For example, the missionaries transformed the Dakota concept of Wakan Tanka into the Christian notion of God. However, there was no concept within Dakota culture for

"God," and no word in English that captured the true meaning of "Wakan Tanka," which denotes a mystery of creation that is beyond human comprehension. In other instances, words and concepts were invented in the Dakota language where they didn't exist, such as crafting the word "Wonega Wakan" for Holy Spirit.[4] The result was the missionaries' complete domination and control over not only what Dakota people read but also how they thought. Their worldview was radically transformed from within, as concepts were recast in the mold of a Christian ideology.

Riggs' efforts were aimed at more than the colonization of Dakota minds. As a translator during Dakota treaty negotiations, he also participated in colonizing their lands. During negotiations, the meaning of Dakota and English words were changed, and parts of the 1851 Treaty of Traverse des Sioux, which was translated into both languages, were mistranslated or withheld. The words Riggs used for "cede" and "sale" were, respectively, "erpeyapim [sic]" (which he translated "to throw away, to put aside, to leave, to forsake, and to lose") and "wiyopekiya [sic]" (which he translated "to reprove, chide, to correct, punish, to trade for something else, exchange"). Forever alienating land by selling it or exchanging it for material things was a foreign concept to Dakota people. "What understanding would the Dakota [people] have had of how one might abandon the land considered to be a relative?" ask Gwen Westerman and Bruce White. "Sale" and "cede" are words inextricably linked with property rights. Thus, it might not have been possible, Westerman and White observe, "to find a word in Dakota which adequately conveyed [their] meaning since the Dakota [people] did not recognize the idea of property rights."[5] In the Dakota-language version of the treaty, Riggs omitted the language in Article 4 that set aside $1.36 million in trust for Dakota people as payment.[6] After the Dakota leaders had signed the treaty, they were directed to sign "traders papers" that weren't translated but handed over Dakota money to traders like Andrew Myrick in payment of alleged debts accrued by Dakota people. The 1851 Treaty of Mendota followed the Treaty of Traverse des Sioux, which together ceded more than 24 million acres of Dakota territory. Once the traders took their cut, the Dakota people were paid pennies per acre and removed from their land except for a ten-mile strip running 140 miles on the south shoreline of the Minnesota River.

Colonizers imposed the prose of property relations onto Dakota people and territory. When the very language and concepts used to define Dakota existence had been purposefully distorted, Dakota people resorted to the poetics of resistance. Setting a trader's building aflame or killing settlers are forceful acts not easily mistranslated. If an X-mark on a treaty or a ledger book was a symbol that came to signify assent, cooperation, and agreement, these were its opposites.

The first acts of Dakota writing were nearly synonymous with amassing debt. The root word of wicazo, the Dakota word for pen or pencil, is icazo, which carries two definitions. The first is to buy something on credit, to owe. The second is to mark something or to make a line.[7] The late Dakota scholar Elizabeth Cook-Lynn explained this original meaning to me when telling how she chose the name Wicazo Sa for the American Indian studies journal she cofounded. Wicazo Sa roughly translates into "red pen" or "red pencil." It is both an affirmation of intellectual sovereignty and an act of correction. Red (or sa) is a popular color, with many meanings and associations among Oceti Sakowin people and American Indians. Oglala Lakota writer Ivan Star describes red as the color of the north associated with perseverance and endurance. A buffalo faces the north wind in the dead of winter in an act "indicative of astuteness in the face of adversity," Star writes.[8] The act of Native writing carries on the history of enduring and resisting the onslaught of settler colonialism, its erasures and distortions. Red has become the color most associated with American

Indians of the Western Hemisphere, epitomized by the Lakota name Oyate Kin Luta—"the Red Nation" or "the Red People." A red pen is also the instrument of correction. Before the primacy of word processors, editors marked a page with red ink, correcting errors, inaccuracies, and bad writing. A wicazo sa thus is an affirmation of American Indian sovereignty that writes our own stories and corrects the settler colonial narratives that have colonized our language and our relations with the land.

Our History Is the Future, first published in 2019, attempted to bridge the intellectual tradition of "writing back" with the traditions of resistance that gave life to what can be described as the era of the Water Protector. I took my lead from the Indigenous people struggling to break colonialism's shackles. My goal was to narrate that struggle with honesty not just for academic and historical analysis but with the hope that it would bolster the confidence of people seeking to transform their worlds. I wrote for people in struggle, especially Indigenous people, who can see themselves as not just observers but makers of history. My aim was to show that social movements are legitimate sites of knowledge production and social theory that build upon the millions of small actions made by ordinary people that lead to extraordinary events.

Much has been written about the historic uprising at Standing Rock in 2016 against the construction of the Dakota Access Pipeline across treaty lands. Very little has contextualized the long tradition of Indigenous resistance, especially among the Oceti Sakowin. Many histories of Native people separate dramatic events of the nineteenth century from the twentieth century, as if the world had ended at Wounded Knee in 1890 after the massacre of Ghost Dancers and began again at Wounded Knee in 1973 during the armed takeover by dissident Oglalas and the American Indian Movement. What happened during the interregnum? And what had happened in our history from the turbulent "AIM days" to the present? Lots, as I have shown in this book. The lack of a media spectacle and a settler society's purposeful forgetting doesn't mean history stopped. Likewise, the #NoDAPL movement didn't end once the camps at the confluence of the Missouri and Cannonball rivers dispersed. It was just the beginning of the era of the Water Protector.

The effects of this new phase are quantifiable and reflect a qualitative shift that has not yet been widely recognized. For instance, a 2021 Indigenous Environmental Network and Oil Change International report found that Indigenous-led movements in the United States and Canada have "stopped or delayed greenhouse gas pollution equivalent to at least one-quarter of annual U.S. and Canadian emissions." That adds up to a remarkable 1.8 billion metric tons of carbon emissions. Indigenous people, who make up about 5 percent of the population in Canada and 2.6 percent of the population in the United States, punch well above their weight class when it comes to combatting global warming. While the report is quantitative and geographic, tracking twenty-six sites of struggle against various fossil fuel projects across all stages, from the nodes of extraction to the spiraling web of pipelines and transportation networks, it is also temporal.[9] Climate change is like a compound debt that, in our modern era, first accelerated during the advent of industrial capitalism. But most of the damage has occurred recently, within the last seven decades when carbon-induced global warming came to be accepted as a scientific reality in Western societies. Thus, halting or challenging carbon emissions now functions like a compound return for future generations. Water Protectors of today and yesterday might not live to see the fruits of their struggle— that is, a cooler and more just planet. But the impacts will resonate long after they are gone.

In a 2018 conversation in Albuquerque, New Mexico, Pueblo scholar and activist Jennifer Marley asked Oohenumpa Lakota activist Madonna Thunder Hawk about why she committed herself to the American Indian Movement and the Red Power movement, participating in the most iconic events such as the occupation of Alcatraz, the Trail of Broken Treaties, the Custer courthouse riot, and the occupation of Wounded Knee. The full-time commitment sometimes put her own family in danger. "We're the ancestors of tomorrow," Thunder Hawk said, "so we act accordingly." Elizabeth Cook-Lynn expressed a similar sentiment that we, as people of the Oceti Sakowin, are here only to ensure the coming of the next generation:

> I had this grandmother who said this to me earlier, "You don't even own your own life, my dear. You're only taking care of it for the next generation." That's fairly profound when you think about it. It is really what the Dakotas think about themselves and the world. It has, on the one hand, been their weakness because it's been exploited. But on the other hand, it is also their strength. It is what will make them, in the end, the winners in this conflagration. We're not protesting so much as we are saying: we have the right to our place in this universe.[10]

The lives of Thunder Hawk and Cook-Lynn bridge the gap between intellectual and activist. They are steeped in a historical tradition that looks to the past for guidance while striving for correct relations with the human and natural worlds. How else should we understand what it means to be a Water Protector? The Standing Rock movement that sprang up to protect Mni Sose from the trespass of the Dakota Access Pipeline and was grounded in anti-capitalist and Indigenous values of being a good relative to present and future generations—that is, the aspiration to be *ancestors of the future*.

§

As I have shown in this book, the tradition of Indigenous resistance draws from global movements for dignity and justice that

266

offer poetic inspiration. African revolutionary Amilcar Cabral once asked his compatriots in the anti-colonial revolution: how did they wage a successful struggle? The common strategy, they responded, was to wage a guerrilla war by taking to the mountains. The most famous example was how Fidel Castro and Che Guevara took to the Sierra Maestra mountains, learning the campesino culture while waging an armed revolution against a US-backed Cuban dictator. Cabral listened to and studied his comrades' suggestions intensely. His West African nation of Guinea-Bissau had its own topography: a coastal region abutting a flat interior. There were no mountains. There were also distinct political, social, economic, and historical conditions that made his country different from the island nation of Cuba. "As for our mountains," Cabral concluded, "we decided that our people had to take their place, since it would be impossible to develop our struggle otherwise. So our people are our mountains."[11] The independence movement would struggle among the people, creating literacy programs and health clinics to meet people's basic needs. Going to the people created a culture of resistance by "return[ing] to the source."

Cabral's ideas resonated with the Red Power movement of the 1960s. For example, a decade of struggle that began with the National Indian Youth Council under the leadership of Clyde Warrior quickly spread to urban and reservation Indian communities. The American Indian Movement formed in Minneapolis in 1968 to promote education, health, and housing programs for urban Natives. The Red Power movement, however, was still looking for its mountains. While allied with other social movements, it was also distinct. The United States wasn't just a racist society. The goal wasn't civil rights or integration but liberation from the colonial system—it was the overturning of colonialism to liberate the land and the people.

Where did the movement derive its strength and power? Sure, it mobilized the frustrations of Indigenous youth disillusioned by the failed policies of urban relocation and termination.

Many desired a return to the culture and spirituality that seemed alienated from them, and often could only be found within reservation communities, where it remained largely intact. As the Wounded Knee occupation in 1973 underlined, AIM increasingly sought guidance from traditional elders or those who still held onto the sanctity of Indigenous sovereignty evidenced through the many treaties made with the United States. In 1974, at the first convening of the International Indian Treaty Council, those treaty people represented AIM's mountains. They were the source of knowledge who said to take the 1868 Fort Laramie Treaty to the United Nations, to get land back in He Sapa and water rights restored for Mni Sose. Armed resistance was never the primary strategy, but a tactic in service of the return to—and defense of—the source. After all, Indigenous people during this time posed almost no military threat to the United States government. Yet, as this book has shown, police repression nearly destroyed the Red Power movement.

The parallels between the crackdowns on the Red Power movement and the continued surveillance, harassment, and repression of Water Protectors are instructive. Throughout its history, the colonial state has imagined the figure of the Indian as the original "terrorist"—that is, the original enemy of empire. Initially, Indian killing appeared synonymous with frontier "defense." Lenape scholar Joanne Barker argues that the terrorist designation of Indigenous resistance became a template later applied to communists, anarchists, and socialists.[12] In this sense, the Indigenous are the targets of the original and oldest Red Scare, and the United States can therefore be understood as the world's leading anticommunist *and* settler-colonial project. The subjugation and genocide of Indigenous peoples in North America is tied to the endless war making against the alternatives to US hegemony.

What has made traditions of Indigenous resistance reach beyond the narrowing confines of the nation-state is solidarity.

The Black radical tradition has profoundly shaped my study of Indigenous movements. Ruth Wilson Gilmore calls this kind of intellectual and political project an "infrastructure of feeling," which is a "consciousness-foundation" that allows us to "select and reselect our liberatory lineages."[13] Not all that falls under the category of "Indigenous" necessarily qualifies as "radical" nor "revolutionary" at all moments or places in time. The tradition is not defined by static notions of the past but a constant dialogue and debate about discernment and politics. Robin D. G. Kelley's *Freedom Dreams* recovered the future worlds Black radicals tried to create, helping me see the long and parallel tradition of Indigenous resistance.[14] It put Black and Indigenous intellectuals in conversation beyond the level of theory, reviving *actual* collaborations. As I wrote in the chapter on internationalism, the friendship between the Black sociologist and activist W. E. B. Du Bois and Dakota medical doctor and writer Ohiyesa (Charles Eastman) had a mostly unrecognized role in helping shape early-twentieth-century American Indian activism. Eastman's *The Soul of the Indian* (1911) was no doubt inspired by Du Bois's *The Souls of Black Folk* (1903). Du Bois was the only non-Native voting member of the Society of American Indians, founded in 1911. And later that year, the two traveled and spoke together at the Universal Races Congress in London. Gilmore's call to select and reselect our liberatory lineages to foreground infrastructures of feeling demonstrates that traditions are not mutually exclusive but often overlapping and intertwined. Theories of change arise from within Indigenous movements, but the power and inspiration to carry out that change extends beyond the Native settler binary and the limitations of the nation-state.

Our History Is the Future has brought me and the stories contained within it across many geographies of resistance. The book has taken on a social life of its own, traveling with me to the terraced olive groves on the rolling hills of Ramallah, Palestine; the Coroní River of Venezuela; La Paz, Bolivia; the mouth of the Amazon in Brazil; the wild rice camps in Keweenaw Bay; the Stop Line 3 camps in Mni Sota Makoce; the streets of Quito, Ecuador; the East Philips neighborhood in Minneapolis; and many other beautiful sites of struggle. More important, the book has brought me to my home near Bdote, a creation site of the Dakota Oyate. What was at first a humble encampment to stop the Dakota Access Pipeline at the confluence of the Missouri and Cannonball rivers sparked a movement, galvanizing the largest gathering of North American Indigenous nations in recent history against the most destructive institution in human history—the fossil fuel industry. It didn't happen in a major urban center. A new climate movement arose in the rural oil state of North Dakota, a place where reactionary politics have been mostly defined against and despite the original peoples of the land. Amid the violent and exclusionary nature of white supremacy, however, a movement forged a new and more grounded political identity—which could also be considered spiritual and cultural—that centered values in defense of water and earth that were not exclusive *just* to the Indigenous. To be a Water Protector isn't to engage in the narrow politics that privilege the closed identity sets of one people and their singular future above all others. Rather, to be a Water Protector is to engage in a universal politics grounded in Indigenous values, pushing for a world in which many worlds fit; it is to fight for collective futures defined by the humble people of the world, not corporations. Access to clean water, after all, isn't only an Indigenous problem but a fundamental human right. It is a problem for everyone, though especially acute for the poor and those bearing the brunt of climate change. This generation of Land Defenders, Water Protectors, Forest Defenders, martyrs, and kai'i found their mountains, literally and figuratively in Cabral's sense, in rivers, forests, urban sprawls, and many other sacred landscapes. The power of the land has animated chains of solidarity across the globe. The earth encompasses us all.

There is a critical link between US settler colonialism and imperialism, which divide humanity. The recent history of struggle shows that the Water Protector movement resonates well beyond rural landscapes and things categorically "Indigenous." It has forced me to confront the limitations and possibilities of the North American Indigenous movements and to resist all political and intellectual attempts to domesticate them within imperial borders. When we recite the verses of our resistance in an international idiom, something snaps into place: the force of our alternative, presaged by courageous acts of solidarity. We are a signal fire to the future: our decolonial movements must also be anti-imperialist.

§

In Palestine I learned that poetry measures distance. "Bint Nakba / And don't you forget it, my grandfather warned me," Jehan Bseiso read from her poem commemorating the Nakba's seventieth anniversary in an East Jerusalem basement theater.[15] We were told the Gazan writers were not allowed to leave the world's largest open-air prison to participate in this year's Palestine Festival of Literature. How far was Gaza? I wondered. Our Indigenous territories seem large and vast, but Palestine seems so small on the map in comparison. The distance to Gaza is measured by security checkpoints, I was told, which can take hours or days to cross if one's lucky. And for millions, the right of return to one's homelands is measured by concrete walls, concertina wire, citizenship status, stamps on a passport, Arabic names, UN resolutions, the Israeli Nation-State Law, and families of settlers occupying Palestinian homes and villages.

In Ramallah, Omar Barghouti, a cofounder of the Boycott, Divestment, and Sanctions movement, told us he was on his way to the United States to attend his daughter's wedding and to speak about the right to peacefully boycott one's occupiers. I told him to meet with American Indian leaders when he arrived, and that he's always welcome in our Lakota homelands as a relative and friend. Those words were useless, however, because days later our occupier denied him access to our home. From Palestine, the distance to Turtle Island is measured by visas and walls, settler laws, and State Department directives. The Great March of Return was also a measure of distance. How far was one willing to travel for freedom? At what cost? Palestinian historian Salman Abu Sitta reminds us that many of the hundreds of villages emptied after the Nakba in southern Palestine are walkable from Gaza.[16] In other words, the right of return for hundreds of thousands is within walking distance. During the Great March of Return, Israeli snipers targeted "the backs of knees to force amputation" as Gazans attempted to cross a perimeter fence. Jehan's poem sticks in my mind: "And if we lose our legs? / we will crawl, / on our hands and elbows."[17] Despite the distances we must travel for freedom, Palestine is always near my heart.

Colonial time creates different temporalities.
It speeds up
and slows down.
It's thick like mud
weighing on the feet of the colonized
—attempting to stick them in place,
in the past,
or in forever negation.
The feet of the colonizer,
on the other hand,
are light and mobile.
The colonizer's time is quick.
A US passport,
the right color skin,
the correct language
(anything but Arabic),
and an entitled jaunt grant fast access

to a world others only dream about. .
A sidewalk.
An access road.
Air.
An ocean.
Yet,
the colonial reality is meant to exaggerate time,
to make its novelty on the historical stage
seem as natural as the olive groves and rolling hills.
Like the ocean or Gaza,
the history of known freedom is just over that hill.
Though it stretches far back into time,
it is familiar to everyone.
A poem.
A song.
A story.
A stone.
You can smell it.
It's the fire that still burns in our hearts
thousands of grasslands
and sacred mountains away
where we also put our feet in the dirt,
grasped our history,
and said no.
And we came crashing down on them
like waves of history.[18]

I wrote this poem, titled "Waves of History," in 2019 after first visiting Palestine. On October 7, 2023, I watched as Palestinians broke through the Gaza perimeter fence as the Al-Aqsa Flood operation began. The world shifted that day. I recalled the words my friends in Ramallah quoted by the martyred fighter-intellectual Bassel al-Araj: "Liberate your mind before the land." The authority of the occupation, my friends argued, drew its power not from its bombs and walls but from occupying the minds of the colonized, haunting their imaginations and their dreams, therefore attempting to curtail what they thought was possible. In 2019, my friend Mahdi Sabbagh described a long list of methods—such as imposing a land, sea, and air blockade, controlling food and water, and preventing people from leaving and returning—by which the occupation has made Gaza uninhabitable. "Why not just call it genocide?" I asked him. Colonialism and genocide, I thought, ought to be easily recognized forms of oppression. But I come from a country that denies it is colonial and has never officially acknowledged its own genocide against Indigenous peoples. There is a similar disavowal by Israel and a national narrative that it is an exceptional country, immune from criticism because it has conflated Jewishness with its national project, despite critiques of this conflation coming from within the Jewish community itself. That narrative has also consistently come undone because active resistance against the theft of land and the ongoing siege has pushed Israel into more obvious and cruel forms of abuse. "I realized that in Palestine," Mahdi wrote me in an email in 2023, three days into the most recent scorched earth campaign in Gaza, "we had been conditioned to downplay our suffering because we are told that it is not the same, that it is less then. We are patronized and told that we couldn't possibly understand and that even if we could[,] we couldn't possibly speak without bias." He had internalized that his oppression was less than the Shoah, less than the centuries of European colonial wars and occupations, and therefore Palestinian freedom was also of secondary concern. That is why he "tactfully avoided the term genocide," a term for which the occupation stands accused before the world, and a term that justifies resistance. "[W]e do not accept this cynical take on the world," Mahdi wrote about the Western compulsion to make Palestinians suffer in silence. "We grew up in a culture that honors life," he wrote, refusing the lens through which Palestinians are only seen as victims or those unworthy of sympathy and solidarity.

Within days of the Al-Aqsa Flood, the occupation intensified its genocidal campaign on Gaza and escalated its attack on the West Bank. Within months, it massacred tens of thousands. After the New Year, South Africa brought the occupation before the International Court of Justice on charges of genocide, breaking the spell of inviolability surrounding the youngest European settler-colonial project. And yet, despite the mass slaughter and the brutal retaliation, the smell of freedom seems closer than it has in generations. An unyielding culture of resistance is still the lodestar of a free Palestine, and a renewed solidarity movement has brought millions to the streets in yet another wave of history.

§

Palestine has shown the world what is possible—and at great expense. The attempt to crush a free Palestine resonates across the globe, especially in South America. "What we are seeing in Gaza is a rehearsal for the future," the president of Colombia, Gustavo Petro, said in his opening statement at the COP28 summit in Dubai, United Emirates. "Hitler is knocking on the European and American middle-class homes' doors," he warned, "and many are letting him in."[19] The comparison between twentieth-century and emergent twenty-first-century fascism was bleak but measured: climate change and US interventions through sanctions and war have helped fuel the exodus of refugees from the south to the north, which now ignites racist polarization that tilts whole polities further rightwards. Petro's indictment was leveled at the liberal democracies of the global North, who, in his estimation, have only succeeded in securing high levels of resource consumption and carbon emissions by hardening their borders. Large, carbon-consuming countries like the United States have allowed and have provided the weapons to systematically kill tens of thousands of Palestinians, much as they have attempted to strangle any alternative to their hegemony. The current solution on offer has held the future hostage. The way forward is to unite the global South with a vision for a more just and sustainable planet. If a free Palestine emerges from the destruction, Petro offered, "we will be able to see a living humanity re-emerge tomorrow in the midst of the remains of the climate crisis."[20]

The climate crisis is one vector through which to analyze imperialism. Missing from many analyses that explore these connections, however, is the importance of Indigenous movements and resistance to US settler colonialism and their connections to movements in the global South. Much like Mahdi's hesitancy to openly identify certain oppressions, there is hesitancy to connect "domestic" Indigenous movements in the global North with alternative political and social projects of the global South. The present global division of humanity concerns those who live with war and suffering and those who live in countries that perpetuate it, a system that is not only divided by racial and imperial designs but also one that enshrines them. The divisions of the world are also present within Turtle Island.

For example, there is a direct link between the ongoing Venezuelan crisis and oil production in North America. When global oil prices fell during the North American oil boom, a crisis ensued in Venezuela. The Bolivarian revolution had increased the political participation and expanded the rights of Indigenous peoples (who prefer the term Original Peoples), women, the LGBTQ community, Afro-descendants, and poor people. In turn, the country's resource wealth had been redistributed among its most marginalized sectors. The oil crisis all but halted that social progress. In the years following the Great Recession, dampened demand and Obama's pro-oil-and-gas energy policies catalyzed the construction of new carbon infrastructure to drill and transport oil from production to market. The boom helped wean the US economy from oil imported from countries like Venezuela. Prices fell precipitously; Venezuelan incomes too. The alternative source of oil sought to replace it was much worse on ecological and social indexes, bringing havoc to and threatening Indigenous territories with the creation of oil pipelines, tar sands "dead zones," fracking rigs, and refineries, locking in settler economies to drill at the expense of Indigenous lands and lives. The most recent standoffs against the construction of oil and gas pipelines at Standing Rock, Bayou Bridge, Line 3, and Unist'ot'en Camp show that the United States and Canada still need to plunder Indigenous lands to make a profit to keep their economies afloat. It follows that Indigenous resistance in North America is at the forefront of combatting imperialist plunder, and our struggles are interconnected with movements of the global South.

Why target Venezuela? The State Department's antagonism is owed, in part, to the country's vast oil reserves. But it also has to do with the perceived threat that Venezuela poses to the United States' influence and power in the region, both as an alternative to neoliberalism and because it remains a lifeline to Cuba, the target of a crushing, decades-long blockade that the United Nations annually votes to end. Venezuela's solidarity has also extended to the Indigenous nations of Turtle Island. In 2007, the late and preeminent Oglala Lakota journalist Tim Giago applauded Hugo Chavez and the Bolivarian revolution for providing heating assistance to hard-hit Indian reservations, which include some of the poorest places in North America, during the harsh winter months. "People have heated their home with dryers. A lot of children have been ill because of cold homes. Tribal programs haven't had heat," Margaret Bad Warrior, a tribal attorney from the Cheyenne River Sioux Tribe, described the situation on her reservation in the winter of 2007.[21] Citgo Petroleum, at the time a Venezuelan state-owned oil company, had for nearly a decade donated millions of dollars in heating assistance not only to reservation communities but also to low-income neighborhoods and homeless shelters. Giago excoriated US hypocrisy for failing to uphold its own treaty obligations to American Indians, while it criticized other countries such as Venezuela, and he hammered away at the failure of capitalist economies on reservations to keep Indigenous people warm and fed. "Where [were] the rich casino-owning tribes?" Giago asked. "Busy counting their money I guess."[22]

My family on the Lower Brule Reservation was a direct beneficiary of Venezuela's heating assistant program. Our lands were dammed and flooded for hydroelectricity in the mid-twentieth century. But our reservations don't control the flow or profit from the power generated from that dispossession. In fact, Native communities most impacted by the Pick-Sloan dams on the Missouri River typically pay the same electricity rates as the average consumer, with the greatest ongoing price paid—the physical loss of land—disproportionately outsourced to reservation communities. Imagine if we had the power to sell that electricity at rates we decided appropriate for the amount of destruction caused to our lands and livelihoods? What if we used those revenues to reinvest into our economies and redistribute the wealth to those, including the land and water itself, most impacted by this environmental destruction?

Venezuela's act of solidarity, small as it may seem, profoundly shaped how I viewed the Indigenous struggle in relation to other movements in the global South. It was then that I first seriously began to study the Bolivarian revolution and the challenges it sought to overcome. Much like Native nations in Turtle Island, nations of the global South are often trapped by an economic system put in place by colonialism, which forces colonized nations into single-commodity production—typically extractivist, such as oil and gas—that are then refined and consumed elsewhere at higher prices.

These nations become resource colonies producing goods and raw materials for the global North. For example, just as much of the Navajo Nation's revenues have historically derived from oil and coal, largely for US consumption, most of Venezuela's export revenues once came from petroleum and gas. Resource nationalism has been a pathway for asserting control over the prices and profits and redistributing that wealth internally. But it has also created vulnerability as social progress has been tied to single-commodity production. This dependence on oil revenues was a weakness the United States exploited when it sanctioned Venezuelan oil companies and global oil prices fell. Instead of collapsing, the Bolivarian project has survived and attempted to diversify its economy.

In October 2019, I attended a gathering of Indigenous peoples from around the world in the state of Bolívar as a delegate for the Red Nation. During the proceedings, we learned of the Indigenous participation in the Bolivarian revolutionary process. The Venezuelan constitution recognizes and protects Indigenous rights to land, culture, and language and guarantees three permanent seats for Indigenous representatives in the National Assembly. Wiphalas, representing the Andean cosmovision of the Pachamama, lined the conference grounds, where breakout groups discussed and debated land and water rights, women's rights, and Indigenous visions of socialism. Conference delegates gave final reports to the gathering as Pémon dancers and Mayan medicine women performed ceremonies at the confluence of the Orinoco and Caroní rivers and the famous Llovizna Falls, which had been dammed in the 1950s. Hydroelectricity is the main source of power in Venezuela, developed through Indigenous displacement and dispossession similar to the Pick-Sloan dams on the Missouri River. Although restricted, the waterfalls flowed with an intensity that reflected the power of the Indigenous gathering. It was during the final ceremonies that I offered a note of gratitude and thanks to the people of Venezuela for providing heating assistance to our reservation communities. I read from a collective statement by the Red Nation:

> Indigenous people are the stream of history, with ancestors pushing us through the present and into the future. Today, we are at the convergence of these beautiful rivers, the power behind our movements driving us forward as we crash down like waves of history. We are the tip of the spear. We are the front lines. And like the crashing and cascading waterfalls, we create mist that refracts rainbows representing all nations trying to throw off the yoke of imperialism. We are a natural force, a solution to this crisis . . . You cannot stop the rain. You cannot stop a tornado. You cannot stop the wind. You cannot stop fire. You cannot stop power because power moves through us.

Before we left Caracas to return to the United States, we had a chance encounter with David Choquehuanca, then general secretary of ALBA, an intergovernmental political and economic alliance promoting Bolivarianism. A dedicated observant of Aymara spirituality and peace advocate, he invited us to a global prayer for peace to be held at Lake Titicaca in Bolivia during the Winter Solstice. But there would be no ceremony. Within days, Choquehuanca went into hiding. A right-wing military coup ousted the Indigenous president of Bolivia, Evo Morales, and began a terror campaign targeting Indigenous peoples and leaders of the Movement Toward Socialism. A year later, I returned to Caracas as an international observer for the National Assembly elections. Morales, having fled Bolivia with his life, gave a speech on the dialogue of civilizations, a concept inspired by the former socialist prime minister Zapatero of Spain. "There was no civilization, only invasion," Morales said of the European conquest of Abya Ayala, the Kuna term for the continents of the Western

Hemisphere. "When they [the European imperialists] strike, it's not solely against Indigenous people," he said of the coup against his government and the social movements that brought him to power. "They strike against our model." Morales said there is a Manichean way to view the current conflicts in the world. There is an "imperialist civilization" and a "people's civilization." "Life is sacred," he concluded, which is "the view of socialism."

The United States' relentless, decades-long, frontal assault on Venezuela was a testament to this statement. Debilitating US sanctions that have affected the imports of medicine and food have been aimed at eviscerating the legacy of Hugo Chavez and the Bolivarian revolution. As a result, there has been mass migration of millions out of Venezuela and an estimated forty thousand deaths from 2017 to 2018, according to a 2019 report by the Center for Economic and Policy Research.[23] Indigenous peoples in Venezuela's Orinoco Mining Arc region have experienced more acutely the economic, social, and environmental devastation because of US aggression. The Venezuelan government calls it a "National Strategic Development Zone" to help diversify the national economy and to regulate mining operations. In the southern state of Bolívar, a once thriving ecotourism economy guided by Indigenous knowledges and practices has been decimated by US sanctions. There are no tourists and therefore no more jobs in tourism. Economic desperation has fueled increased exploitation and violence. Nature reserves that were set aside through Chavez's region for Indigenous management have become enclaves for paramilitaries. Illegal gold mining operations mar the landscape and employ Indigenous miners in dangerous conditions that have seen an uptick in trafficking and violence along the Brazilian border, including deadly clashes with security forces. Amid the chaos, my friends Viviana and Alejandra, two young Pémon matriarchs of the Mapauri community, still consider themselves Chavistas, dedicated to fulfilling the promises of the Bolivarian revolution to Indigenous peoples. The vision they offer stems from a practice of socialism that takes as its starting point the noncapitalist ways of life, economies, culture, and spirituality found in Indigenous cosmovisions. This was not an abstract or idealistic program but one that is continually practiced and maintained daily. Viviana was the head captain of Mapauri, in charge of security and an unarmed volunteer force of *milicianos*, according to a Pémon matriarchal governance system that the Venezuelan constitution recognizes and protects. Alejandra is a community health expert and traditional Pémon healer. She combines her years of training under her community elders with a formal education system that integrates and promotes Indigenous knowledges in the practice of community health. While critical of the government's role in the violence, they are more critical of how US sanctions have strangled their local economy, pushing young Indigenous men to leave the villages to work in the mines or to join paramilitaries.

The two Pémon women also helped lead an international campaign in 2020 to return the Kueka Stone (or Grandmother Stone) that was taken in 1998 by a German sculptor. "The Kueko Stone," the Grandfather Stone, "was sad," Alejandra told me. "His cosmic partner was stolen from him." The Kueko and Kueka stones, two large red granite boulders, play an important role in the origin stories of the Pémon people and represent the longer history of pillage, theft, and destruction of Indigenous lands. More importantly, Alejandra argued that the return of the stone (which is one the largest repatriated Indigenous items in history) has served as a larger story about Indigenous rights in Venezuela and the possibilities of justice. They formed alliances between Indigenous grassroots organizations, environmentalists, European allies, and the Venezuelan government. While largely unremarked as a major win for Indigenous peoples in the Western media, which have also downplayed or ignored the effects of US sanctions on Indigenous peoples, the return of the Kueka Stone was more than a symbolic act. In 2020, the Kueka Stone made its transatlantic journey home with support and pressure from the government of Nicolás Maduro, who called it "a spiritual and cultural treasure." "Reuniting our ancestor stones," Alejandra told me as we offered prayers and tobacco at the Kueko Stone in 2019, "will make us whole again, healing our people and the land."

§

It was the middle of a snowstorm in February 2023. The Minneapolis Police Department blocked off six blocks along Cedar Avenue, which cuts through the Little Earth housing complex. South Minneapolis is one of the most diverse neighborhoods in Minnesota. Seventy percent of residents are people of color, and 30 percent speak a foreign language. It's also home to Little Earth, a large and historic urban Native housing community and the heartbeat of the American Indian Movement of yesterday and today. Residents lined up along a police line with bullhorns and banners. The East Phillips neighborhood is just down the road from the Third Precinct on Lake Street that blazed its way into international headlines in 2020. Although diverse, the community is united in its distrust of the police. The red and blue flashing lights highlighted a poster on a street corner lamppost. It was for an unnamed, young Native woman who had gone missing in the neighborhood. But the police weren't there to tackle the issue of murdered and missing Indigenous women and relatives. They cordoned off the area to ensure people didn't return to the camp they had just cleared.

I was waiting for news about my friends Vinny and Rachel. Police detained and charged them and others with misdemeanor trespassing during the eviction of Camp Nenoocaasi, a tent city erected to stop the demolition of the Roof Depot, a notoriously polluted area in Minneapolis' so-called arsenic triangle. To avoid the bad publicity of arresting Indigenous people at a camp that began in ceremony, police chose to avoid sending people to the Hennepin County Jail, instead dropping them off at a nearby homeless shelter. It must not have occurred to them that the assumption that a homeless shelter was a better place for Indigenous people than a jail cell was equally inflammatory. Minneapolis has a disproportionately high Native houseless population, painfully visible during the winter months and whose winter camps are frequently targeted with evictions.

Camp Nenoocaasi, though evicted by police, effectively stopped the demolition, which, according to local activists, could have potentially released a toxic arsenic plume in an area already reeling from the effects of air pollution. The Minnesota Pollution Control Agency found that air pollution in the Twin Cities Metro Area accounts for 10 percent of all Minneapolis and St. Paul deaths—that's 1,600 people a year.[24] East Phillips had other plans for the Roof Depot. Indigenous community organizers brought together a coalition of environmentalists and labor unions to successfully halt the demolition. Plans are underway to rehabilitate the Roof Depot building and site into a large-scale urban farm with affordable, low-income housing. Most Native people don't live on Indian reservations. Many live in cities like Minneapolis. The Stop the Demo movement showed that Water Protectors and Land Defenders are everywhere, especially in our major metropolitan areas.

After the police killing of George Floyd, Minneapolis became the epicenter of the uprisings against property. Floyd, after all, was murdered after allegedly trying to buy cigarettes at a convenience store with a counterfeit $20 bill. He was tackled to the ground only one hundred miles from where another store owner once told starving Dakotas to "eat grass." Three days after, the Third Precinct burned. The fort of killer cops who called themselves "cowboys" was destroyed.

According to a 2023 report by the Department of Justice, these "cowboys" of the Third Precinct and East Phillips neighborhood used force 49 percent more often when stopping Black people and 69 percent more often when stopping Native people than when stopping white people, unholstering or pointing their guns at Black and Native youth at rates 13.5 and 19.6 times higher, respectively, per capita than white youth, and 4.7 and 6.8 times higher than white adults.[25] While inflicting terror on Black and Native youth, Minnesota police applications for "permanent disability benefits due to post-traumatic stress disorder skyrocketed" from 2019 to 2022, according to the *Star Tribune*, resulting in staggering financial costs to the public.[26]

The George Floyd uprisings in 2020 have reverberated around the globe. Police and prosecutors have taken special notice as the Water Protector movement has expanded and grown, articulating a distinct abolitionist vision. On August 29, 2023, Georgia prosecutors charged fifty-seven individuals from the Stop Cop City movement in Atlanta with RICO charges. The indictment cited May 25, 2020—the day Derek Chauvin murdered George Floyd—as the beginning date for their investigation into "racketeering activity." The charges come amid a growing onslaught of anti-protest legislation protecting "critical infrastructure" and punishing "energy discrimination" such as divesting from fossil fuel companies. Modeled after anti-BDS legislation supported by ALEC that passed in Texas in 2019, the fossil fuel bills criminalizing dissent are promoted as sending "a strong message that the states will fight back against woke capitalism."[27] The backlash is a response to the successes of the Water Protector movement that has qualitatively and quantitatively changed the climate justice movement. Indigenous resistance has challenged 1.8 billion metric tons of CO_2 emissions from Canada and the United States, a 2021 report by the Indigenous Environmental Network and Oil Change International found.[28] That number translates into profits lost and resources used to crush the Water Protector movement. Water Protectors have given us new language and, more importantly, new poetry.

On July 3, 2020, the Oceti Sakowin gathered in He Sapa, the Black Hills, where we emerged from the earth and first became human. It was a protest against Donald Trump's visit to our sacred landscape and Mount Rushmore, a monument to white supremacy. Lakota land defenders spray-painted a poem on a riot shield as the police line advanced. It read, "LAND BACK." The words were unequivocal, the action unambiguous. Whereas Indigenous relations with the land are based on reciprocity and responsibility, white relations are governed by property. And those relations are overturned when that property is destroyed or taken back. When it concerns the land, the past hasn't already happened. The seizure of a continent isn't a fait accompli. History must be retold, reestablished, again and again.

Ignoring what came before the United States treats the original people as "a people without history." The Indigenous have been treated as specters haunting the Americas. In 1890, left with only ghosts of their many dead, they communed with them through the prophetic Ghost Dance. It was called "apocalyptic" by whites, because the central tenet of the vision was land back to the Indigenous. But these were not ghosts; these were ancestors of the future.

ACKNOWLEDGMENTS

All knowledge is produced through relationships. This book tells our history in the past, present, and future tense as it was related to me by numerous individuals. It doesn't belong to only me. Any or all mistakes contained therein are also not solely my responsibility. That is pure bourgeois individualism. The accountability required to tell a story of this magnitude is always a collective process. With regard to its shortcomings, I am the first to admit that others can tell this story the better than me. After all, our tradition of storytelling is a collective and intergenerational process. Our history, as the Oceti Sakowin, is one in which many truths and many worlds fit. I look forward to this story, or ones like it, being told and retold for generations to come.

The inspiration for this book in its present form came from a breakfast conversation in Park City, Utah in January 2017. Bobbi Jean Three Legs, Melanie Yazzie, LaDonna Bravebull Allard, Miles Allard, and myself shared a rental to attend a screening of films about the Standing Rock movement, which followed the lives of Bobbi and LaDonna. Over coffee, we discussed history and the profound meaning it had taken during the #NoDAPL struggle. I wrote this book for young people like Bobbi. I wrote it for my sixteen year-old self who needed theory as a weapon and history as a guide growing up in white supremacist border towns like Chamberlain, South Dakota. This is a story of the prophesied Seventh Generation. They have lit the fires of resistance, and those flames cannot be put out. I hope this history helps produce the confidence necessary in our people, and those who are allied to our cause, to turn back the forces of destruction.

I wrote the bulk of this book in four weeks sitting on a couch. My aunt Mary Alice and my uncle Dave were kind enough to open their home to me, which sits along our river, Mni Sose, the Missouri River, in Chamberlain—two places I had to be mentally and physically to finish the writing. Most of the history of our people, the Kul Wicasa, comes from my father Ben. His father Andrew and his grandfather Ruben entrusted it with him, and he entrusted it with me. The broader history of our people draws from conversations with Lewis Grassrope and LaDonna, both of whom I admire for their deep historical knowledge. (As a methodological note, I avoided sharing any ceremonial or privileged cultural knowledge that wasn't already published; and I did not share what was not mine to share.) For a year, Melanie patiently listened to me rant and read passages. She also supported me through times of terrible danger and times of radical profundity. For that I am profoundly thankful to her as a comrade. A complete list of interlocutors for the oral histories would be a complete failure. So I would like to thank all of our knowledge-keepers who selflessly share the stories and traditions with our young people. "Remember the stories," more than one elder has told me. "Your life doesn't belong to you. You're only here to ensure the coming generation," I was also told. Those are humble directions that I take to heart.

In October 2016, my dear friends Jordan Camp and Christina Heatherton gave me the confidence to write this book. They introduced me to Andrew Hsiao and the wonderful Verso comrades. My friend and mentor, Alex Lubin, who was the chair of our department at the time, encouraged me to suspend my current dissertation project and to finish the book. So I did. Parts of the abandoned dissertation eventually became parts of this book, and the other parts are a story for another time. As my dissertation chair, Jennifer Denetdale, an enduring inspiration as an Indigenous historian, mentor, and freedom-fighter in her own right, refused to accept anything less than a solid manuscript with solid prose. I am forever indebted to her. Alyosha Goldstein and David Correia, who also sat on my committee, patiently helped me sharpen my analytics and writing. And Christina stepped in and helped me finish. Jordan, Christina, and Manu Karuka workshopped the manuscript for Barnard College's New Direction in American Studies Project. Jaskiran Dhillon, Roxanne Dunbar-Ortiz, and K-Sue Park generously read the manuscript. Audrea Lim provided the final feedback and finishing touches. All of them are wonderful comrades. Without them, you wouldn't be reading this.

Walter Johnson offered me Harvard University's American Democracy Fellowship (2017–2018) at the Charles Warren Center for Studies in American History. During that time, I finished book edits and learned a great deal about history and t-shirts from Walter. While in Cambridge, Massachusetts, I gained a greater appreciation for our Wampanoag relatives in so-called "New England" and the true history of Thanksgiving, a National Day of Mourning for Indigenous peoples. I will never forget. I would also like to acknowledge and thank the archival staff and researchers at the South Dakota Oral History Center at the University of South Dakota, the archivists at the Center for Southwest Research at the University of New Mexico, and the staff and archivists at the Newberry Library in Chicago. Since this project began in 2016, I have slept on numerous couches and floors, in one car, and too many camping tents. To everyone who has ever opened your home to me, shared food, or cared, thank you for being a good relative. Pilamayaye, Stacy, Delane, and Tyrell for opening the door. The Red Nation comrades—Jennifer, Hope, Demetrius, Andrew, Kyon, Melissa, Kiley, Brandon, Radmilla, Majerle, Ua, and Cheyenne—granted me the time away and the courage to finish this project. Thank you for picking up my slack and for being good people of the earth. You will never know how humbly inspired I am by all of you.

A couple weeks before our first trip to Standing Rock in August 2016, we mourned the police killing of Loreal Tsingine. I remember that hot day in Winslow, Arizona—not a cloud in the sky. It began to rain. Loreal's cousin said it was a female rain, cool and gentle, a blessing. The same rain fell that September day when we took the streets in Chicago to protest the Army Corps of Engineers after Dakota Access unleashed the attack dogs on the anniversary of the Whitestone Hill Massacre. After I found out Miles had passed, a light snow fell in Toronto, and I mourned with relatives. Mni Wiconi! We remember everyone that we have lost on the road to justice and freedom. My mother Angela and my grandparents Joyce and Andrew did not get to witness the glory of our people in those fine hours, days, and weeks. But our ancestors live on through us and in the stories we tell. We are never truly alone, and they are never truly gone. As the Dakota scholar Ella Deloria once wrote, "I am not afraid; I have relatives."

Lastly, I thank the Water Protectors, past and present, for your sacrifice that we may live. You knew your duty and the price you had to pay. Pilamayaye ota! They cannot take away the dream of beauty that Crazy Horse gave to us. Like him, we will live forever. Mitakuyapi Bliheiciyapo!

NOTES

Prologue: Prophets

1 Quoted in Alleen Brown, Will Parrish, and Alice Speri, "Leaked Documents Reveal Counterterrorism Tactics used at Standing Rock to 'Defeat Pipeline Insurgencies,'" *Intercept*, May 27, 2017, theintercept.com.

2 Altwin Grassrope, *Tatanka Mazaskazi: Golden Buffalo* (Lower Brule, SD: Lower Brule Sioux Tribe, 2000), 7.

3 Quoted in Gyasi Ross, "Native Grandmothers Defend Mother Earth: Faith Spotted Eagle Kicks SERIOUS Knowledge About Keystone XL," *Indian Country Today*, April 4, 2017, indiancountrymedianetwork.com.

4 Nicholas Black Elk, *The Sixth Grandfather: Black Elk's Teachings Given to John G. Neihardt*, ed. Raymond J. DeMallie (Lincoln, NE: University of Nebraska Press, 1985), 289.

5 See Ardalan Raghian, "Newly Released Documents Show Dakota Access Pipeline Is Discriminatory Against Indigenous Peoples," *Truthout*, January 22, 2018, truthout.org.

6 Michael L. Lawson, *Dammed Indians Revisited: The Continuing History of the Pick-Sloan Plan and the Missouri River Sioux* (Pierre, SD: South Dakota Historical Society Press, 2009), 52–3.

7 Ibid., 163.

8 Frank C. Estes, *Make Way for the Brules* (Lower Brule, SD: Lower Brule Sioux Tribe, 1963).

9 Quoted in George C. Estes and Richard R. Loder, *Kul-Wicasa-Oyate* (Lower Brule, SD: Lower Brule Sioux Tribe, 1971), front matter.

10 Albert White Hat Sr., *Life's Journey – Zuya: Oral Teachings from Rosebud*, ed. John Cunningham (Salt Lake City, UT: University of Utah Press, 2012), 44.

11 Josephine Waggoner, *Witness: A Húnkpapha Historian's Strong-Heart Song of the Lakotas*, ed. Emily Levine (Lincoln, NE: University of Nebraska Press, 2013), 57.

12 Vine Deloria, Jr., "Foreword" in John G. Neihardt, *Black Elk Speaks* (Lincoln, NE: University of Nebraska Press, 1979), xv.

13 Neihardt, *Black Elk Speaks*, 207.

14 Black Elk, *The Sixth Grandfather*, 43.
15 Ella Deloria, *Speaking of Indians* (Lincoln, NE: University of Nebraska Press, 1998), 25.
16 Kim TallBear, "Badass (Indigenous) Women Caretake Relations: #NoDAPL, #IdleNoMore, #BlackLivesMatter," Hot Spots, *Cultural Anthropology*, December 22, 2016, culanth.org.
17 Marcella Gilbert, "A Lesson in Natural Law," forthcoming.

1. Siege

1 Chief Arvol Looking Horse, "Important Message from Keeper of Sacred White Buffalo Calf Pipe," *Indian Country Today Media Network*, September 7, 2017, newsmaven.io/indiancountrytoday.
2 Quoted in Nick Estes, "Declaring War on KXL: Indigenous Peoples Mobilize," *Mass Dissent*, summer 2014, nlgmasslawyers.org. Unless otherwise cited, I draw heavily from my participation, observation, and notes of the events and interviews with key participants documented in this chapter.
3 Wayne Frederick, interview by Ed Schultz, *The Ed Show*, MSNBC, April 3, 2014.
4 See Zoltán Grossman, *Unlikely Alliances: Native Nations and White Communities Join to Defend Rural Lands* (Seattle: University of Washington Press, 2017), 177–87.
5 TransCanada, *Keystone XL Pipeline Project, South Dakota Public Utilities Commission Quarterly Report*, June 30, 2011, 4.
6 Edward C. Valandra, "Stolen Native Land," *Themedes*, June 2014.
7 Jess Gilbert, Spencer D. Wood, and Gwen Sharp, "Who Owns the Land? Agricultural Land Ownership by Race/Ethnicity," *Rural America* 17:4, 2002, 55–62.
8 See Village Earth, "Food Insecurity and Agriculture Income for Native vs. Non-Native Producers," villageearth.org; US Department of Agriculture, *2012 Census of Agriculture: American Indian Reservations*, 2014, vol. 2, pt. 5, agcensus.usda.gov.
9 Ted Turner Enterprises, "Ted Turner Ranches FAQ," Ted Turner official website, tedturner.com.
10 See Cedric Robinson, *Black Marxism: The Making of the Black Radical Tradition* (Chapel Hill, NC: University of North Carolina, 2000).
11 Sylvia McAdam (Saysewahum), "Armed with Nothing More than a Song and a Drum: Idle No More," in *The Winter We Danced: Voices from the Past, the Future, and the Idle No More Movement* (Manitoba: ARP, 2014), 67.

12 Jesse Cardinal, "The Tar Sands Healing Walk," in *A Line in the Tar Sands: Struggles for Environmental Justice*, ed. Toban Black et al. (Toronto: Between the Lines and PM Press, 2014), 131.

13 Ibid., 129.

14 Ibid., 131.

15 Sâkihitowin Awâsis, "Pipelines and Resistance Across Turtle Island," in *A Line in the Tar Sands*, 255.

16 Mary Annette Pember, "On National Day of Awareness for Missing and Murdered Native Women, Here's What We Don't Know," *Rewire*, May 4, 2018, rewire.news.

17 Ashifa Kassam, "Guatemalan Women Take On Canada's Mining Giants Over 'Horrific Human Rights Abuses,'" *The Guardian*, December 13, 2017, theguardian.com.

18 See Matthew Frank, "Over a Barrel: The Boom and Bust, the Promise and Peril, of the Bakken," *Mountain West News*, March 14, 2016, mountainwestnews.org.

19 Damon Buckley, "Firsthand Account of Man Camp in North Dakota from Local Tribal Cop," *Lakota Country Today*, May 5, 2014, lakota countrytimes.com.

20 Emily Arasim and Osprey Orielle Lake, "Women on the Front Lines Fighting Fracking in the Bakken Oil Shale Formations," *EcoWatch*, March 12, 2016, ecowatch.com.

21 Kandi Mossett, interview by Amy Goodman, "We are Sacrifice Zones: Native Leader Says Toxic North Dakota Fracking Fuels Violence Against Women," *Democracy Now!*, December 11, 2015, democracynow.org.

22 Quoted in Cherri Foytlin, Yudith Nieto, Kerry Lemon, and Will Wooten, "Gulf Coast Resistance and the Southern Leg of the Keystone XL Pipeline," in *A Line in the Tar Sands*, 184.

23 "Transcript of President Obama's remarks in Cushing, Okla., March 22, 2012," *Oklahoman*, March 22, 2012, newsok.com.

24 See Scott Parkin, "When We Fight, We Fuck Shit Up: Keystone XL and Delegitimizing Fossil Fuels," *CounterPunch*, November 9, 2015, counterpunch.org.

25 Naomi Klein, *This Changes Everything: Capitalism vs. the Climate* (New York: Simon & Schuster, 2014), 294–5.

26 Lower Brule Sioux Tribe, "Resolution Authorizing Chairman Jandreau to Sign Letter to President Obama and Secretary John Kerry Stating the Lower Brule Sioux Tribe's Prospective Benefits and Working Relationship with TransCanada Development of a Community Investment Program Between the Lower Brule Sioux Tribe and TransCanada," res. doc. no. 14-007, November 12, 2013.

27 "Mother Earth Accord," Indigenous Environmental Network, ienearth.org.

28 In 2011, White Plume had been arrested along with hundreds of others protesting KXL in front of the White House. In March 2012, she and members from Owe Aku stopped "heavy hauls" carrying KXL construction materials through Pine Ridge. For several years, Owe Aku led direct action trainings called "Moccasins on the Ground," that played a pivotal role against KXL and the Dakota Access Pipeline in 2016.

29 See Ernst Schusky, *The Forgotten Sioux: An Ethnohistory of the Lower Brule Reservation* (Chicago, IL: NelsonHall, 1975).

30 See Michael L. Lawson, *Dammed Indians Revisited: The Continuing Legacy of the Pick-Sloan Plan and the Missouri River Sioux* (Pierre, SD: South Dakota State Historical Society, 2009), 232–3.

31 See "Timeline of Events," Lower Brule Sioux Tribe official website, lowerbrulesiouxtribe.com.

32 Kul Wicasa Ospiye, "Declaration," May 11, 2015, available at <docs.wixstatic.com/ugd/5ecd07_d78df4fe77584b9bab995 a40d9d9716f.pdf>.

33 Quoted in "Lower Brule Sioux Tribe Rejects Keystone XL, Calls for Immediate Removal of TransCanada from Treaty Lands," Press Release, *Lakota Voice*, April 29, 2015.

34 See "DAPL," Lower Brule Sioux Tribe official website.

35 See Amy Dalrymple, "Pipeline Route Plan First Called for Crossing North of Bismarck," *Bismarck Tribune*, Aug 18, 2016, bismarcktribune.com.

36 Unless otherwise noted, the following quotes and draws from the audio recording found here: "Sept 30th DAPL Meeting with SRST," filmed September 2014, YouTube video, 1:08:17, posted by Standing Rock Sioux Tribe, December 6, 2016, youtube.com.

37 Liz Hampton, "Sunoco, Behind Protested Dakota Pipeline, Tops US Crude Spill Charts," *Reuters*, September 23, 2016, reuters.com.

38 Alleen Brown, "Five Spills, Six Months in Operation: Dakota Access Track Record Highlights Unavoidable Reality—Pipelines Leak," *Intercept*, January 8, 2018, theintercept.com.

39 *Constitution of the Standing Rock Sioux Tribe*, available at indianaffairs.nd.gov.

40 See Jeffrey Ostler and Nick Estes, "'The Supreme Law of the Land': Standing Rock and the Dakota Access Pipeline," *Indian Country Today*, January 16, 2017, indiancountrymedianetwork.com.

41 Quoted in Kris Maher, "Dakota Pipeline's Builder Says Obstacles Will Disappear Under Donald Trump," *The Wall Street Journal*, November 16, 2016, wsj.com.

42 Quoted in *Standing Rock Sioux Tribe v. US Army Corps of Engineers*, 16-cv-1534, D.E. 22-1 (2016), earthjustice.org.

43 See Ardalan Raghian, "Newly Released Documents Show Dakota

Access Pipeline Is Discriminatory Against Indigenous Peoples," *Truthout*, January 22, 2018, truthout.org.

44 Associated Press, "North Dakota Officials Borrow $4M, Slam Feds on Protest Cost," *Argus Leader*, November 1, 2016, argusleader.com.

45 Dave Archambault II, "Taking a Stand at Standing Rock," *New York Times*, August 24, 2016, nytimes.com.

46 Quoted in *Standing Rock Sioux Tribe v. US Army Corps of Engineers*.

47 I draw this insight from conversations with Harsha Walia. See Harsha Walia, "A Truly Green Economy Requires Alliance between Labour and Indigenous People," *System Change Not Climate Change*, June 3, 2015, systemchangenotclimatechange.org.

48 Standing Rock Sioux Tribe, "Archambault on Presidential Visit: A Day Focused on Native Youth," *Indian Country Today*, June 24, 2014, indiancountrymedianetwork.com.

49 Tariq Brownotter, "Letter to Obama," Rezpect Our Water, official website, July 23, 2016, rezpectourwater.com.

50 See "Standing Rock Chair: Obama Could Stop the Dakota Pipeline Today and Preserve Indigenous Sacred Sites," *Democracy Now!*, November 3, 2016, democracynow.org.

51 Ibid.

52 Seth Kreshner, "Police Are Still Getting Surplus Army Gear—And They're Using it to Crack Down on Standing Rock," *In These Times*, November 2, 2016, inthesetimes.com.

53 Curtis Walman, "Police Across the Country Looked at Standing Rock as a Sort of Law Enforcement Laboratory," *MuckRock*, January 11, 2017, muckrock.com.

54 Kristen Simmons, "Settler Atmospherics," Dispatches, *Cultural Anthropology*, November 20, 2017, culanth.org.

55 "Why Is North Dakota Strip-Searching Dakota Access Pipeline Protesters Charged with Misdemeanors?" *Democracy Now!*, October 18, 2016, democracynow.org.

56 Jenni Monet, "I was Strip-Searched, but my White Cellmates were not," *Indian Country Today*, May 3, 2017, indiancountrymedianetwork.com.

57 "It's a Whole New Ball Game Now," *My Next Guest Needs No Introduction*, season 1, ep. 1, Netflix, January 12, 2018.

58 "Protestor: 'It will be a Battle,'" Faith Spotted Eagle, interview by CNN, November 1, 2016, cnn.com.

59 Gyasi Ross, "Voices from The Front Lines in Standing Rock V.2: Alayna Eagle Shield and Educating a New Generation of Revolutionaries," *Indian Country Today Media Network*, October 7, 2016, indiancountrymedianetwork.com.

60 Sandy Grande, "The Future of US Education is Standing Rock," *Truthout*, July 4, 2017, truth-out.org.
61 Molly Larkeyin, "Meet the Leader of the Two-Spirit Camp at Standing Rock," *GoMag*, January 13, 2017, gomag.com.
62 For more information visit Water Protector Legal Collective, water-protectorlegal.org.

2. Origins

1 Elizabeth Cook-Lynn, "'There Are No Two Sides to This Story': An Interview with Elizabeth Cook-Lynn," interview by Nick Estes, *Wicazo Sa Review* 31:1, 2016, 40.
2 Robert Kelley Schneiders, *Unruly River: Two Centuries of Change Along the Missouri* (Lawrence, KS: University of Kansas Press, 1999); John E. Thorson, *River of Promise, River of Peril: The Politics of Managing the Missouri* (Lawrence, KS: University of Kansas Press, 1994); Henry C. Hart, *The Dark Missouri* (Madison, WI: University of Wisconsin Press, 1957).
3 Quoted in John C. Ewers, "Intertribal Warfare as the Precursor of Indian-White Warfare on the Northern Great Plains," *Western Historical Quarterly* 6:4, 1975, 397.
4 See Nick Estes, "Why a Team Name is More than a (Racist) Word," *High Country News*, December 22, 2017, hcn.org.
5 Richard White, "The Winning of the West: The Expansion of the Western Sioux in the Eighteenth and Nineteenth Centuries," *Journal of American History* 65:3, 1978, 319–43. See also Gary Clayton Anderson, "Early Dakota Migration and Intertribal War: A Revision," *Western Historical Quarterly* 11: 1, 1980, 17–36.
6 See Heidi Kiiwetinepinesiik Stark, "Criminal Empire: The Making of the Savage Land," *Theory and Event* 19:4, 2016.
7 Lakota winter counts are typically viewed as a nineteenth-century innovation, and the Lakotas themselves as a relatively new social group. The Battiste Good winter count, however, documents Lakota history as early as the tenth century and contends that the Dakota people were a people living in their homelands long before this. See Candace S. Greene and Russell Thornton, eds., *The Year the Stars Fell: Lakota Winter Counts at the Smithsonian* (Lincoln, NE: University of Nebraska Press, 2007), 292–7.
8 See, for example, Elizabeth R. P. Henning, "Western Dakota Winter Counts: An Analysis of the Effects of Westward Migration and Culture Change," *Plains Anthropologist* 27:95, 1982, 57–65.
9 Gwen Westerman and Bruce White, *Mni Sota Makoce: The Land of*

the Dakota (St. Paul, MN: Minnesota Historical Society Press, 2012), 22.

10 I have added "nation" to each of these names because the various divisions, while forming a whole political organization of a single nation, saw themselves also as distinct smaller nations. For a description of the Oceti Sakowin political divisions and the origins of each name, see Josephine Waggoner, *Witness: A Húnkpapha Historian's Strong-Heart Song of the Lakotas*, ed. Emily Levine (Lincoln, NE: University of Nebraska Press, 2013), 39–52.

11 Luther Standing Bear, *Land of the Spotted Eagle* (Lincoln, NE: University of Nebraska Press, 1978), 124–6.

12 Craig Howe, Lydia Whirlwind Soldier, and Lanniko L. Lee, eds., *He Sapa Woihanble: Black Hills Dream* (St. Paul, MN: Living Justice Press, 2011); N. Scott Momaday, *The Way to Rainy Mountain* (Albuquerque, NM: University of New Mexico Press, 1976); Jeffrey Ostler, *The Lakotas and the Black Hills* (New York: Viking, 2010), 3–27.

13 Luther Standing Bear, *My Indian Boyhood* (Lincoln, NE: University of Nebraska Press, 2005), 2.

14 "Jefferson's Instructions to Lewis," *Journals of the Lewis and Clark Expedition*, vol. 7, 293.

15 The expedition called this band of the Lakotas the "Tetons." They most likely encountered a subdivision of the Tintonwan (the Tetons), the Sicangu (the Brules). Today, the Sicangus are split between the Lower Brule Sioux Tribe and the Rosebud Sioux Tribe.

16 Quoted in John Ordway, "September 25, 1804," *Journals of the Lewis and Clark Expedition*, (Lincoln, NE: University of Nebraska), available at <lewisandclarkjournals.unl.edu>.

17 "Jefferson's Instructions to Lewis," 250. For an explanation on the expedition's hostage-taking, see Craig Howe, "Lewis and Clark among the Tetons: Smoking Out What Really Happened," *Wicazo Sa Review* 19(1) (2004): 47–72.

18 Quoted in Meriwether Lewis and William Clark, *The Travels of Capts. Lewis and Clarke* (London: Longman, 1806), 171–2.

19 See Kim TallBear, "Stephen Ambrose's *Undaunted Courage*: A White Nationalist Account of the Lewis and Clark Expedition," in *This Stretch of the River: Lakota, Dakota, and Nakota Responses to the Lewis and Clark Expedition and Bicentennial*, eds. Craig Howe and Kim Tallbear (Sioux Falls, SD: Pine Hill Press, 2006), 45–57.

20 Lewis and Clark, *Travels*, 171.

21 Ibid., 55.

22 Jeffrey Ostler, "'Just and Lawful War' as Genocidal War in the (United States) Northwest Ordinance and Northwest Territory, 1787–1832," *Journal of Genocide Research* 18:1, 2016, 3.

23 Emphasis added. Ibid., 1.
24 Steven Newcomb, *Pagans in the Promised Land: Decoding the Doctrine of Christian Discovery* (Golden, CO: Fulcrum, 2008), 104.
25 Tonya Gonnella Frichner, *Preliminary Study on the Impact on Indigenous Peoples of the International Legal Construct Known as the Doctrine of Discovery*, United Nations Economic and Social Council, Permanent Forum on Indigenous Issues, New York, April 19–30, 2010, E/C.19/2010/13, 11.
26 See Walter Johnson, *River of Dark Dreams: Slavery and Empire in the Cotton Kingdom* (Cambridge, MA: Harvard University Press, 2013).
27 Bernard W. Sheehan, *Seeds of Extinction: Jeffersonian Philanthropy and the American Indian* (New York: Norton, 1973), 245.
28 Jeffrey Ostler, *The Plains Sioux and US Colonialism from Lewis and Clark to Wounded Knee* (Cambridge: Cambridge University Press, 2004), 21.
29 Ibid., 28–9.
30 William R. Swagerty, "History of the United States Plains Until 1850," in *Handbook of North American Indians*, vol. 13, *Plains*, pt. 1, eds. Raymond J. Demallie and William C. Sturtevant, 261–70.
31 See Vine Deloria Jr., *Red Earth, White Lies: Native Americans and the Myth of Scientific Fact* (Golden, CO: Fulcrum, 1997).
32 Ibid., 276.
33 David D. Smits, "The Frontier Army and the Destruction of the Buffalo, 1865–1883," *Western Historical Quarterly* 25:3, 1994, 312–38.
34 Waggoner, *Witness*, 461–2.
35 For buffalo population estimates and the causes of their destruction, see Andrew C. Isenberg, *The Destruction of the Bison* (Cambridge, MA: Cambridge University Press, 2000); M. Scott Taylor, "Buffalo Hunt: International Trade and the Virtual Extinction of the North American Bison," *American Economic Review* 101:7, 2011, 3162–95.
36 Roxanne Dunbar-Ortiz, *An Indigenous Peoples' History of the United States* (Boston: Beacon, 2014), 9.
37 Virginia Driving Hawk Sneve, *Completing the Circle* (Lincoln: University of Nebraska Press, 1998), 25.
38 See Women's Earth Alliance and Native Youth Sexual Health Network, Violence on the Land, Violence on Our Bodies: Building an Indigenous Response to Environmental Violence, official website, landbodydefense.org.
39 Virginia Driving Hawk Sneve, *Completing the Circle* (Lincoln, NE: University of Nebraska Press, 1998), 25; *Sioux Women: Traditionally Sacred* (Pierre, SD: South Dakota Historical Society Press, 2016), 23–6.

40 For a comparative study of different historical experiences among Dakota and Ojibwe marriages with white traders and the institution of coverture, see Catherine J. Denial, *Making Marriage: Husbands, Wives, and the American State in Dakota and Ojibwe Country* (St. Paul, MN: Minnesota Historical Society Press, 2013).

41 Driving Hawk Sneve, *Completing the Circle*, 25.

42 Thwaites, *Journals of the Lewis and Clark Expedition*, vol. 2, 282–3.

43 Ibid., 349.

44 Quoted in F. A. Chardon, *Journal at Fort Clark, 1834–1839*, ed. Annie H. Abel (Pierre, SD: State of South Dakota, 1932), 271n258.

45 Sarah Deer, *The Beginning and End of Rape: Confronting Sexual Violence in Native America* (Minneapolis: University of Minnesota Press, 2015), xvii.

46 Dian Million, *Therapeutic Nations: Healing in an Age of Indigenous Human Rights* (Tuscon, AZ: University of Arizona Press, 2013), 7.

47 The exclusion of Indigenous women from the realm of European diplomacy, treaty making, and trade was a common imperial practice. See Linda Tuhiwai Smith, *Decolonizing Methodologies: Research and Indigenous Peoples*, 2nd ed. (London: Zed, 2012), 9.

48 For an explanation and interpretation of Indigenous "assent," "consent," and treaty making, see Scott Richard Lyons, *X-Marks: Native Signatures of Assent* (Minneapolis: University of Minnesota Press, 2010).

49 See Cathleen D. Cahill, *Federal Fathers and Mothers: A Social History of the United States Indian Service, 1869–1933* (Chapel Hill, NC: University of North Carolina Press, 2011).

50 See Sandy Grande, *Red Pedagogy: Native American Social and Political Thought* (Lanham, MD: Roman & Littlefield, 2004), 129–32; Margaret D. Jacobs, *White Mother to a White Race: Settler Colonialism, Maternalism, and the Removal of Indigenous Children in the American West and Australia, 1880–1940* (Lincoln, NE: University of Nebraska Press, 2009).

51 See Demaillie and Parks, "Tribal Traditions and Records," 1070–1; Greene, "Battiste Good's Earlier Entries," in *The Years the Stars Fell*, 293–4.

52 Indigenous women often participated in activities, such as war making, traditionally labeled as "male roles" in European societies. See Beatrice Medicine, "'Warrior Women': Sex Role Alternatives for Plains Indian Women," in *The Hidden Half: Studies of Plains Indian Women*, ed. Patricia Albers and Beatrice Medicine (Lanham, MD: University Press of America, 1983), 267–80.

53 See Mishuana Goeman, *Marking My Words: Native Women Mapping Our Nations* (Minneapolis: University of Minnesota Press, 2013).

54 Jaskiran Dhillon, "'This Fight Has Become My Life and It's Not

Over': An Interview with Zaysha Grinnell," Hot Spots, *Cultural Anthropology*, December 22, 2016, culanth.org.

55 S. Lyman Taylor, *A History of Indian Policy*, (Washington, DC: United States Department of Interior, Bureau of Indian Affairs, 1973), 42-4; Francis Paul Prucha, *American Indian Treaties: The History of a Political Anomaly* (Berkeley: University of California Press, 1994), 6–7.

56 R. G. Robertson, *Rotting Face: Smallpox and the American Indian* (Caldwell, ID: Caxton Press, 2001), xi.

57 Chardon, *Journal at Fort Clark*, 126.

58 George Catlin, *North American Indians*, vol. 2 (Edinburgh: John Grant, 1926), 2.

59 Quoted in Lewis and Clark, *The Travels of Capts. Lewis & Clarke*, 27. Although Lewis and Clark brought with them a form of cowpox, it is doubtful the sample they carried survived by the time they reached the Mandan village.

60 Clyde D. Dollar, "The High Plains Smallpox Epidemic of 1837–1838," *Western Historical Quarterly* 8:1, 1977, 23–4; Ostler, *The Plains Sioux*, 31.

61 James Mooney, *The Aboriginal Population of American North of Mexico* (Washington, DC: Government Printing Office, 1928), 12–3.

62 For an example of the now widely circulated "middle ground" thesis, see Richard White, *The Middle Ground: Indians, Empires, and Republics in the Great Lakes Region, 1650–1815* (New York: Cambridge University Press, 1991).

3. War

1 Quoted in James Mooney, *The Ghost-Dance Religion and Wounded Knee* (New York: Dover, 1973), 1072, author's translation.

2 Patrick Wolfe, "Settler Colonialism and the Elimination of the Native," *Journal of Genocide Research* 8:4, 2006, 387.

3 "While colonial leaders were often responsible for dictating policies that supported colonial expansion," Dakota historian Waziyatawin writes. "Civilian populations of settlers had much to gain from helping to implement those policies. For example, scorch and burn was a tactic used in the earliest stages of American colonisation, prompting the Seneca victims of his policy to name George Washington, one of America's most famous founding fathers, Town Destroyer. Major General John Sullivan's army carried out Washington's orders by razing Haudenosaunee orchards and ripening fields of corn and beans. Washington's troops and their families were later rewarded

for their service with title to Indigenous lands." "Malice Enough in their Hearts and Courage Enough in Ours: Reflections on US Indigenous and Palestinian Experiences under Occupation," *Settler Colonial Studies* 2:1, 2012, 176.

4 Andrew J. Birtle, *US Army Counterinsurgency Operations Doctrine, 1860–1941* (Washington, DC: Center for Military History, 2009), 27.

5 Byrd, *Transit of Empire*, xxxv.

6 Laleh Khalili, *Time in the Shadows: Confinement in Counterinsurgencies* (Palo Alto, CA: Stanford University Press, 2013), 18.

7 I draw my definition of sovereignty—as arising from the "colonial encounter"—from Antony Anghie, *Imperialism, Sovereignty and the Making of International Law* (New York: Cambridge University Press, 2007).

8 Many treaties during the early nineteenth century contained this exact language. See Vine Deloria Jr. and Raymond Demallie, *Documents of American Indian Diplomacy: Treaties, Agreements and Conventions, 1775–1979*, vol. 1 (Norman, OK: University of Oklahoma Press, 1999).

9 Raymond J. Demaillie, "The Great Treaty Council at Horse Creek," in *Nation to Nation: Treaties Between the United States and American Indian Nations*, ed. Suzan Shown Harjo (Washington, DC: National Museum of the American Indian, 2014), 91–4.

10 For an excellent analysis of the role Fort Laramie played in the Powder River country and during the ensuing Plains wars, see Dunbar-Ortiz, *An Indigenous Peoples' History* (Boston, MA: Beacon, 2014), 186–91.

11 Francis Paul Prucha, *American Indian Treaties: The History of a Political Anomaly* (Berkeley, CA: University of California Press, 1994), 237–40.

12 Demaillie, "The Great Treaty Council," 111.

13 Ostler, *The Plains Sioux The Plains Sioux and US Colonialism from Lewis and Clark to Wounded Knee* (Cambridge: Cambridge University Press, 2004), 378.

14 Josephine Waggoner, *Witness: A Húnkpapha Historian's Strong-Heart Song of the Lakotas*, ed. Emily Levine (Lincoln, NE: University of Nebraska Press, 2013), 332–3.

15 *Annual Report of the Commissioner of Indian Affairs*, 33rd Cong., 1st sess., 1853–54, 122.

16 Doreen Chaky, *Terrible Justice: Sioux Chiefs and US Soldiers on the Upper Missouri, 1854–1868* (Norman, OK: University of Oklahoma Press, 2012), 32–3.

17 "Wasicu" is a term more associated with criminal behavior than it is considered a descriptor for race.

18 Edwin Thompson Denig, *Five Indian Tribes of the Upper Missouri: Sioux, Arikaras, Assiniboines, Crees, Crows*, ed. John C. Ewers (Norman, OK: University of Oklahoma Press, 1961), 26–7.

19 Chaky, *Terrible Justice*, 34–5.

20 The defeat of Grattan is to this day still referred to as "the Grattan Massacre" by the US military.

21 Ostler, *The Plains Sioux*, 42.

22 Quote from Susan Bordeaux Bettelyoun and Josephine Waggoner, *With My Own Eyes: A Lakota Woman Tells Her People's History*, ed. Emily Levine (Lincoln, NE: University of Nebraska Press, 1998), 64, 155n12.

23 Joseph Marshall III, *The Journey of Crazy Horse: A Lakota History* (New York: Penguin, 2005), 68.

24 Ostler, *The Plains Sioux*, 42; Marshall, *The Journey of Crazy Horse*, 68–9.

25 Paul N. Beck, *Columns of Vengeance: Soldiers, Sioux, and the Punitive Expeditions* (Norman, OK: University of Oklahoma, 2013), 11–13. See also Paul N. Beck, *Inkpaduta: Dakota Leader* (Norman, OK: University of Oklahoma Press, 2008).

26 Waziyatawin, *What Does Justice Look Like?: The Struggle for Liberation in Dakota Homeland* (St. Paul: Living Justice Press, 2008), 32–7.

27 Quoted in Duane Schultz, *Over the Land I Come: The Great Sioux Uprising of 1862* (New York: St. Martin's Press, 1992), 28.

28 See Jennifer Nez Denetdale, *Reclaiming Diné History: The Legacies of Chief Manuelito and Juanita* (Tucson, AZ: University of Arizona Press, 2007).

29 See Carol Chomsky, "The United States–Dakota War Trials: A Study in Military Injustice," *Stanford Law Review* 43, 1990, 13–98.

30 Beck, *Columns of Vengeance*, 45–9.

31 Ladonna Bravebull Allard, "Why the Founder of Standing Rock Sioux Camp Can't Forget the Whitestone Massacre," *Yes! Magazine*, September 3, 2016, yesmagazine.org.

32 Beck, *Columns of Vengeance*, 166–7.

33 As Ostler points out, technically, the 1851 Treaty did allow for the construction of roads through Lakota territory. The construction of the Bozeman Trail, however, could be viewed as violating "the spirit of the 1851 agreement, which they [Lakotas, Cheyennes, and Arapahos] believed permitted travel on the North Platte road alone." Ostler, *The Plains Sioux*, 45.

34 Marshall, *The Journey of Crazy Horse*, 45–51.

35 Quoted in Craig Howe, Lydia Whirlwind Soldier, and Lanniko L. Lee, eds., *He Sapa Woihanble: Black Hills Dream* (St. Paul: Living Justice Press, 2011), 22–3.

36 The Oceti Sakowin still reunites annually for sun dances, powwows, and basketball games. For example, the Lakota Nation Invitational basketball tournament brings tens of thousands of the Oceti Sakowin to He Sapa in December. Although basketball tournaments are celebrations of sorts, tribal councils frequently schedule their meetings at the tournament.

37 See Marshall, *The Journey of Crazy Horse*, 37.

38 See Beatrice Medicine, "Oral History" in *The Great Sioux Nation Sitting in Judgement on America, An Oral History of the Sioux Nation and Its Struggle for Sovereignty*, ed. Roxanne Dunbar-Ortiz (Berkeley, CA: International Indian Treaty Council, 1977), 121–3.

39 See Ella Deloria, *The Dakota Way of Life* (Rapid City, SD: Mariah Press, 2007), 8–15.

40 W. E. B. Du Bois, *Black Reconstruction in America, 1860–1880* (New York: Free Press, 1998), 708.

41 See Vine Deloria Jr. and Clifford M. Lytle, *The Nations Within: The Past and Future of American Indian Sovereignty* (Austin: University of Texas Press, 1984), 16–27.

42 Patrick Wolfe, *Traces of History: Elementary Structures of Race* (New York: Verso, 2016), 160.

43 Jeffrey Ostler, *The Lakotas and the Black Hills* (New York: Viking, 2010), 62.

44 For the text of the 1868 Treaty, Francis Paul Prucha, ed., *Documents of United States Indian Policy*, 3rd ed., (Lincoln, NE: University of Nebraska Press, 2000), 109–13.

45 David D. Smits, "The Frontier Army and the Destruction of the Buffalo," *Western Historical Quarterly* 25:3, 1994, 322–3.

46 Red Cloud, "I Was Born a Lakota," in *Lakota Belief and Ritual*, eds. Raymond J. Demallie and Elaine A. Jahner (Lincoln, NE: University of Nebraska Press, 1991), 139.

47 Joseph Marshall III, *The Day the World Ended at Little Bighorn: A Lakota History* (New York: Penguin, 2007), 38.

48 Chalkley M. Beeson, "A Royal Buffalo Hunt," *Transactions of the Kansas State Historical Society* 10, 1908, 577.

49 Terry Mort, *Thieves' Road: The Black Hills Betrayal and Custer's Path to Little Bighorn* (New York: Prometheus, 2015), 67–8.

50 Richard Slotkin, *The Fatal Environment: The Myth of the Frontier in the Age of Industrialization, 1800–1890* (Norman, OK: University of Oklahoma Press, 1985), 358–70. See also Ostler, *The Plains Sioux*, 59–60.

51 Marshall, *The Journey of Crazy Horse*, 201–2.

52 Quoted in Richard G. Hardorff, ed., "Moving Robe Woman Interview," *Lakota Recollections of the Custer Fight* (Lincoln, NE: University of Nebraska Press, 1997), 93.

53 See Martin J. Kidston, "Northern Cheyenne Break a Vow of Silence," *Helena Independent Record*, June 28, 2005, helenair.com.

54 Hardorff, "Moving Robe Woman Interview," 96.

55 Prucha, *Documents of United States Indian Policy*, 146.

56 See Sidney L. Harring, *Crow Dog's Case: American Indian Sovereignty, Tribal Law, and United States Law in the Nineteenth Century* (Cambridge, UK: Cambridge University Press, 1994).

57 Ostler, *Lakotas and the Black Hills*, 101. For a detailed account of the efforts to address the theft of the Black Hills, see Mario Gonzalez and Elizabeth Cook-Lynn, *The Politics of Hallowed Ground: Wounded Knee and the Struggle for Indian Sovereignty* (Urbana, IL: University of Illinois Press, 1998); Edward Lazarus, *Black Hills/ White Justice: The Sioux Nation versus the United States, 1775 to the Present* (Lincoln, NE: University of Nebraska Press, 1999).

58 Suzanne Shown Harjo, "Introduction," in *Nation to Nation*, 4–6.

59 Standing Bear, *Land of the Spotted Eagle*, 132.

60 Prucha, *Documents of United States Indian Policy*, 179. See also Frederick E. Hoxie, *The Campaign to Assimilate the Indians, 1880–1920* (Lincoln, NE: University of Nebraska Press, 1984).

61 Ostler, *The Plains Sioux*, 54–5.

62 "Letter from the Secretary of the Interior Transmitting . . . In response to Senate resolution of December 13, 1888, report relative to opening part of the Sioux Reservation," 50th Cong., 2nd sess., Senate, ex. doc. no. 17, December 17, 1888, 79.

63 "Message from the President of the United States . . . Transmitting Reports relative to the proposed division of the great Sioux Reservation, and recommending certain legislation," 51st Cong., 1st sess., Senate, ex. doc. no. 51, February 10, 1890, 67. Henceforth, "Crook report."

64 Quoted in Ostler, *The Plains Sioux*, 236.

65 Crook report, 222.

66 Quoted in Ella Deloria, *Speaking of Indians* (Lincoln, NE: University of Nebraska Press, 1998), 81–3.

67 Ostler, *The Plains Sioux*, 262.

68 Mooney, *The Ghost-Dance Religion*, 777.

69 Ostler, *The Plains Sioux*, 250.

70 Ibid., 277–8.

71 Mooney, *The Ghost-Dance Religion*, 819–20.

72 Ostler, *The Plains Sioux*, 351.

73 Quoted in Robert M. Utley, "The Ordeal of Plenty Horses," *American Heritage* 26:1,1974, americanheritage.com.

74 See Dunbar-Ortiz, *An Indigenous Peoples' History*, 156–7.

4. Flood

1 "Joe Thompson Statements before the Subcommittee of the Committee on Public Works," February 16, 1959, M. Q. Sharpe papers, box 184, Chilson Collection, University of South Dakota, Vermillion, South Dakota.

2 Quoted in Francis Paul Prucha, ed., *Documents of United States Indian Policy*, 3rd ed., (Lincoln: University of Nebraska Press, 2000), 234.

3 Edward C. Valandra, *Not Without Our Consent: Lakota Resistance to Termination, 1950–59* (Urbana, IL: University of Illinois Press, 2010), 48.

4 Graham D. Taylor, *The New Deal and American Indian Tribalism: The Administration of the Indian Reorganization Act, 1934–45* (Lincoln, NE: University of Nebraska Press, 1980), 13–14.

5 John Collier, *America's Colonial Record* (London: Victor Gollancz, 1947), 31.

6 Vine Deloria Jr., "This Country Was a Lot Better Off When the Indians Were Running It," *New York Times*, March 8, 1970.

7 Vine Deloria Jr., introduction to Michael L. Lawson, *Dammed Indians Revisited: The Continuing History of the Pick-Sloan Plan and the Missouri River Sioux* (Pierre, SD: South Dakota State Historical Society Press, 2009), xv.

8 D'Arcy McNickle, "Introduction" in *Dams and Other Disasters: A Century of the Army Corps of Engineers in Civil Works*, Arthur E. Morgan (Boston: P. Sargent, 1971).

9 Ruben Estes to Francis Case, May 16, 1937, folder 157, Francis Case papers, special collections, Dakota Wesleyan University, Mitchell, South Dakota. Ruben Estes is the great-grandfather of the author.

10 *Chamberlain Register*, November 7, 1935; Ernst Schusky, *The Forgotten Sioux: An Ethnohistory of the Lower Brule Reservation* (Chicago: NelsonHall, 1975), 191.

11 Schneiders, 158–60.

12 Case to Estes, June 1, 1937, Case papers.

13 Case to John Herrick, June 12, 1940, Case papers.

14 Case to J. W. Jackson, July 12, 1940, Case papers.

15 Schneiders, 159; Lawson, 7

16 *Winters v. US*, 207 US 564 (1907), 576.

17 See Willima H. Veeder, "Winters Doctrine Rights: Keystone of National Programs for Wester Land and Water Conservation and Utilization," *Montana Law Review* 19, 1965, 149–72.

18 See Jeffery Ostler and Nick Estes, "'The Supreme Law of the Land': Standing Rock and the Dakota Access Pipeline," *Indian Country Today*, January 16, 2017, indiancountrymedianetwork.com.

19 Ibid.

20 See Dunbar-Ortiz, *An Indigenous Peoples' History*, 15–31.

21 Lanniko L. Lee, "Ways of River Wisdom," in *Shaping Survival: Essays by Four American Indian Tribal Women*, ed. Charles L. Woodard (Lanham, MD: Scarecrow, 2001), 25.

22 Melanie K. Yazzie, "Unlimited Limitations: The Navajos' Winters Rights Deemed Worthless in the 2012 Navajo–Hopi Little Colorado River Settlement," *Wicazo Sa Review* 28:1,2013, 26–37.

23 See James B. Hedges, "The Colonization Work of the Northern Pacific Railroad," *Mississippi Valley Historical Review* 13:3, 1926, 311–42.

24 Thomas M. Shapiro, *The Hidden Cost of Being African American: How Wealth Perpetuates Inequality* (New York: Oxford University Press, 2005), 190.

25 Char Miller, "Welcome to the Era of Scarcity" in *Water In the 21st-Century West: A High Country Reader*, ed. Char Miller (Corvallis, OR: Oregon State University Press, 2009), 303.

26 Quoted in Lawson, *Dammed Indians*, 102.

27 M. Q. Sharpe, "History of the Missouri River States Committee," n.d., M. Q. Sharpe papers, folder 2, box 151, Richardson Collection, University of South Dakota, Vermillion, South Dakota.

28 Lawson, *Dammed Indians*, 9.

29 Thurston, *River of Promise*, 82.

30 John Ferrell, "Developing the Missouri: South Dakota and the Pick-Sloan Plan," *South Dakota History* 19, 1989, 309–315; Lawson, *Dammed Indians*, 41–3.

31 US Department of the Interior, Bureau of Indian Affairs, *Damage to Five Reservations from Three Missouri River Reservoirs in North and South Dakota* (Billings, MO: Missouri River Investigation Project, 1954), 22a.

32 Lawson, *Dammed Indians*, 52–3.

33 Ibid., 47.

34 Lee, "Ways of River Wisdom," 37.

35 Ibid., 40–1.

36 E. Y. Berry, "Statements Before Congress," *Congressional Record*, 83rd Cong., 2nd sess., 1954, 13160.

37 Ibid.

38 US Department of the Interior, Bureau of Indian Affairs, Missouri River Basin Investigation, *The Indian and the Pick-Sloan Plan* (Billings, MO: Missouri River Investigation Project, 1954), 4–5

39 Ibid., 9.

40 Ibid., 9.

41 US Department of Interior, Bureau of Indian Affairs, *Damage to Five Reservations from Three Missouri River Reservoirs in North and*

South Dakota (Billings: Missouri River Investigation Project, 1954), 71.

42 Mary Annette Pember, "Mouse Beans: More than a Reliable Food Source," *Indian Country Today*, August 29, 2017, indiancountry-medianetwork.com.

43 US Congress, House Subcommittee on Indian Affairs, Committee on Interior and Insular Affairs, *Compensation to Indians of the Standing Rock Sioux Reservation* (unpublished hearing), 85th Cong., 2nd sess., 1958, 239–40.

44 Lisa Jones, "A Dam Brings a Flood of Diabetes to Three Tribes," *Indian Country Today*, July 6, 2011, indiancountrymedianetwork.com.

45 Quoted in Edward Lazarus, *Black Hills/White Justice: The Sioux Nation versus the United States, 1775 to the Present* (Lincoln, NE: University of Nebraska Press, 1999), 121.

46 Lower Brule Sioux Tribe, Congressional Hearings, 1955, statement of Richard LaRoche Jr., before House Committee on H. R. 3544 (S. 953), 23 June 1955, Sharpe papers, box 184.

47 *Damage to Five Reservations*, 13.

48 George Estes and Richard Loder, *Kul Wicasa Oyate* (Lower Brule, SD: Lower Brule Sioux Tribe, 1971), 70.

49 *Compensation to Indians of the Standing Rock Sioux Reservation*, 239–40.

50 *Damage to Five Reservations*, 8.

51 Ibid., 11.

52 *The Indian and the Pick-Sloan Plan*, 7.

53 Lawson, *Dammed Indians*, 182.

54 Minutes from "Joint Meeting of the Lower Brule and Crow Creek Tribal Councils," June 22, 1951, Sharpe papers, box 184.

55 Alice H. Jandreau to Sharpe, November 17, 1951, Sharpe papers, box 184.

56 Dillon S. Myer to E. Y. Berry, August 31, 1951, E. Y. Berry papers, Black Hills State University, Spearfish, South Dakota.

57 Brule county commissioner's motion, December 5, 1951, Berry papers.

58 Edward C. Valandra, *Not Without Our Consent: Lakota Resistance to Termination, 1950–59* (Chicago, IL: University of Illinois Press, 2006), 79.

59 Melcher to Berry and Case, April 14, 1954, Berry papers.

60 Herbert Wounded Knee to E. Y. Berry, Crow Creek Sioux Tribe, "Resolution Opposing Moving the Agency" and draft of "Resolution Urging Prompt Opening of Negotiations with the Crow Creek Tribe," August 27, 1951, Berry papers.

61 Valandra, *Not Without Our Consent*, 221–30.

62 Charles Wilkinson, *Blood Struggle: The Rise of Modern Indian Nations* (New York: Norton, 2005), 123–5.

63 Rob Nixon, *Slow Violence and Environmentalism of the Poor* (Cambridge, MA: Harvard University Press, 2013), 2.

5. Red Power

1 John Trudell, "We Are Power," *History Is a Weapon*, historyisaweapon.com/defcon1/trudellwearepower.

2 Quoted in Sarah Sunshine Manning, "The Power of Oceti Sakowin Women," *Indian Country Today*, August 30, 2017, indiancountrymedianetwork.com.

3 Quoted in Elizabeth A. Castle et al., "'Keeping One Foot in the Community'": Intergenerational Indigenous Women's Activism from the Local to the Global (and Back Again)," *American Indian Quarterly* 27:2, 2003, 847.

4 Quoted in Daniel M. Cobb, *Native Activism in Cold War America: The Struggle for Sovereignty* (Lawrence, KS: University of Kansas Press, 2008), 8.

5 McNickle, D'Arcy McNickle, *They Came Here First: The Epic of the American Indian* (New York: Harper & Row, 1975), 284.

6 Daniel M. Cobb, "Asserting a Global Indigenous Identity: Native Activism Before and After the Cold War," in *Native Diasporas: Indigenous Identities and Settler Colonialism in the Americas*, eds. Gregory D. Smithers and Brooke N. Newman (Lincoln, NE: University of Nebraska Press, 2014), 443.

7 For more on the history of NIYC, see Bradley G. Shreve, *Red Power Rising: The National Indian Youth Council and the Origins of Native Activism* (Norman, OK: University of Oklahoma Press, 2011).

8 For an overview of Vine Deloria's career and life, see Frederick E. Hoxie, *This Indian Country: American Indian Activists and the Place They Made* (Penguin: New York, 2012), 337–92. For a family history of the Delorias, see Vine Deloria Jr., *Singing for a Spirit: A Portrait of the Dakota Sioux* (Santa Fe, NM: Clearlight, 1999).

9 Deloria, "This Country Was a Lot Better Off When the Indians Were Running It," *New York Times*, March 8, 1970.

10 Vine Deloria Jr., "We Were Here as Independent Nations," in *Say We Are Nations: Documents of Politics and Protest in Indigenous America Since 1887*, ed. Daniel M. Cobb (Chapel Hill: University of North Carolina Press, 2015), 134, 137.

11 Vine Deloria Jr., *Custer Died for Your Sins: An Indian Manifesto* (Norman, OK: University of Oklahoma Press, 1988), 180.

12 Vine Deloria Jr., *We Talk, You Listen: New Tribes, New Turf* (Lincoln, NE: Bison, 2007), 145–7.

13 Arthur V. Watkins, "Termination of Federal Supervision: The Removal of Restrictions over Indian Property and Person," *Annals of the American Academy of Political and Social Science* 311, 1957, 55.

14 Deloria, *Custer Died for Your Sins*, 183.

15 Vine Deloria Jr., *Behind the Trail of Broken Treaties: An Indian Declaration of Independence* (Austin: University of Texas Press, 1985), 3.

16 Clyde Warrior, "We Are Not Free," in *Red Power: The American Indians' Fight for Freedom*, 2nd ed., eds. Alvin M. Josephy Jr., Joane Nabel, and Troy Johnson (Lincoln, NE: University of Nebraska Press, 1999), 17.

17 Ibid., 21.

18 See LaNada Boyer, "Reflections of Alcatraz," in *American Indian Activism: Alcatraz to the Longest Walk*, eds. Troy Johnson, Joane Nagel, and Duane Champagne (Urbana, IL: University of Illinois Press, 1997), 88–103.

19 Indians of All Nations, "Our Children will know Freedom and Justice," in *Say We Are Nations*, 158–9.

20 We Will Remember, pamphlet, Roger A. Finzel papers, Center for Southwest Research, University of New Mexico, box 1, folder 2.

21 See Julie L. Davis, *Survival Schools: The American Indian Movement and Community Education in the Twin Cities* (Minneapolis: University of Minnesota Press, 2013), 88–91; Brenda J. Child, *Holding Our World Together: Ojibwe Women and the Survival of Community* (New York: Viking, 2012), 156, 160; Elizabeth A. Castle, "'The Original Gangster': The Life and Times of Red Power Activist Madonna Thunder Hawk," in *The Hidden 1970s: Histories of Radicalism*, ed. Dan Berger (New Brunswick, NJ: Rutgers, 2010), 272–5.

22 Madonna Thunder Hawk, "Native Organizing Before the Non-Profit Industrial Complex," in *The Revolution Will Not Be Funded: Beyond the Non-Profit Industrial Complex*, ed. INCITE! Women of Color Against Violence (Cambridge, MA: South End, 2007), 101.

23 Quoted in Manning, "The Power of Oceti Sakowin Women."

24 Quoted in Castle, "The Original Gangster," 275.

25 Quoted in Lorelei Means, "Women of All Red Nations," in Josephy et al., *Red Power*, 52.

26 Dennis Banks with Richard Erdoes, *Ojibwa Warrior: Dennis Banks and the Rise of the American Indian Movement* (Norman, OK: University of Oklahoma Press, 2004), 64.

27 See Josephy et al., *Red Power*, 44–7.

28 Dunbar-Ortiz, *An Indigenous Peoples' History of the United States* (Boston: Beacon, 2014), 185.

29 Paul Chaat Smith and Robert Allen Warrior, *Like a Hurricane: The Indian Movement from Alcatraz to Wounded Knee* (New York: The

New Press, 1996), 171–93.

30 Ibid., 112–26.

31 Stew Magnuson, *The Death of Raymond Yellow Thunder: And Other True Stories from the Nebraska-Pine Ridge Border Town* (Lubbock: Texas Tech University Press, 2010), 4.

32 Quote from "reservation, n.," Oxford English Dictionary, September 2016, *OED Online*, oed.com.

33 See Winona LaDuke and Sean Aaron Cruz, *The Militarization of Indian Country* (East Lansing, MI: Makwa Enewed, 2013); Dunbar-Ortiz, *An Indigenous Peoples' History*, 133–61.

34 Audra Simpson, "Settlement's Secret," *Cultural Anthropology* 26:2, 2011, 205–17.

35 Smith and Warrior, *Like a Hurricane*, 179; James E. Emery interview by Stephen R. Ward, July 11, 1972, SDOHP 0527, transcript, South Dakota Oral History Project, South Dakota Oral History Center, University of South Dakota, Vermillion, South Dakota, 11.

36 Emphasis added. Quote from US Congress, *Constitutional Rights of the American Indian*, 603

37 US Congress, Senate Committee on Public Works, *To Investigate the Adequacy and Effectiveness of Federal Disaster Relief Legislation*, part 2., 93rd Cong., 1st sess., March 30 and 31, 1973, 291, 297.

38 Quoted in Calvin Kentfield, "A Letter from Rapid City," *New York Times*, April 15, 1973.

39 US Congress, *Federal Disaster Relief Legislation*, 452.

40 Ibid.

41 Ibid., 455.

42 Mary F. Berry, "Homesteading: New Prescription for Urban Ills," *Challenge*, January 1974, 2.

43 Quoted in Kentfield, "A Letter from Rapid City."

44 Ibid.

45 Don V. Bartlett, interview by E. Hausle, July 30, 1973, SDOHP 0952, transcript, South Dakota Oral History Project, South Dakota Oral History Center, University of South Dakota, Vermillion, South Dakota, 11.

46 Ibid., 13, 14.

47 Ibid., 11, 16–9.

48 Quoted in Warrior and Smith, *Like a Hurricane*, 198.

49 Excerpted in Brian Glick, *War at Home: Covert Action Against US Activists and What We Can Do About It* (Boston, MA: South End Press, 1989), 77.

50 John Grenier, *The First Way of War: American War Making on the Frontier, 1607–1814* (Cambridge, UK: Cambridge University Press, 2005), 12.

51 See D'Arcy McNickle, *They Came Here First*.

52 See, "Pine Ridge Reservation Deaths to Be Reinvestigated," *Weekend Edition*, NPR, August 18, 2012, npr.org.

53 Jordan T. Camp, *Incarcerating the Crisis: Freedom Struggles and the Rise of the Neoliberal State* (Berkeley, CA: University of California Press, 2016), 7.

54 Quoted in Peter Matthiessen, *In the Spirit of Crazy Horse: The Story of Leonard Peltier and the FBI's Ware on the American Indian Movement* (New York: Penguin, 1992), 107.

55 South Dakota Criminal Justice Initiative Work Group, *South Dakota Criminal Justice Initiative: Final Report 2012* (Pierre, SD: State of South Dakota, 2012).

56 US Census Bureau, Department of Commerce, *Poverty Rates for Selected Detailed Race and Hispanic Groups by State and Place: 2007–2011*, by Suzanne Macartney and Kayla Fontenot, issued February 2013.

57 Pennington County Sheriff's Office, *Annual Report, 2012*, issued 2013; Nick Estes, "Off the Reservation: Lakota Life and Death in Rapid City, South Dakota," *Funambulist* 5, May–June 2016, thefunambulist.net; Nick Estes, "Racist City, SD: Life is Violent, and Often Deadly in Rapid City," *Indian Country Today*, September 5, 2014, indiancountrymedianetwork.com.

58 "The Counted: People Killed by the Police in the US," *The Guardian*, June 1, 2015, theguardian.com.

59 Quoted in *Oyate Wicaho* January 1981, Finzel Papers, Box 4.

60 See Black Hills Alliance, *The Keystone for Survival*; Miners for Safety, Yellow Thunder Camp press release, April 17, 1981, Roger A. Finzel papers, Center for Southwest Research, University of New Mexico, box 2, folder 19.

61 Bartlett interview, 20.

6. Internationalism

1 Larry Red Shirt, "Concluding Ceremony September 23," International Indian Treaty Council, *The Geneva Conference: International NGO Conference on Discrimination Against Indigenous Peoples*, Palais des Nations, Geneva, Switzerland, September 20–23, 1977, 32.

2 First International Indian Treaty Council, "Declaration of Continuing Independence," iitc.org/about-iitc/the-declaration-of-continuing-independence-june-1974.

3 For a history of AIM's internationalism, see Roxanne Dunbar-Ortiz, "How Indigenous Peoples Wound Up at the United Nations," in *The*

Hidden 1970s: Histories of Radicalism, ed. Dan Berger (New Brunswick, NJ: Rutgers, 2010), 115–34; for a history of the COINTEL program, see Ward Churchill and Jim Vander Wall, *Agents of Repression: The FBI's Secret Wars Against the Black Panther Party and the American Indian Movement* (Boston, MA: South End, 1990).

4 See Daniel M. Cobb, "Asserting a Global Indigenous Identity: Native Activism before and after the Cold War," in *Native Diasporas: Indigenous Identities and Settler Colonialism in the Americas*, eds. Gregory D. Smithers and Brooke N. Newman (Lincoln, NE: University of Nebraska Press, 2014), 443–72.

5 See also Leanne Betasamosake Simpson, *As We Have Always Done: Indigenous Freedom Through Radical Resistance* (Minneapolis, MN: University of Minnesota Press, 2017), 55–70. Here, she writes about Nishnaabeg internationalisms between and among human, nonhuman, and other-than-human relations and nations, and the definition of Indigenous territories.

6 See Cobb, "Asserting a Global Indigenous Identity."

7 D'Arcy McNickle, *They Came Here First: The Epic of the American Indian* (New York: Lippincott, 1949), 275.

8 See David Martinez, *Dakota Philosopher: Charles Eastman and American Indian Thought* (St. Paul, MN: Minnesota Historical Society Press, 2009); Raymond Wilson, *Ohiyesa: Charles Eastman, Santee Sioux* (Urbana, IL: University of Illinois Press, 1983).

9 Tadeusz Lewandowski, *Red Bird, Red Power: The Life and Legacy of Zitkala-Ša* (Norman, OK: University of Oklahoma Press, 2016), 16.

10 Lazarus, *Black Hills/White Justice*, 128.

11 Quoted in Society of American Indians, *Report of the Executive Council on the Proceedings of the First Annual Conference of the Society of American Indians* (Washington, DC: Society of American Indians, 1912), 11.

12 Charles A. Eastman, *The Indian Today: The Past and Future of the First American* (New York: Doubleday, 1915), 101.

13 Charles A. Eastman, "Justice for the Sioux," *American Indian* 7:2, Summer 1919, 79.

14 Ibid., 148.

15 Society of American Indians, *Proceedings of the First Annual Conference of the Society of American Indians*.

16 W. E. B. Du Bois, *The Souls of Black Folks: Essays and Sketches* (Chicago, IL: McClurg, 1903), 1, 3, 13.

17 Ibid., 112–14, 123.

18 Charles A. Eastman, *The Soul of the Indian* (Boston, MA: Houghton Mifflin, 1911), 22–3.

19 Gustav Spiller, ed., *Papers on Inter-Racial Problems, Communicated to the First Universal Races Congress Held at the University of London,*

July 26–29 (Boston, MA: World's Peace Foundation, 1911), xiii–ix.

20 Ibid., 374.

21 Eastman, *From the Deep Woods of Civilization* (New York: Dover, 2003 [1916]), 106.

22 John W. Larner, "Society of American Indians," in *Native America in the Twentieth Century*, ed. Mary B. Davis (New York: Garland, 1994), 604.

23 Zitkala-Ša, "Editorial Comment," *American Indian* 7:3, July–September 1918, 114.

24 Quoted in Frederick E. Hoxie, ed., *Talking Back to Civilization: Indian Voices from the Progressive Era* (Boston, MA: Bedford and St. Martin's, 2001), 126.

25 "Editorial Comment," *American Indian* 6:1, January–March 1918, 19–20. See also Roxanne Dunbar-Ortiz, *Red Dirt: Growing* (Norman, OK: University of Oklahoma Press, 1997), 14–19.

26 Editorial, "Break the Shackles Now, Make Us Free," *American Indian* 5:4, October–December 1917, 213–21.

27 Zitkala-Ša, "Red Man's America," *American Indian* 5:1, October–December 1917, 64.

28 Zitkala-Ša, "Red Man's America," 230.

29 Charles Eastman, "The Sioux of Yesterday and Today," *American Indian* 5:1, October–December 1917, 234.

30 Editorial, "Editorial Sanctum: The Sioux Number of Our Magazine," *American Indian* 6:1, winter 1918, 41.

31 Zitkala-Ša, "Editorial Comment," *American Indian Magazine* 7:1, spring 1919, 6.

32 Ibid.

33 Zitkala-Ša, "Editorial Comment," *American Indian* 6:4, winter 1919, 161.

34 Carlos Montezuma, "Another Kaiser in America," in *Say We Are Nations: Documents of Politics and Protest in Indigenous America Since 1887*, ed. Daniel M. Cobb (Chapel Hill, NC: University of North Caroline Press, 2015), 34–5.

35 Charles A. Eastman, "The Indian's Plea for Freedom," *American Indian* 6:4, winter 1919, 163–5.

36 Zitkala-Ša, "Our Sioux People," Unpublished manuscript, Box 1, Folder 5, Gertrude and Raymond Bonnin Collection, L. Tom Perry Special Collections, Harold B. Lee Library, Brigham Young University, Provo, Utah.

37 Lewandowski, *Red Bird, Red Power*, 182–3.

38 Quoted in Ibid., 187.

39 Standing Rock Council Resolution, March 26, 1974, Finzel papers, box 2, folder 21.

40 Oglala Treaty Council Resolution, March 1974, Finzel papers, box

2, folder 21.

41 Russell Means with Marvin J. Wolf, *Where White Men Fear to Tread: The Autobiography of Russell Means* (New York: St. Martin's, 1995), 324–5.

42 International Workgroup on Treaties, June 13, 1974, Finzel papers, box 2, folder 21.

43 International Workgroup on Treaties, June 10, 1974, Finzel papers, box 2, folder 21. At this time, Jimmie Durham claimed to be "Cherokee," but Cherokee Nation enrollment officers and officials have recently discredited his claims. See guest editorial, "Dear Suspecting Public, Jimmie Durham is a Trickster," *Indian Country Today*, June 26, 2017, indiancountrymedianetwork.com.

44 International Treaty Council Meeting, June 14, 1974, Finzel papers, box 2, folder 21.

45 See Amilcar Cabral, *Return to the Source: Selected Speeches of Amilcar Cabral* (New York: African Information Service, 1973).

46 International Treaty Council Meeting, June 14, 1974, final papers, box 2, folder 21.

47 See John William Sayer, *Ghost Dancing the Law: The Wounded Knee Trials* (Cambridge, MA: Harvard University Press, 1997).

48 Russell Means' testimony, cited in *The Great Sioux Nation*, 45.

49 Vine Deloria Jr., "The United States Has No Jurisdiction in Sioux Territory," in *The Great Sioux Nation*, 146.

50 Emphasis added.

51 Dunbar-Ortiz, in *The Great Sioux Nation*, 13.

52 Judge Warren Urbom, "Excerpts from the Decision," in *The Great Sioux Nation*, 197.

53 See Robert A. Williams Jr., *The American Indian in Western Legal Thought: The Discourses of Conquest* (New York: Oxford University Press, 1990).

54 Urbom, "Excerpts from the Decision," in *The Great Sioux Nation*, 198.

55 John Thorne, "Excerpts from the Defense Summary Argument," in *The Great Sioux Nation*, 194.

56 Urbom, "Excerpts from the Decision," in *The Great Sioux Nation*, 197.

57 See Alyosha Goldstein, "Thresholds of Opposition: Liberty, Liberation, and the Horizon of Incrimination," in *Poverty in Common: The Politics of Communal Action During the American Century* (Durham, NC: Duke University Press, 2012), 199–243.

58 International Indian Treaty Council, "Decolonization, Liberation and the International Community," *Treaty Council News*, December 1977, 3, Finzel papers, box 4.

59 International Indian Treaty Council, "Red Paper," Finzel papers, box 2, folder 21.

60 "Indian Delegation Visits Soviet Union," *Treaty Council News*, November 1977, 3, Finzel papers, box 4.

61 Sherry Means, "These Countries Believe Strongly in Human Rights," *Treaty Council News*, November 1977, 4.

62 György Ferenc Tóth, *From Wounded Knee to Checkpoint Charlie: The Alliance for Sovereignty between American Indians and Central Europeans in the Late Cold War* (Albany, NY: State University of New York Press, 2016), 117–40.

63 Means, *Where White Men Fear to Tread*, 399.

64 Quoted in John K. Cooley, "American Indians Bring Message: 'No Shah, No Hostages,'" *Christian Science Monitor*, January 21, 1980.

65 "Final Notes on the Treaty Council's Participation in the Hostage Mail Exchange," *Oyate Wicaho*, February–March 1981, 7, Finzel papers, box 4.

66 Quote from Elizabeth Cook-Lynn, "'There Are No Two Sides to This Story,'" 42.

67 Yasser Arafat, "A Discussion with Yasser Arafat," *Journal of Palestine Studies* 11:2, 1982, 14.

68 Vine Deloria Jr., *Behind the Trail of Broken Treaties: An Indian Declaration of Independence* (Austin: University of Texas Press, 2000), 183, 185.

69 See Steven Salaita, *The Holy Land in Transit: Colonialism and the Quest for Canaan* (Syracuse, NY: Syracuse University Press, 2006).

70 Alex Lubin, *Geographies of Liberation: The Making of the Afro-Arab Political Imaginary* (Chapel Hill, NC: University of North Carolina Press, 2014), 7–9.

71 Dunbar-Ortiz, "How Indigenous Peoples Wound Up at the United Nations," 123, 132n14. As part of the 1993 Oslo Accords, Zionism was unclassified as a form of racism.

72 See International Indian Treaty Council, *The Geneva Conference: International NGO Conference on Discrimination Against Indigenous Peoples*.

73 International Indian Treaty Council, *The Geneva Conference: International NGO Conference on Discrimination Against Indigenous Peoples*, 25–6.

74 Dunbar-Ortiz, "How Indigenous Peoples Wound Up at the United Nations," 126.

75 All of these nations have since reversed their opposition by qualifying their decisions to uphold the declaration as simply a "non-binding" agreement.

76 United Nations Commission on Human Rights, *Study on Treaties, Agreements and Other Constructive Arrangements Between States and Indigenous Populations*, final report by Miguel Alfonso Martinez, special rapporteur, Working Group on Indigenous Peoples, July 1997, 24.

77 *United States v. Sioux Nation of Indians*, 448 US 371, 1980.

78 Quote from US Commission on Civil Rights, South Dakota Advisory Committee, *Native Americans and the Administration of Justice in South Dakota*, transcript of a community forum held December 6, 1999, 86–7.

79 Zoltán Grossman, *Unlikely Alliances: Native Nations and White Communities Join to Defend Rural Lands* (Seattle: University of Washington Press, 2017).

80 Walter Echo-Hawk, *Into the Light of Justice: The Rise of Human Rights in Native America and the UN Declaration on the Rights of Indigenous Peoples* (Golden, CO: Fulcrum, 2013), 16.

81 Department of Defense Appropriations Act of 2010, Title 8, sec. 8113, 45–7.

82 Echo-Hawk, *Into the Light of Justice*, 276.

83 Department of Defense Appropriations Act of 2010, 45–6.

84 United Nations Human Rights Council, *The Situation of Indigenous Peoples in the United States of America*, submitted by S. James Anaya, special rapporteur, United Nations General Assembly, 21st sess., No. A/HRC/21/47/Add. 1, August, 2012, 11.

7. Liberation

1 Fred Moten and Stefano Harney, *The Undercommons: Fugitive Planning and Black Study* (New York: Minor Compositions, 2013), 17.

2 Audra Simpson, *Mohawk Interruptus: Political Life Across the Borders of Settler States* (Durham, NC: Duke University Press, 2014).

3 Christopher Schano, "North Dakota Department of Corrections and Rehabilitation emails re: protests, September 7–18 2016," *MuckRock*, September 19, 2016, muckrock.com.

4 Ruth Wilson Gilmore, "Abolition Geography and the Problem of Innocence," in *Futures of Black Radicalism*, eds. Gaye Theresa Johnson and Alex Lubin (New York: Verso Books, 2017).

5 See Linda Tabar and Chandni Desai, "Decolonization is a Global Project: From Palestine to the Americas," *Decolonization: Indigeneity, Education and Society* 6:1, x.

6 See Katie Mazer, *Mapping a Many Headed Hydra: The Struggle Over the Dakota Access Pipeline*, Infrastructure Otherwise Report no. 1, October 2017, available at <infrastructureotherwise.org/DAPL_Report_20170921_FINAL.pdf>.

7 See Keeanga-Yamahtta Taylor, *From #BlackLivesMatter to Black Liberation* (Chicago, IL: Haymarket, 2016).

8 Kim Tallbear, "The US-Dakota War and Failed Settler Kinship," *Anthropology News*, November 2016, sfaa.net.

Afterword: Ancestors of the Future

1 Mark K. Tilsen, *It Ain't Over Until We're Smoking Cigars on the Drill Pad: Poems from Standing Rock and the Frontlines* (Minneapolis, MN: self-pub., Smart Set, 2021), 102.

2 Layli Long Soldier, *Whereas* (Minneapolis, MN: Graywolf Press, 2017), 54.

3 Sarah Hernandez, *We Are the Stars: Colonizing and Decolonizing the Oceti Sakowin Literary Tradition* (Tucson: University of Arizona Press, 2023).

4 Ibid.

5 Gwen Westerman and Bruce M. White, *Mni Sota Makoce: The Land of the Dakota* (St Paul: Minnesota Historical Society Press, 2012), 174.

6 Ibid., 178.

7 For translations and definitions of wicazo and -icazo, see Eugene Buechel and Paul Manhart, *Lakota Dictionary: Lakota-English/ English-Lakota, New Comprehensive Edition* (Lincoln: University of Nebraska Press, 2002).

8 Ivan Star, "Sharing Lakota Perspectives and Meanings of Color," *Native Sun News*, December 23, 2014, https://indianz.com/ News/2014/12/23/ivan-star-sharing-lakota-persp.asp.

9 Indigenous Environmental Network and Oil Change International, *Indigenous Resistance against Carbon*, August 2021, https://www. ienearth.org/indigenous-resistance-against-carbon/.

10 Elizabeth Cook-Lynn, "'There Are No Two Sides to This Story,'" 35.

11 Amílcar Cabral, *Our People Are Our Mountains: Amilcar Cabral on the Guinean Revolution* (London: Committee for Freedom in Mozambique, Angola and Guiné, 1972), 12.

12 See Joanne Barker, *Red Scare: The State's Indigenous Terrorist* (Berkeley: University of California Press, 2021).

13 Ruth Wilson Gilmore, *Abolition Geography: Essays Toward Liberation* (New York: Verso, 2022), 490.

14 See Robin D. G. Kelley, *Freedom Dreams: The Black Radical Imagination* (Boston: Beacon, 2022).

15 Jehan Bseiso, "Bint Nakba," *Psychoanalytic Activist*, https://psycho-analyticactivist.com/70th-anniversary-of-nakba-bint-nakba/.

16 Salman Abu Sitta, "I Could Have Been One of Those Who Broke Through the Siege on October 7," *Mondoweiss*, January 4, 2024, https://mondoweissnet/2024/01/i-could-have-been-one-of-those -who-broke-through-the-siege-on-october-7/.

17 Jehan Bseiso, "Bint Nakba."

18 Nick Estes, "Waves of History," 2019 (unpublished).

19 Gustavo Petro Urrego, "The Unleash of Genocide and Barbarism on

the Palestinian People Is What Awaits the Exodus of the Peoples of the South Unleashed by the Climate Crisis," (statement, COP28 High Level Segment National Statements Opening, Dubai, UAE, December 1, 2023), https://petro.presidencia.gov.co/prensa/Paginas/President-Petro-The-unleash-of-genocide-and-barbarism-on-the-Palestinian-people-is-what-awaits-the-exodus-231201.aspx.

20 Ibid.

21 Quoted in Jodi Rave, "Tribes Receive Heating Assistance," *Indianz. com*, February 19, 2007, https://indianz.com/News/2007/000956.asp.

22 Tim Giago, "Hugo Chavez Steps up for Native Americans and the Poor," *Huffpost*, March 16, 2007, https://www.huffpost.com/entry/hugo-chavez-steps-up-for_b_43630.

23 Mark Weisbrot and Jeffrey Sachs, "Economic Sanctions as Collective Punishment," Center for Economic and Policy Research, April 2019, https://cepr.net/images/stories/reports/venezuela-sanctions-2019-04.pdf.

24 "Life and Breath Report," Minnesota Pollution Control Agency, 2022, https://www.pca.state.mn.us/air-water-land-climate/life-and-breath-report#:~:text=We%20found%20that%20air%20pollution,for%20heart%20and%20lung%20problems.

25 Department of Justice, "Justice Department Finds Civil Rights Violations by the Minneapolis Police Department and the City of Minneapolis," June 16, 2023, https://www.justice.gov/opa/pr/justice-department-finds-civil-rights-violations-minneapolis-police-department-and-city.

26 Randy Furst, "Police Disability Retirements Stressing Communities, Sending State Pension Costs Soaring," *Star Tribune*, March 25, 2023, https://www.startribune.com/police-disability-retirements-stressing-communities-sending-state-pension-costs-soaring/600261973/.

27 Meg Cunninghan, "Model Legislation Targets Banks that Divest from Fossil Fuel Companies," ABC News, https://abcnews.go.com/Politics/model-legislation-targets-banks-divest-fossil-fuel-companies/story?id=81865813.

28 Indigenous Environmental Network and Oil Change International, *Indigenous Resistance against Carbon*.

INDEX